POETRY IS NOT

"THE BEST WORDS

IN THE BEST ORDER";

FOR LANGUAGE

IT IS THE HIGHEST

FORM OF EXISTENCE.

—JOSEPH BRODSKY

F A R R A R
S T R A U S
G I R O U X

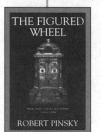

THE FIGURED WHEEL
New and Collected Poems 1966–1996
Robert Pinsky

UNCOLLECTED POEMS
Rainer Maria Rilke
A Bilingual Edition
Translated by Edward Snow

LIFE OF A POET
Rainer Maria Rilke
Ralph Freedman

New paperbacks

THE INFERNO OF DANTE
A Bilingual Edition
Translated by Robert Pinsky

CORA FRY'S PILLOW BOOK
Rosellen Brown

RED SAUCE, WHISKEY AND SNOW
August Kleinzahler

AFTER OVID
New Metamorphoses
Edited by Michael Hofmann
and James Lasdun

PIER PAOLO PASOLINI: POEMS
Selected and Translated by
Norman MacAfee
with Luciano Martinengo

TO THE CENTER OF THE EARTH
Michael Fried

CHICKAMAUGA
Charles Wright

SELECTED VERSE
Federico García Lorca
A Bilingual Edition
Edited by Christopher Maurer

PARNASSUS

POETRY IN REVIEW

VOLUME 21, No. 1 & No. 2

Parnassus: Poetry in Review, Vol. 21, Nos. 1 & 2. Published semiannually. Editorial offices, 205 W. 89th St. #8F, N.Y., N.Y. 10024. Tel: (212) 362-3492. Copyright © 1996 by Poetry in Review Foundation. All rights reserved. No part of this journal may be reproduced without the consent of the publisher. Advertising inquiries should be directed to the publisher. Subscription rates: $27.00 1 year, $46.00 2 years (individuals); $46.00 1 year, $88.00 2 years (libraries). Foreign rates: add $2.00 per issue. Back issues are available. All unsolicited manuscripts must be accompanied by a stamped, self-addressed envelope. Subscribers are requested to notify the publisher of any change of address.

ISSN: 0048-3028

Publication of this magazine has been made possible by grants from the National Endowment for the Arts in Washington, D.C., a Federal agency created by Act of Congress in 1965; the Middlecott Foundation; and the New York State Council on the Arts.

Table of Contents

Cover: SIDNEY GOODMAN
Luke's Dream, pastel and charcoal on paper. 1993–94. *Courtesy of the Terry Dintenfass Gallery*

We are pleased to announce
that the winner of the fourth annual
$500 Terrence Des Pres Prize
for Excellence in Reviewing or
Poetry Criticism is
MARJORIE PERLOFF
for her essay-review
"What to Make of a Diminished Thing,"
which was published
in *Parnassus: Volume 19, Number Two*

Judges: PAMELA WHITE HADAS, LAWRENCE JOSEPH, CYNTHIA MACDONALD

THIS ISSUE OF PARNASSUS is dedicated to the memory of Stanley Elkin, Stanley Lewis, and Sherman Paul. Stanley Elkin was a virtuoso whose instrument was the English language; his ear for American speech rhythms was peerless. I'll never forget playing softball against Stanley in 1971. Nobody could imitate his style of controlled abandon, or demonic intensity; in much the same spirit his imagination—zany, sardonic, melancholy, spelunking, original, exacting—ruled his fiction. There are no saints in Stanley's work: His characters, whether crooks or bailbondsmen, rabbis or d.j.s or widows, hustle for survival in the Vanity Fair that is American society, escaping at times with a tarnished grace. Stanley proved that, in the hands of a prose master, the road of tragicomic excess can lead to the palace of pleasure.

Stanley Lewis, the founding publisher of *Parnassus,* loved everything about books, from their verbal alchemy to their typography and binding. When he was a boy, somebody must have slipped a potion into his milk which cast a lifelong spell that was the music of his soul. In the early 1970s, long before Hélène Cixous and Maurice Blanchot became vogue figures in the academy, David Lewis Publisher (Stan's pioneering small press) brought out important books by them. And the Parnassus Bookshop was a haven for bibliophiles to browse in or chat with the proprietor who was often wreathed in a halo of pipe smoke. When Stan closed the shop, many people keenly felt the loss of a precious literary amenity. *Parnassus: Poetry in Review* would not have existed without Stan's willingness to venture into the Bermuda Triangle of literary magazines with a novice editor at the helm.

Sherman Paul was a scholar-critic whose books on Emerson and Thoreau earned him a justifiably fine reputation. What set Sherm apart from most of his colleagues was his refusal to settle cozily into the role of specialist. Driven by an abiding passion for American poetry, he wrote about the work of Robert Duncan, Robert Creeley, and Gary Snyder (and the architect Louis Sullivan) with as much relish as he elucidated Hart Crane's *The Bridge* and William Carlos Williams' *The Desert Music.* I'm sure I was just one of many people who benefitted from Sherm's unfailing generosity, civility of spirit, wise counsel, and friendship.

Collecteds

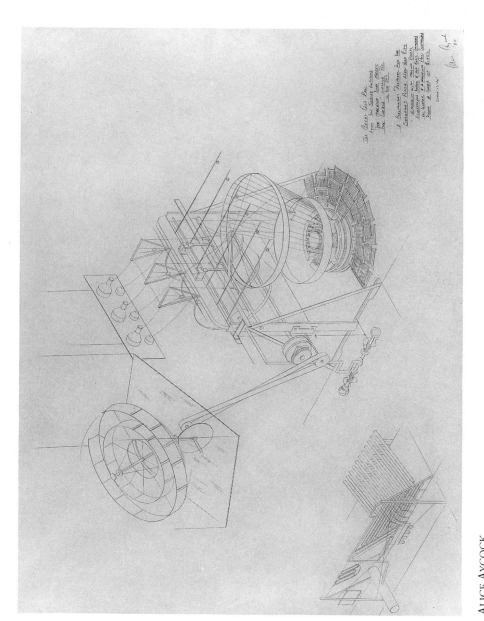

ALICE AYCOCK
The Great God Pan

A Torchlight Procession of One

Christopher Murray Grieve took the pseudonym Hugh MacDiarmid in 1922 and between then and his death in 1978 turned himself into one of the most excessive writers of the twentieth century. His *Complete Poems,* in two volumes, run to some 1,500 pages and represent only a fraction of his total output; the prose is more voluminous still, for MacDiarmid was a journalist and controversialist from his teenage years and made his living by producing copy for newspapers and undertaking commissions for a variety of full-length books. The work as a whole reveals a disconcerting unevenness, but the quality of his best poetry and the historic importance of his whole career mean that MacDiarmid deserves more attention than he has received outside his native Scotland.

MacDiarmid's position in Scottish literature and culture is in many respects analogous to that of Yeats in Ireland, and the liberationist ambitions of Irish writers were always of great importance to him. His linguistic overweening was hugely encouraged by the example of Joyce, while Yeats and other post-Revival writers continued to be highly influential in his program of cultural nationalism. One could even say that MacDiarmid achieved for Scotland what the combined efforts of the Gaelic League and the Literary Revival achieved for Ireland: First of all, he effected a reorientation of attitudes to the country's two indigenous languages, the Scots Gaelic of the Highlands and Islands and the vernacular Scots of the Borders and Lowlands. And secondly, MacDiarmid more or less single-handedly created a literature in one of these languages, and acted as an inspiration for the poet who was to change the course of poetry in the other.

In the 1920s, MacDiarmid himself emerged fully fledged as a writer of lyric genius in the language he had invented and which he called Synthetic Scots; in the 1930s, his friendship with Sorley MacLean helped MacLean to fare forward and become the redemptive genius of modern poetry in Gaelic. Within the contemporary conditions, in other words, MacDiarmid demonstrated the artistic possibilities of the indigenous speech and in so doing brought to the fore what he called "lapsed or unrealized qualities" in the two linguistic heritages which corresponded "to 'unconscious' elements in a distinctive Scottish psychology." All in all, his practice and example have had an inestimable influence on the history of Scottish writing in particular, and Scottish culture in general, over the last fifty years. There is a demonstrable link between MacDiarmid's act of cultural resistance in the Scotland of the 1920s and the literary self-possession of writers such as Alasdair Gray, Tom Leonard, Liz Lochead, and James Kelman in the 1980s and 1990s. He prepared the ground for a Scottish literature that would be self-critical and experimental in relation to its own inherited forms and idioms, but one that would also be stimulated by developments elsewhere in world literature.

MacDiarmid, then, was an inspirational writer whose artistic achievement remains problematic. He was a Communist and a nationalist, a propagandist and a plagiarist, a drinker and a messer, and he carried out all these roles with immense panache. He made enemies with as much flair as he made friends. He was a Stalinist and a chauvinist, he was Anglophobic and arrogant, but the very excessiveness which he constantly manifested, the exorbitant quality that marked everything he did, also charged his positive achievements and gave them real staying power. To put it another way, MacDiarmid possessed that "forcibleness" which Sir Philip Sidney judged to be the ultimately distinguishing mark of poetry itself, although it was a forcibleness which revealed itself as unmistakably in the aggravations and affronts of his work as in its triumphs.

So the negative things that can be said about MacDiarmid's poetry do not invalidate his achievement, nor would they have greatly disturbed the poet himself. He was very clearheaded about his productions and in the 1960s wrote to a BBC producer as follows: "My job, as I see it, has never been to lay a tit's egg, but to erupt like a volcano, emitting not only flame, but a lot of rubbish." From a person of less abundant capacity and with a less compulsive appetite for overdoing things, this could have sounded like an excuse; from MacDiarmid, however, it emerges as a boast. With him, the speech from the dock is sure to be a roar of defiance. No wonder Norman MacCaig suggested that the anniversary of his death should be marked each year by the observance of two minutes of pandemonium. "He would walk into my mind," MacCaig said at the graveside in Langholm in 1978, "as if it were a town and he a torchlight procession of one, lighting up the streets. . . ."

Still, although his vitality was epoch-making, MacDiarmid has probably written more disconcertingly than any other major twentieth-century poet. Anybody who wishes to praise the work has to admit straightaway that there is an un-get-roundable connection between the prodigality of his gifts and the prodigiousness of his blather. The task for everybody confronted with the immense bulk of his collected verse is to make a firm distinction between the true poetry and what we might call the habitual printout. And then there are the questions that arise because of his magpie habits of composition (or is it modernist collage?): the silent incorporation into his own text of the texts of others, sometimes of a technical nature, sometimes discursive, sometimes even literary, the most notorious example being the eight-line "Perfect," which can be regarded as either a found poem or a plagiarism from a story by Glyn Thomas—all depending on how much of a critical Malvolio you want to be. Even if that mileage of earnest, pedantic, and variously plagiaristic verse does not disqualify him from the league of the major talent, it does prevent him from being regarded as "a master." If we call a writer a master, it suggests an oeuvre with a kind of roundedness and finish that MacDiarmid did not even aspire to. He was more devoted to opening salvos than finishing touches; and even though he did once quote with approval the apothegm that "every force evolves its form," he was one of those whose faculties more naturally rallied to the banner of force.

So the volcanic image he used about himself was entirely appropriate, and in fact, MacDiarmid the poet was himself the result of an eruption. In 1922, he emerged like a new and fiery form out of the agitated element of Christopher Grieve's imagination; or it could be said with equal justification that he emerged from the awakened energies of the Scots language itself. These had been long dormant as a literary resource until they were stirred into fresh activity when Grieve encountered a learned monograph entitled *Lowland Scotch as Spoken in the Lower Strathearn District of Perthshire* and wrote his first poem in a new version of that old speech. And it was at this moment that he took the pseudonym Hugh MacDiarmid, as if he knew instinctively that he had been born again, as if his boydeeds as a literary figure were now over and he had discovered his heroic name and destiny. MacDiarmid arrived as a fully developed phenomenon, one who both produced and was produced by the language he wrote in, henceforth to be known variously as Synthetic Scots or Vernacular Scots or the Doric. And the first poem of the new language was called "The Watergaw":

> Ae weet forenicht i' the yow-trummle
> I saw yon antrin thing,
> A watergaw wi' its chitterin' licht
> Ayont the on-ding;
> An' I thocht o' the last wild look ye gied
> Afore ye deed!
>
> There was nae reek i' the laverock's hoose
> That nicht—an' nane i' mine;
> But I hae thocht o' that foolish licht
> Ever sin' syne;
> An' I think that mebbe at last I ken
> What your look meant then.

The poet's biographer, Alan Bold, records how these lines came about, when Grieve focused upon two pages of Sir James Wilson's researches in the book I have just mentioned:

> Most of the words in "The Watergaw" . . . came from two pages of Wilson's work. Yow-trummle ("cold weather in July after shearing"), watergaw ("indistinct rainbow") and on-ding ("beating rain or snow") are all on one page; the first phrase of the second stanza "There was nae reek i' the laverock's hoose / That nicht' appears in Wilson's list of Proverbs and Sayings . . . where it is glossed as "There's no smoke in the lark's house to night" (said when the night is cold and stormy).

The use Grieve made of these found elements was a far cry from the kind of busy transcription out of dictionaries and reference books which would disfigure so much of his later work in English. In 1922, however, what the recorded words and expressions did was to stretch a trip wire in the path of Grieve's auditory imagination so that he was pitched headlong into his linguistic unconscious, into a network of emotional and linguistic systems that had been in place since childhood. The common speech of his subcultural life as a youngster in Dumfriesshire was suddenly ratified by the authority of scholarship. His little self, the dialect creature at the core of his adult speech, began to hear itself amplified within a larger historical acoustic. Grieve turned into MacDiarmid when he realized that his writing identity depended for its empowerment upon his securing an ever deepening access to those primary linguistic strata in his own and his country's memory. And this sense of a nascent truth, of a something not quite clearly apprehended but very definitely experienced, is exactly what is embodied in "The Watergaw." Its real subject is the uncanny. The watergaw, the faint rainbow glimmering in chittering light, provides a sort of epiphany, and MacDiarmid connects the shimmer and weakness and possible revelation in the light behind the drizzle with the indecipherable look he received from his father on his deathbed. But how the poem sounds is probably more important than what it sees. What constitutes the true originality here is the combined sensation of strangeness and at-home-ness which the words create. Each expression, each cadence, each rhyme is as surely and reliably in place as stones on a hillside. The words themselves are uncanny: Whether or not their dictionary meaning is understood, it is hard to resist their phonetic allure, their aura of a meaning which has been intuited but not yet quite formulated. Just as the dying father's look transmitted a definite if mysterious promise of revelation, so, on the verge of its disappearance as a living speech, the old language rallies and delivers a new poetry for the future.

What happened in "The Watergaw," of course, and in other famous lyrics that followed it, such as "The Eemis Stane" and "Wheesht, Wheesht" and "The Bonnie Broukit Bairn," was what typically happens in lyric poetry of the purest sort. Suddenly the thing chanced upon comes forth as the thing predestined: The unforeseen appears as the inevitable. The poem's words seem always to have belonged together and to have enjoyed a distinct existence apart from all other words. Here, for example, is another one of those lyrics upon which MacDiarmid's fame rests, a very short one called "The Bonnie Broukit Bairn." The bairn or baby in question is the earth itself, which is distinguished here from other planets by its ability to "greet," which is to say its ability to weep or cry like an infant. The crimson aura of Mars and the green luminosity of Venus represent one kind of beauty. But earth's beauty is different, since earth is the site of human suffering, and this gives it a more grievous and vulnerable presence in the firmament than any of the other planets. "Crammasy" means crimson, "gowden" feathers are golden feathers, "wheen o' blethers" is a pack of nonsense, "broukit bairn" is a neglected baby, and the "haill clanjamfrie" is the whole bloody lot of them.

> Mars is braw in crammasy,
> Venus in a green silk goun,
> The auld mune shak's her gowden feathers,
> Their starry talk's a wheen o' blethers,
> Nane for thee a thochtie sparin',
> Earth, thou bonnie broukit bairn!
> —*But greet, an' in your tears ye'll droun*
> *The haill clanjamfrie!*

When he wrote this poem, Grieve was thirty-one years of age, a working journalist with an intense commitment to cultural and political renewal within Scotland, which for him boiled down to resisting and reversing the influence and impositions of English standards and English ways. Born in 1892 in the town of Langholm in Dumfriesshire, he was the first child of a postman father who had died young in 1910. His mother came from farming stock and had revealed her own gift for the demotic when she described the newborn poet as "an eaten and spewed lookin' wee thing wi' een like twa burned holes in a blanket." After being educated locally and having read, by his own account, everything in the local Carnegie Library, Grieve went at the age of sixteen to a teacher-training college in Edinburgh, an institution from which he was forced to withdraw because of an escapade involving the theft of the headmaster's books. From then on, he made his living as a migrant journalist, although it has to be admitted that the migrancy was helped along by Grieve's innate gift for falling out with bosses and his rapidly developing capacity as a whiskey drinker. Be that as it may, between January 1911 (when he quit college in Edinburgh) and July 1915 (when he joined the British army and went off to serve with the Medical Corps in Salonika), Christopher Grieve had worked with *The Edinburgh Evening Despatch*, *The Monmouthshire Labour News*, *The Clydebank and Renfrew Press*, *The Fife Herald*, and *The Fife Coast Chronicle*. He had also read voraciously and had contributed articles to the journal which was to be central to his whole intellectual development, A. R. Orage's *The New Age*. Through contact with Orage and his magazine, he was led to read, among others, Nietzsche and Bergson, and was as deeply susceptible to the Nietzschean injunction "Become what thou art" as he was to Bergson's claim that it was creative urge rather than natural selection which promoted the evolutionary process. But for Grieve to become what he was would mean becoming MacDiarmid, which in turn would mean achieving a Scottish identity long repressed by Anglocentric attitudes and Standard English speech: The evolutionary process would have to be creative at both the personal and political levels.

He returned from the war with a gradually clarifying program and developed into a propagandist for a new Scottish Idea, something that would take off from and reflect in literary terms Whitman's democratic American idea and Yeats's cultural nationalism; while in the political sphere, the project for a new Scotland would be fired by Lenin's Communism and by a vestigial but emotionally decisive predisposition to the Christian way of redemption through self-sacrifice. Grieve, moreover, had been initiated into the rough-and-tumble of politics during a miners' strike in Wales in 1911, and after that through his contacts with socialist activists in Scotland, people like John MacLean and James Maxton; so naturally he was deeply stirred by the Easter Rising in Dublin in 1916 and the Bolshevik Revolution in Russia the following year, two events which had a powerful impact on the way he would henceforth imagine the future, both nationally and internationally.

There was generosity as well as ferocity in MacDiarmid's espousals, and it is well to be reminded that behind his habitual self-promotions, there was a constant desire to be of service. As Douglas Sealy observed in a recent review, he had a calling which he served rather than a career which he worked at. By 1922, at any rate, Christopher Grieve had perfected his idiom as a polemicist and propagandist and was ready for pupation into Hugh MacDiarmid, a creature he would later describe as the "stone among the pigeons" and "the catfish that vitalizes the other torpid denizens of the aquarium." Here he is, getting into his stride in an editorial in the first number of *The Scottish Chapbook,* a journal edited by Grieve and devoted to the creation of a new movement in Scottish literature:

> Scottish literature, like all other literatures, has been *written* almost exclusively by blasphemers, immoralists, dipsomaniacs, and madmen, but, unlike most other literatures, has been *written about* almost exclusively by ministers, with, on the whole, an effect similar to that produced by the statement (of the worthy Dr. John McIntosh) that "as a novelist, Robert Louis Stevenson had the art of rendering his writings interesting," and "his faculty of description was fairly good."

This prose was fired off in 1922 and represents Grieve in typically provocative form: zesty, head-on, fiercely devoted to eliciting a response. His polemical writings employed all the troublemaking tactics of a dangerman in a bar, stripped to his shirtsleeves and squaring up to anyone and everyone. Protest and crusade rather than nostalgia and pathos were the hallmarks of his new commitment to the old words. There was nothing backward-looking in the impulse, for MacDiarmid was very consciously organizing a new movement in literature and revealing the ambitions of an experimenter: He could never have been accused of subscribing to some form of arrested linguistic development. Synthetic Scots was not simply meant to give audiences the pleasures of self-recognition, for that could lead to the sentimentality and self-indulgence which MacDiarmid wanted to banish from the culture altogether. Nor was his first purpose to proclaim the superior vitality of the local language over the compromised and compromising idiom of standardized modern English. These things might be incidental to his effort, but central to it was the challenge of jump-starting a language interrupted by history (as Douglas Dunn has called it) and getting it into modern running order. In fact, MacDiarmid's ways with the old words were as revolutionary and self-conscious as the young Ezra Pound's ways with a diction based upon archaism and a translatorese derived from Anglo-Saxon, Latin, and Chinese originals. And there was also something in his practice which corresponded to the poetics of Robert Frost, insofar as the thing that MacDiarmid was after in the deep Scottish ear resembled what Frost called "the sound of sense," a phonetic patterning which preceded speech and authenticated it, a kind of preverbal register to which the poetic voice had to be tuned.

What gave these ideas and hopes credibility was not, however, MacDiarmid's forcible personality, but rather the astonishing poem which he published in 1926 called *A Drunk Man Looks at the Thistle*. The title tells all that a reader needs to know before plunging in: This is an encounter between an intoxicated imagination and everything which that imagination can invent by meditation upon the national symbol of Scotland. At one moment, for example, the thistle has a mainly domestic and negative meaning, and is perceived by the drunk man as part and parcel of Scottish kitsch, of a piece with tartan for tourists, Burns suppers, haggises, Harry Lauder, and every kind of Caledonian corniness. But at another moment, it becomes the *yggdrasil*, the worldtree, a cosmic symbol that allows for poetry that is more visionary than satiric, a poetry of great sweep and intellectual resonance which nevertheless keeps its ear to the native ground. In these lines toward the end of the poem, for example, you can hear the reassuring democratic measure of the ballad stanza; but you can also hear something more stately and deeply orchestrated. There is a stereophonic scope to the music, as if the *gravitas* of the medieval Scots poet William Dunbar were echoing within the stellar reaches of Dante's *Divine Comedy*. (The word "hain" here, incidentally, means to keep or preserve, and "toom" to empty out, but what is more important than these details of sense is the verity of the tone of the whole passage.)

> The stars like thistles' roses floo'er
> The sterile growth o' space ootour,
> That clad in bitter blasts spreids oot
> Frae me, the sustenance o' its root.
>
> O fain I'd keep my hert entire,
> Fain hain the licht o' my desire,
> But ech, the shinin' streams ascend,
> And leave me empty at the end.

> For aince it's toomed my hert and brain
> The thistle needs maun fa' again.
> —But a' its growth'll never fill
> The hole it's turned my hert intill!
>
> Yet hae I silence left, the croon o' a'.

Through the deep reach of this poem's music, through its associative range and its inclusion of haunting translations from Russian and French sources, MacDiarmid served notice that his sympathies and concerns were not confined to the local scene, and that his outrage at the condition of Scotland was just an aspect of his longing for a totally transformed life for all human beings on the planet. In other words, if MacDiarmid did have a nostalgia, it was the one that Osip Mandelstam embraced, "a nostalgia for world culture."

And yet *The Drunk Man* could hardly be described as a solemn bid in the high-cultural stakes. On the contrary, what distinguishes it is its inspired down-to-earthness. It has a huge improvisational energy and is driven forward by an impetuous antiestablishment urge. Even though this impetuousness is an effect of the poem's style, it seems paradoxically to manifest an impatience with the very idea of style per se. The overriding impression is that the poem has too much business to get through to be bothered with merely literary considerations. It can be as close to doggerel as to Dante—and get away with it. Here, for instance, are a few lines from a rough-and-tumble section where the drunk man has a vision of the great cosmic wheel, where Scotland and the dramatis personae of Scottish history are at once set up and cut down within the perspectives of infinity:

> I felt it turn, and syne I saw
> John Knox and Clavers in my raw,
> And Mary Queen o' /Scots ana',
>
> And Robbie Burns and Weelum Wallace
> And Carlyle lookin' unco' gallus,
> And Harry Lauder (to enthrall us).

And as I looked I saw them a',
A' the Scots baith big and sma',
That e'er the braith o' life did draw.

"Mercy o' Gode, I canna thole
Wi sic an orra mob to roll."
—*Wheesht! It's for the guid o' your soul!*

. . . .

But in this huge ineducable
Heterogeneous hotch and rabble
Why am I condemned to squabble?

A Scottish poet maun assume
The burden o' his people's doom,
And dee to brak' their livin' tomb.

Mony hae tried, but a' ha'e failed.
Their sacrifice has nocht availed.
Upon the thistle they're impaled!

The mixture of passion and irreverence is everywhere in *A Drunk Man* and relates it to Irish masterpieces like Brian Merriman's *The Midnight Court* and Patrick Kavanagh's *The Great Hunger,* poems which similarly combine the expression of poetic high spirits, personal outrage, and social protest. Merriman's metrical vitality and insinuating intelligence remind me of parallel qualities in the MacDiarmid poem; and Kavanagh's rawer expression of personal and social trauma is also akin to much that is going on in the Scottish work. Yet perhaps the main point is that none of these poems is directly confessional; all of them are more than simply therapeutic. They do get something aggrieved out of their authors' systems, but their purpose is as public as it is personal. They act like their society's immunity systems, attacking whatever unhealthy or debilitating forces are at work in the body politic. And in this, they manifest poetry's high potential, its function as an agent of possible transformation, of evolution toward that more radiant and generous life which the imagination desires.

This poem is MacDiarmid's masterpiece. Even if his political program failed to materialize, even if the nationalism and socialism which he espoused found themselves unrealized and unpopular, even if his vernacular republic did not attain constitutional status, the fact is that *A Drunk Man Looks at the Thistle* did achieve the redress of poetry. MacDiarmid created a fully realized, imaginatively coherent work, one that contained such life-enhancing satire, such emotional weight, and such specific imaginative gravity that it could be placed in the mind's scales as something both equal to and corrective of the prevailing conditions. It was a magnificent intervention by creative power into a historical situation. Its force was the force of the glimpsed alternative, and it still gives credence to MacDiarmid's wonderfully stirring affirmation in another context that poetry is human existence come to life. In the year of its publication, it may have sold only ninety-nine copies, but already it was on its way to that most important audience of all, "the reader in posterity." It released in the Scots language what MacDiarmid also accurately called a *vis comica,* a capacity for comedy in the widest sense; it was both a deluge and an overflow, so much so that we might say the poem introduced an almost magical element into Scottish life, the kind represented by the crane bag in old Irish mythology.

The crane bag belonged to Manannan, the god of the sea, and contained every precious thing that he possessed. And "when the sea was full, all the treasures were visible in it; but when the fierce sea ebbed, the crane bag was empty." Similarly, *A Drunk Man Looks at the Thistle* contains all the treasures that might or might not become radiant within the personal and national life of Scotland. Indeed, there are moments when the drunk man himself seems to have intimations that the poem he is speaking relates to the crane bag myth. In the following stanza, for example, he says that his "harns" or brains respond to the ebb and flow of inspiration as seaweed responds to the ebb and flow of tides. And the poem itself will be forever correspondingly susceptible to the changing capacities of its audience. Like Manannan's marvelous sporran, it will reveal or retain its treasures, depending upon the fullness or emptiness of the imaginative world in which it subsists:

> My harns are seaweed—when the tide is in
> They swall like blethers and in comfort float,

But when the tide is oot they lie like 'gealed
And runkled auld bluid vessels in a knot.

The tidal wave of MacDiarmid's verse in Vernacular Scots was to keep running long after he completed *A Drunk Man Looks at the Thistle,* and it sustained him through many other astonishing performances, such as "Water Music" and "Tarras" and the title poem of the volume in which these appeared in 1932, *Scots Unbound.* In that book, the poet is in his element, hitting the note and holding the tune with all his old resource and exhilaration. But at this point I must take my leave of MacDiarmid, the Scots maker *redivivus,* and turn, too briefly and in conclusion, to the problematic status of MacDiarmid's vast output of verse in English during the remainder of his always amazing writing life.

I was once told about the entry procedures to be followed at a hospital run by a fundamentalist religious group in Tulsa, Oklahoma: Incoming patients are asked to fill out a form which requires them to declare, among other things, the date of their birth, and then, the date of their rebirth. For Grieve, there would have been no problem with this: birth, 1892; rebirth, 1922. But the fact of the matter is that MacDiarmid *qua* MacDiarmid could have come up with two sets of dates also, insofar as he was born in Synthetic Scots in 1922 and reborn in English sometime around 1933.

Personally, I find this period the most moving in the whole of MacDiarmid's life. These were the years when he lived with his second wife, Valda Trelyvn, and his newborn son, Michael, on the small island of Whalsay in the Shetlands. In retreat. Over the top and out of sight, so to speak, both physically and psychologically. Drink, the strain of breaking up with his first wife, political hassles, financial troubles, the tension of personal enmities—in the early 1930s, all of these things brought MacDiarmid to the stage of a nervous breakdown. But he survived, and his survival had to do with his getting down to the bedrock of his own resources, a bedrock which was reinforced at the time by contact with the stoical fishermen of the Shetland Islands and by his feeling of being imaginatively at home in the bleakness of the actual geological conditions. Racked by the huge ambitions he had imagined for himself, he now endured the beginnings of an ordeal in his poetic being, one in which the megalomaniac and the marvel-worker vied for the voice of the bard; where the blether of William McGonagall sporadically overwhelmed the strains of Hugh MacDiarmid; where the plagiarist too readily gained an upper hand over the poet; where the sureness of tone and dramatic inevitability which pervade his master-piece deserted him and a disconcerting unreliability entered his poetic voice. This is the MacDiarmid who breaks the heart because he so often and so enragingly fumbles the job, the poet who can at one moment transport a reader's ear and body into a wonderfully sustaining element, a language pure as air or water, a language which carries the reader (as the truest poetry always does) into the sensation of walking on air or swimming free—but then the air fails or the water drains, a disastrous drop occurs in the vocal and metrical pressure, what was fluent becomes flaccid, what was detail becomes data, and what was poetry becomes pedantry and plagiarism. Such letdowns keep happening at crucial turns in poems which are elsewhere full of lovely clarity and temperate, steady wisdom, poems such as "Island Funeral" or "Lament for the Great Music" or "Direadh III." And the failure derives in the main from three typical aspects of MacDiarmid's later writing: his increasingly propagandist stance, the uncertainty of his ear outside his native Scots, and his more and more compulsive habit of transcription (perhaps in the end a better term than plagiarism, since his habits were by then so well known to his readership and regarded with such indulgence).

When he wrote *A Drunk Man Looks at the Thistle,* MacDiarmid was less tied to the Communist party line than he would be in years ahead, although there was already a strong admixture of Leninism to corroborate his natural sympathy with the underdog. As time went on, however, Lenin's dream of world revolution gradually became associated in MacDiarmid's mind with the boundary-crossing powers of a new world language, one which he took to be foreshadowed in the experimental, meaning-melting ventures of Joyce's *Finnegans Wake.* Joyce's move from the baby-babble of a Dublin infant at the beginning of *A Portrait of the Artist as a Young Man* to the dream-speak of a world-embracing, multilingual consciousness in *Finnegans Wake* was, for MacDiarmid, a pattern of the way local speech could exfoliate into an all-inclusive world idiom and be fundamental to the evolution of that higher intellectual and imaginative plane which the revolution would promote. In practice, however, these two writers differed greatly insofar as Joyce's linguistic virtuosity was radically pleasure-seeking and absolved of any didactic purpose, whereas MacDiarmid's attempts at philological inclusiveness were doctrinaire and strenuously politically correct. Unfortunately, too, his identification of himself with the great prophets and projects of modernism led to an astounding self-inflation and to a verse that eventually strayed into megalomaniac fantasy. It even attained a certain monstrous dimension in poems like the "First Hymn to Lenin," where MacDiarmid declares that the murderous activities of the Cheka (the secret police of the USSR) are a fair price to have to pay for the maintenance of that evolutionary momentum which he and his hero prized so much:

> As necessary, and insignificant, as death
> Wi' a' its agonies in the cosmos still
> The Cheka's horrors are in their degree;
> And'll end suner! What maitters 't wha we kill
> To lessen that foulest murder that deprives
> > Maist men o' real lives?

Doctrinal extremism marred both the nationalist and internationalist strain in MacDiarmid's thinking all through his life. His Anglophobia, for instance, can be both salubrious and strategic, a natural and allowable consequence of opposition to imperialism, and another consequence of his ambition to relocate the focus and idiom of Scottish literature. But unless it is exercised in the service of his more broadly transformative vision of world language and the Communist order, the Anglophobia only massages a kind of vindictive nativism, the very opposite of the liberated consciousness he intended to promote. And it can, of course, pass beyond the stage of mere prejudice to arrive at the lunacy of something like the following, taken from one of the late poems in English:

> So every loveliness that Scotland has ever known
> Or will know, flies into me now,
> Out of the perilous night of English stupidity,
> As I lie brooding on the fact
> That perchance the best chance

Of reproducing the ancient Greek temperament
Would be to "cross" the Scots with the Chinese.

This flawed poetry of the 1930s and 1940s, with all its technical
vocabularies, its Joycean revel in the words and ways of other languages,
its insistence on the possibility of harnessing a future-oriented dream of
Scottish life to the Gaelic and medieval Scots heritages, its ache to
produce a seismic poetry that might include every thing and every
language and every discipline—this poetry wanted to go so far beyond
the proprieties of English literature that it would come right out the
other side of orthodox expression. Yet it is only occasionally that the
eerily beautiful, deliberately arcane words with which he confronts the
reader attain the kind of inevitability which I praised earlier on in the
Scots lyrics. Poems such as "On a Raised Beach" and "In a Cornish
Garden" do surprise by a fine excess, and word by word they possess a
unique multitudinous accuracy and psychedelic richness. Even they,
however, totter close to self-parody and only get by through the huge
appetite their author displays for matching the multiplicity of the
phenomena with a correspondingly cornucopian vocabulary. More
often, alas, neither MacDiarmid's lavishness nor his originality can move
the data across the frontier of writing. Skewed rhythms, egregious
diction, encyclopedic quotation, sheer monotony—MacDiarmid certainly gave his detractors plenty to work with.

Before I end, therefore, I want to suggest very briefly a way of both
respecting and admitting the failure of MacDiarmid's immense epic
effort, in projects such as "Cornish Heroic Song" and "In Memoriam
James Joyce." Historically, it's worth thinking of these works as being
all of a piece with the awesome and sometimes terrible projects of
twentieth-century Soviet Communism; they are like those gigantic dams
and steelworks and tyrannically organized communal farms, every one
of them the result of cruel effort, every one a breathtaking conception
surviving in the world as something both spectacular and uncherished,
evidence of actions at once heroic and doomed. If I exaggerate, it is partly
to emphasize the huge amount of MacDiarmid's poetry that remains
unread and unassimilated. The journalist and the activist in him would
not be quieted, and when there was no outlet for them in prose, they

invaded the verse without compunction. Sooner or later, however, what happened to Wordsworth will happen to MacDiarmid: The second phase of his career will be rendered down to a series of self-contained, self-sustaining passages of genuine poetry, disentangled at last from the editorials and encyclicals he launched so indefatigably for more than forty years upon the unresponsive world.

Still, MacDiarmid was right to make the leap toward the impossible. With the publication of his short lyrics in the collections called *Sangschaw* and *Penny Wheep* (in 1925 and 1926 respectively), then *A Drunk Man* in 1926, not to mention *To Circumjack Cencrastus* and *Scots Unbound* in the early 1930s—with the publication of all this work he not only had created a language but within a decade had endowed it with enough literature to be going on with. But then, in poetry, enough is never enough. To find its true measure, creative talent must exert itself beyond the limit. If MacDiarmid were to continue with the exploration and experiment that had characterized his great decade, he had to get through the barrier of the very excellence he had created. He had to find an idiom that would not make a fetish of the local but would rather transpose the parochial into the planetary. He therefore strove for an all-inclusive mode of utterance, and wrote a loose-weave, discursive, digression-filled verse, prone to off-loading miscellaneous information and opinions, constantly punctuated by disconcerting and abrupt shifts of tone. Although his reasons for this were outlined with exhilarating force in "The Kind Of Poetry I Want"—"Poetry of such an integration as cannot be effected / Until a new and conscious organization of society / Generates a new view / Of the world as a whole," and so on—it did not work. These later poems in Synthetic English generally don't have the intensity or oddity or uncanny inevitability of the early work in Scots, even if here and there they do manage to create that double sensation of surefooted homecoming and light-headed expedition which only the highest poetry achieves. It is surely time, for example, that anthologies of twentieth-century verse—which almost invariably print W. H. Auden's "In Praise of Limestone"—should also carry something from the luminous, almost biblical reveries of "On a Raised Beach." Philip Larkin's *The Oxford Book of Twentieth Century English Verse* ignores it, and Larkin's *Selected Letters* gives us his candid assessment of MacDiarmid in one sentence, as follows: "I am so averse from his work I can hardly bring my eyes to the page." That comes in a letter to Dan Davin at the Oxford University Press, and a couple of weeks later Larkin is asking Anthony Thwaite: "Is there any bit of MacDiarmid that's noticeably less morally repugnant and aesthetically null than the rest?" Thwaite may have given him a few tips, but unfortunately he doesn't seem to have directed his attention to lines like these:

> Nothing has stirred
> Since I lay down this morning an eternity ago
> But one bird. The widest door is the least liable to intrusion,
> Ubiquitous as the sunlight, unfrequented as the sun.
> The inward gates of a bird are always open.
> It does not know how to shut them.
> That is the secret of its song,
> But whether any man's are ajar is doubtful.
> I look at these stones and I know little about them,
> But I know their gates are open too,
> Always open, far longer open, than any bird's can be,
> That every one of them has had its gates wide open far longer
> Than all birds put together, let alone humanity,
> Though through them no man can see,
> No man nor anything more recently born than themselves
> And that is everything else on the Earth.
> I too lying here have dismissed all else.
> Bread from stones is my sole and desperate dearth,
> From stones, which are to the Earth as to the sunlight
> Is the naked sunlight is for no man's sight.
> I would scorn to cry to any easier audience
> Or, having cried, lack patience to await the response.

This scorning to cry to an easy audience is, of course, the secret of MacDiarmid's best work. When he was at his most durable, his appeal was made to an imagined authority, a court of higher spiritual attainment and more illuminated understanding than any he could find around him. And in this, he fulfilled a poetic demand which always precedes and survives the demands of technique and artistic skills. This is the demand that the artist sacrifice himself or herself to an envisaged standard, and what it entails was expressed with great eloquence and persuasiveness by Richard Ellmann when he wrote of the good poetic example of W. B. Yeats: According to Ellmann, in much of his work "Yeats wishes to show how brute fact may be transmogrified, how we can sacrifice ourselves . . . to our imagined selves which offer far higher standards than anything offered by social convention. If we must suffer, it is better to create the world in which we suffer, and this is what heroes do spontaneously, artists do consciously, and all [others] do in their own degree."

For all his intellectual arrogance and poetic megalomania, MacDiarmid was an approachable and companionable man. The exorbitance and willfulness of his poetic persona were partly self-inflationary, but they did arise from his conception of the large prophetic role which poetry had to fulfill in Scotland, and in the world of the future. He did not, however, confuse the greatness of the office with the dimensions of his own life as a citizen. When I met him in his later years, he and Valda lived modestly in their cottage in Biggar in Lanarkshire. Their hospitality was very moving, and they had attained a composure which seemed right after the buffeting they had both undergone forty years earlier, when their extreme poverty only intensified what was already an emotional and vocational ordeal. But then and always MacDiarmid was sustained by a faith older and simpler than the one he professed in Marxism. Lenin's utopian vision was undeniably inspirational for him, but deep down in the consciousness of this child of the Bible-reading Scottish Borders, Christ's commandment to people to love one another was surely equally powerful.

SEAMUS HEANEY

That Strength

That strength. Mother, dug out. Hammered, chained,
dislocated, weeping, sweeping, tossed with its
groaning, hammered, hammering bolts
off death. Shaken and damming
stars. Unjudgeable. Knife. Un
breakable on grindstones
that strength,
Mother
Broke.

Methinks the Poor Town Has Been Troubled Too Long

Light on the brick wall and a north wind whipping the branches
    black.
Shadow draws the thread of the light out flat against its palm.
Eat your soup, Mother, wherever you are in your mind.
Winter noon is on the rise. Weak suns yet alive
are as virtue to suns of that other day.
For the poor town dreams
of surrender, Mother
never untender,
Mother gallant
and gay.

Visit

Rose-ice winter fog over the bridges of the town.
Living with my mother in an old-age home is
the end of a lot of roads for us. Living?
She cannot sleep or eat. Angers trail
off. Red buzzers in the hall make
her eyelids jump. I am backed
up against the ice-wall. She
is coming towards me.
There is nowhere
left in "living"
that she can
live. She
will
have to go through me to get to the other place.

Dumas is crying because Dumas has tears, said Alexandre Dumas aged six when asked by his mother why
he was crying.

ANNE CARSON

Epitaph on 23rd Street: The Poetics of James Schuyler

James Schuyler. *Collected Poems of James Schuyler*. Farrar, Straus & Giroux 1993. 446 pp. $35.00 $23.00 (paper)

Byron: "I hate tasks."

. . . .

Quoth a plaque on Manhattan's 23rd Street: "DEDICATED TO THE MEMORY / OF JAMES SCHUYLER / POET AND PULITZER PRIZE WINNING / AUTHOR OF THE MORNING OF THE POEM AMONG / OTHER WORKS, WHO LIVED AT THE CHELSEA HOTEL / FROM 1979 UNTIL HIS DEATH IN 1991 / PRESENTED BY / FARRAR, STRAUS & GIROUX / JULY 1993." On a public epitaph, words divided into centered lines, broken, resemble poetry, if only visually.

. . . .

His *Collected Poems* dropped into the reading universe and met a familiar silence, the void that usually greets poetry, particularly if its monumentality is of the disguised, offbeat kind. The plaque substitutes for the acclaim his work deserves; makes a connection between residence and poem; asks that we, readers and pedestrians, remember where Schuyler lived and what he lived for; rebukes us for having taken his incarnation, in a hotel at once sleazy and legendary, for granted. The *Collected Poems* communicates pathos of a covert "Eroica": craggy masterwork of the deaf, misunderstood, unlovely shut-in. The silence surrounding Schuyler was not as immense or discouraging as the neglect encircling most dead or living poets. After all, he won a Pulitzer. He stayed in the country homes of wealthy friends. Influential figures championed him;

and he used silence—the state of being ignored—as ore and material. Catatonia of an indifferent public was an atmospheric buzz against which his protected, hothouse verse could become audible to itself.

. . . .

Rumble that contributes to the Schuyler-enabling room hum is the white noise of adjacent typewriting, including the posthumous critic's, the fellow poet's, or the boardinghouse crazy's: "From the next room / the friendly clatter of / an electric typewriter." How characteristic of Schuyler to interpret the neighbor's typing as amicable not competitive. It is pleasant to write when you think that a comrade, equally anonymous, is making a literary racket in the next room.

. . . .

If you read the *Collected* as one long poem, a narrative of a troubled, hypersensitive soul's evolution, then you will believe, as I do, that with age Schuyler grew to like—or tolerate—himself; that self-loathing warmed into self-knowledge.

. . . .

Stopping and starting: Poetry's favorite device is the line break, which prose shuns. At the line break, the poem engages in self-regard, echo, hesitation; it eddies. A prose reader begins to fall asleep; a poetry-lover feels a rising blush. For with the line break, a poem has revealed its chant stigmata. The line break is, aesthetically, an endangered species. In the neglect surrounding poetry, hear the death of the line break; hear a culture's decreasing solicitude toward the line break's fortunes. The lost line break is a little match girl, a degraded relic. For Schuyler, it is ballast: The heart of his poetics is erratic, tender, skittering enjambment. Truism—each line break is a little death, which Schuyler faces stoically and serenely. Imagine that the verse line is a jump rope; Schuyler skips rope, pondering the break when his feet are midair. He is both light on his feet, and performatively clumsy—a kind of oafishness which, like Chaplin's, is a high variety of grace. From "The Bluet": "Unexpected /

as a tear when someone / reads a poem you wrote / for him: 'It's this line / here.' That bluet breaks / me up, tiny spring flower / late, late in dour October." The line break before "reads" reminds us of reading's oddness, reminds us that our hands are a reader's. The line break after "unexpected" warns that every line break had better deliver a surprise if it wants any supper. "It's this line / here": The fleshy finger points, saying, "Here, reader, the line breaks." "[B]reaks / me up": Line's schism demolishes "me," also induces the aesthete's admiring tears. How late in the day I am noticing these tiny miraculous instances.

. . . .

Schuyler's lines are tight and nervous but also sometimes long and self- and universe-loving. Certainly he grew to forgive his own silence as well as his own overflow. He wrote fat poems, but also skinny poems; for the fat ones, he surmounted the line-ending's curtailment and succumbed to a physiological, shameful explosion: ". . . when my bladder flashed the message that I had to go and / I had to go *now,* not in two minutes. . . ." This is how "The Morning of the Poem" ends: he remembers urine gushing forth, "piss all over Paris, not / To mention my shirt and pants, light sun tans: why couldn't it / have been the depths of winter, and me in heavy / Dark overcoat?" To write a fat, long poem, he must surrender to the memory of flood and embarrassment.

. . . .

"What a long time since I wrote a poem" (Schuyler, in "Four Poems," dedicated to Frank O'Hara). The time between poems is always a long time, as the time of the poem is always short, or long, or concerned with the difference (negligible) between abbreviated and endless.

. . . .

Schuyler commonly and lazily uses the verb "to be"; he identifies. This is this. "The scars upon the day / are harsh marks of / tranquility." Do not oppose scar and happiness.

. . . .

He thinks (and transcribes and dignifies) "Mme. de Sévigné / -type thoughts," and what thoughts would not yearn for such an isolate and opal pedigree? By calling them "-type thoughts" he acknowledges derivativeness, eagerness to mimic the great lady, satisfaction in being a copy. He must have loved Proust's taste for Mme. de Sévigné: I, too, adore the exiled éclat of a woman who, far from the loved one, must be satisfied with sent commonplaces.

. . . .

Like Hart Crane, Schuyler is fond of the word "bluet," repeats it, and therefore repossesses it. He indulges the words he loves, as he wishes each passing day would pamper him. Some typical titles: "June 30, 1974." "Dec. 28, 1974." "February 13, 1975." "August first, 1974." Each day is an eclectic collection of moods and circumstances, potentially catastrophic; toward a ruined day's end, cheerfulness sometimes breaks through. The movement of his thought owes more to the diary's or letter's amplitudes than to the poem's parsimonies. And Schuyler's politics—if he had any—found body in formalist questions. Adorno would have deplored Schuyler's gorgeous sentimentality but would have appreciated his resistance to the received and the manufactured, even if his poetic manipulations strive to look like onanism crossed with haiku. Schuyler opens up "poem" to gay air; changes the dull wallpaper; lets light fall on a neglected corner; solves the question of garbage collection—how to handle a day's waste, how to convert indolence into literature.* Indolence is more than a temperament. It is a religion. The indispensable poets have cultivated it. Byron: "I smoke and Stare at Mountains." Schuyler: "A nothing day full of / wild beauty. . . ." Nothing days are collected poetry. Any day I read Schuyler or try to write this essay becomes a nothing day. Keats wrote: "this morning I was writing with one hand, and with the other holding to Mouth a Nectarine . . ." A few days later, Keats will fill "To Autumn" with mythic fruit, but so

---

*See Willard Spiegelman's new study, *Majestic Indolence: English Romantic Poetry and the Work of Art*, published by Oxford University Press.

much richer is the letter's inclusion of the actual, accidental, adjacent Nectarine! Schuyler's poems, like Keats's letters, include the contiguous object, the Nectarine in the sinister hand.

. . . .

To include the fruit beside the blank page, the page on which one is about to write a sentence, is to be indolent enough to notice wild beauty, to stare at it, to wonder what words might begin to be useful in a description of it, but to stop several steps short of actually writing the words down.

. . . .

His one ostensibly political poem, about Vietnam, is a failure. ("May, 1972.") He writes: "The war / must end. It goes on." He raises his voice to an unaccustomed public pitch; generally comfortable with things that "go on" (beauty, langour, moods), he cannot enjoy war's ongoingness.

. . . .

Breakdown, mental illness, social withdrawal: In "A Few Days," Schuyler admits to having sat wordless at a dinner party chez Ashbery. Why are his poems, then, so voluble? Paradoxical, that this most socially inept of writers should have composed poems that play the peerless hostess, charming posthumous guests.

. . . .

Fifteen years ago, I would have been praising Frank O'Hara, and my love for his poems would have included a desire, physically, to embrace or incorporate his glamour. Now (approaching middle age, or inhabiting it), I write about Schuyler, the least physically "cute" of the so-called New York School.

. . . .

His poems include the perception and the moment of the perception's correction, when he discovers it to have been mistaken, wrongsighted: "Tearing and tearing / ripped-up bits of paper, / no, it's not paper / it's snow." He loves to mis-identify. But on the crest of an identification (*this is a poem*) he is content to say "no" (*this is not a poem*), and stop. Hence his respect for silence: his more than merely rhetorical or perfunctory gesture of making room for catatonia, failure, and indolence within the ripped-up poem's vise. The silence he incorporates is sage *and* incompetent—the quietness of "writer's block," the dolor of deep trance. Turning away from the poem he is in the midst of writing, he stares, dumbly, at the wall.

. . . .

His prose diaries, published only by small presses, fed the poems. Two indispensable treasures are the DIA Art Foundation's chapbook of diary entries from 1968 and 1969, plainly titled *James Schuyler,* and The Figures's compilation of journal entries, *Early in '71*. Logically the *Collected Poems* should include these prose-poem sketches. (I await—I demand—their publication in a single handsome volume.) Framed, above my desk, is a typescript page of a Schuyler journal (Memorial Day, 1988), including the following paragraph, which is a poem because it exposits and then corrects itself ("Maybe not"), and which also, because of the way Schuyler typed it, visually resembles poetry. I reproduce his exact lineation:

> Last night, after dinner in that agreeable res-
> taurant in Housatonic, where the poet brothers Gizzi
> wait table, I had a passionate desire for some-
> thing forbidden—not what the others were having
> and I was not: a martini, wine, the kind of dessert
> called something like "Chocolate Suicide"—
> a cigarette, one lousy cigarette. Does this go
> on forever? Maybe not: right this minute, I do
> not want a cigarette.

The war goes on, but does this desire for a cigarette (a word he repeats, happily, three times) go on? Yes and no. He hovers between moving on and stopping. "Go / on" is a kind of line break, lost in prose, as is "I do / not want." It's possible that Schuyler considered his prose diaries to be mildly broken into poetic lines but lacked the energy to decide about all the breaks so left the entries in prose paragraphs whose arrangement on his typed page was nonetheless fastidious. Evidently he perceived continuity between his prose and poetry, for he combined the two in his sweetly anomalous *Home Book,* published by Z Press, which features such precious oddities as "The Infant Jesus of Prague," "The Custard Sellers," and "Shopping and Waiting," all absent from the *Collected—* which, to its credit, does include "The Fauré Ballade," defined in an epigraph as "An anthology of [prose and poetry] quotes, misquotes, and (no doubt) misremembered remarks." Stein told Hemingway that remarks are not literature. One "remark" that, *pace* Stein, Schuyler considers luminous is Thoreau's "I am a parcel of vain strivings." Acknowledgment of writing's vanity and necessary incommunicativeness underlies Chelsea Hotel and Walden Pond, twinned symbolic residences. Also in Chelsea Hotel, some years earlier: Robert Mapplethorpe, fellow gatherer, collecting tricks and flowers.

. . . .

Schuyler's love affair with the fragment led not only to chains of miniatures, but, repeatedly, to long poems that recall Keats's defense, in a letter, of the extended poem as bazaar, playground, wilderness: "Do not the Lovers of Poetry like to have a little Region to wander in where they may pick and choose, and in which the images are so numerous that many are forgotten and found new in a second Reading: which may be food for a Week's stroll in the Summer?" Of this genre—the many-acred playpen, crib, or continent; the pasture for grazing, for marveling at the freak acrobatics of an indolent poet expanding and contracting the line's bellows, creating the sine curve of remembering and forgetting—Schuyler's masterpieces are "Hymn to Life," "The

Crystal Lithium," "The Morning of the Poem," and "A Few Days." I do not overstate: there are few poems I know in English (*The Prelude* and *Flow Chart* are two) that successfully achieve this degree of openness to the grace of fact and accident, and the felicities that come only from receptivity to failure. Greatest among Schuyler's long works is "The Morning of the Poem"—because it spins into prose, or totters on the brink of it, and therefore secures a foothold in the vertigo-land called poetry; because it amply folds in details of his life, and thereby admits Mme. de Sévigné-type thoughts into the otherwise autistic field of "poem"; because it is long as hell; because it staggers, like a good drunk; because it embodies happiness and yet is extremely eloquent about unhappiness. I repeat: If I encourage students to read and write poetry, if I write and read and review poetry and think about poetry while walking down the street or before falling asleep, it is at least in part because of the example set by "The Morning of the Poem," even if, when I first read it, in 1981, I took its extraordinary effects for granted, as if such extravagances as Schuyler offered were poetry's norm. Then, I assumed that there were branches full of fruit as plump as "The Morning of the Poem," ready to be plucked. Now I know how few, and how difficult to find. Happily this poem's splendors defy unpacking. Schuyler piles up questions ("Whoever knows what a painter is think-ing?") and impossibilities ("I wish / I could send you a bundle of orange lilies / To paint"). If he could send the lilies, he wouldn't need to write the poem.

. . . .

"Hymn to Life" ends: " 'What are the questions you wish to ask?'"— leaving us with the silence of the many, many questions the *Collected* asks of a life, that my life and other interested lives ask of his *Collected*. His long poems, in Dada mode, stun the artistic enterprise into silence ("I hate tasks," "I smoke and Stare at Mountains").

. . . .

Silence: "Is this the moment? / No, not yet. / When is the moment? / Perhaps there is none. / Need I persist?"

. . . .

"Sitting. Staring. Thinking blankly."

. . . .

Against blankness, these creamy particulars: "Cazenovia Creek," "moth-wing strokes of Sviataslov Richter's / steady fingers," "A tall cold glass of Vichy," "A brown that isn't purple, gamboge, celadon lined / with jade." These details, sonorous, could have been James Merrill's. Schuyler signs them with a self-correcting "isn't": "A brown that *isn't* purple." Why point out what brown isn't? Because he respects description's failure; he admires brown's likeness to purple and the urge to equate the two colors, but he prefers the last-minute realization that they are not identical.

. . . .

He knows the names of flowers, forgets their names, remembers them—the drama of retrieval and amnesia that Proust brought to long prose's fore: "Pink rose of Marion, I / wish I knew your name." We congregate in literature's arbors because we want to fall asleep, and to wake from sleep with the names of flowers on our lips; we want to drift away from known words and then rediscover them.

. . . .

His first book, *Freely Espousing,* was published in 1969, the year of Stonewall. (Frank O'Hara was already dead.) Then, after this belated debut, the work came quickly: *The Crystal Lithium* (1972), *Hymn to Life* (1974), *A Nest of Ninnies* (co-written with John Ashbery, 1976), *The Home Book* (1977), *What's for Dinner?* (1978), the great *Morning of the Poem* (1980). And then *A Few Days* (1985). The meaning of this sudden flowering is mysterious and I won't question it too closely, but I would be a clod not to mention that the 1970s was a decade of gay explosive-ness, and that certainly Schuyler's poetics must have been warmed by that flame. (I almost called the flame "collective," but nothing in

Schuyler's work speaks to the communal spirit—only to the communion of writer and writer, reader and reader.) An aesthetic history of the gay 1970s needs to address not only the explicit (Mapplethorpe's sexual collections) but the arch and the adjacent (Merrill's ecstatic séance gatherings, Schuyler's temperamental potpourris).

. . . .

Perhaps his single most memorable (or liable to be anthologized) poem: "Salute," from *Freely Espousing*. The poem concerns collecting, the failure to collect, and the desire to include failure in the poem.

> Past is past, and if one
> remembers what one meant
> to do and never did, is
> not to have thought to do
> enough? Like that gather-
> ing of one of each I
> planned, to gather one
> of each kind of clover,
> daisy, paintbrush that
> grew in that field
> the cabin stood in and
> study them one afternoon
> before they wilted. Past
> is past. I salute
> that various field.

Noticeable line breaks: "is / not to have thought to do / enough?" Break certainty in half; disturb the finality of "is" with a cancelling "not." "Like that gather- / ing of one of each I / planned." Disturb the relation between subject and object by dividing "I" from the verb "planned": Nothing can be planned, or one must leap across the line hole to make the posited event happen. Split the word "gathering"; disembowel it. Therefore inspire the reader to tread *across* the line breaks, to regather what has been dismembered.

. . . .

Keats on the verge of death wrote a letter only because he feared that later he would not be able and would regret not having done so while he had the strength: "I thought I would write 'while I was in some liking' or I might become too ill to write at all and then if the desire to have written should become strong it would be a great affliction to me." Half the urge to write is the premonition that later the thought I am now having might disappear, so I had better write it down while I have the inclination, however overshadowed this desire is by indolence. Thoughts disappear. Sometimes it is fine if they vanish. Schuyler remembers an act of poetic collecting he wanted to perform, and then tells us that he never accomplished it, but of course in so telling us of his omission, he commits the lost act. Not all poems need to be written. Part of the beauty of the lyric enterprise is that one can stare at verse from across a rift of silent inaction and remark on the unwritten poems. Sometimes it *is* enough to have thought to do. The act of saluting suffices. Anyway, gatherings can't be planned; collections must be spontaneous. (If one obeys that dictum, it is impossible ever to write.) What do Jean Rhys, Robert Creeley and James Schuyler have in common? They alter and truncate thoughts: "Is / not." The line break is the cancellation stamp.

. . . .

Imagine Schuyler committing the act of study that he postulated but never rose to. Picture the poet holding the flower, scrutinizing it. What does it mean to "study" a flower or a poem? It is particularly difficult to examine Schuyler's poems, because they are at once "studied" (mannered) and spontaneous: Shiny and easy (but also, in their sleight-of-hand syntax, baffling), they deflect the interpreter's wiles. Does any meaningful segment of a nation, queer or otherwise, study Schuyler? Do we salute Schuyler? Isn't "salute" an implicitly patriotic gesture? If so, what hybrid patriotism includes Schuyler's isolated stammering, his Ponge-like quest to uncover a flower's unreproducible *sine qua non?* Schuyler salutes the poems he never wrote, the thoughts he never had, the lovers he never adequately cherished, and the vocation he imagines he never entirely occupied. The literature I pursue is deathbed utterance: written—and read—on a figurative border of sentience and extinction, the moment you say to yourself, "I lacked the temerity, diligence, and inspiration to pick those flowers and study them. Past is past. I salute the art I never made, the artifacts I never sufficiently appreciated." The plaque on 23rd Street salutes Schuyler. In *Freely Espousing,* his apolitical book, which broaches the possibility that this alone yet befriended poet might espouse a creed, or (homoerotically) find a male spouse, or (like a lady gardener) cultivate flowers, he silently acknowledges a field whose blossoms he was too distracted, lazy, or burdened to gather. If the "field" is American poetry as a living art; if America, as Richard Howard has recently suggested, is no better than its poetry; then the field I salute, by extolling Schuyler, is a recklessly utopian *vers libre* approximating thought's freedom, the democracy of "a commingling sky" (the first words of his first book), of solitudes assembled in taboo congregations ("Marriages of the atmosphere / are worth celebrating"). He advocates accuracy: "the sinous beauty of words like allergy." "[O]n the other hand I am not going to espouse any short stories in which lawn mowers clack." Thus Schuyler's poems are at once photographically hyperreal, and *symboliste* as Pan's pipe.

. . . .

One can enter Schuyler's creed of *freedom to espouse* through his least free poem, his divinely flat villanelle, self-consciously yet humbly titled "Poem," which I read (arbitrarily?) as an implicit address to John Ashbery, or to the aesthetic of voluptuous opacity that Ashbery was at the time championing. Imagine Ashbery and Schuyler as two participants in a Socratic—Wildean, Yeatsian, Gidean—dialogue about words and meaning, transparency and secrecy. Here is Schuyler's half of the debate, rendered in a form, the villanelle, which traffics in paired puzzled refrains:

> I do not always understand what you say.
> Once, when you said, across, you meant along.
> What is, is by its nature, on display.
>
> Words' meanings count, aside from what they weigh:
> poetry, like music, is not just song.

I do not always understand what you say.

You would hate, when with me, to meet by day
what at night you met and did not think wrong.
What is, is by its nature, on display.

I sense a heaviness in your light play,
a wish to stand out, admired, from the throng.
I do not always understand what you say.

I am as shy as you. Try as we may,
only by practice will our talks prolong.
What is, is by its nature, on display.

We talk together in a common way.
Art, like death, is brief; life and friendship long.
I do not always understand what you say.
What is, is by its nature, on display.

Think of Elizabeth Bishop's famous "One Art" (also, significantly, a villanelle): "One Art" and "Salute" are two great postmodern statements of the poetics of the closet. Bishop wrote: "though it may look like (*Write it!*) like disaster." Simile ("like") is about to happen; self-consciousness (or writing block) interrupts the line. Similarly, Schuyler hiccups between "what is" and "is by its nature." Is, is. Like, like. At the center of definition, exposition, or declaration, lies a stuttering repetition.

. . . .

A prose paraphrase of Schuyler's "Poem": *I thought I was your aesthetic opposite, J.A., but actually we're allies, alongside. Sometimes I can't understand your poems. Why not "display" yourself? And yet even masks can't help but disclose. We reveal, against our will. J.A., principle of hiddenness, you permit by night what you shirk by day. Is it our "nature" to display, to flaunt? Is our "nature" natural? I love the natural world though I am a man of interiors (hotels, indolences). J.A., why do you wish to stand out, admired, from the throng of poets—to attract acclaim by virtue of your fear of display? Our poems are conversations with each other's. I am display, you are secrecy;*

my poems can't be read apart from yours, nor yours apart from mine, nor
ours apart from Frank O'Hara's, who displayed everything, by night and
day. We use common speech. We also follow a shared— communitarian—
path. If what is, is by its nature, on display, then why bother writing poems?
Won't the world display itself, without our earnest boosterism?

. . . .

Hearing Ashbery and Schuyler read together at New York's Poetry
Center at the 92nd Street Y, in the late 1980s (the evening marked
Schuyler's return, after years of no public readings), I observed separated
corpuses converging, as both writers described atmospheres, cloud
cover, the "changeable / silk" of sky and mood. Ashbery had never
seemed more concerned with the comic, the gracile; Schuyler had never
seemed more metaphysical.

. . . .

Long and short lines alternate in "The Morning of the Poem," producing a sexed rush. "Our" culture forbids the line break by ignoring it. I
mean, poetry is what social critics would call "marginalized," and public
discourse takes place in prose, as if the line break, terrifying and other,
had the power to convert sensible democratic speech into anarchic
blather. In "Morning," Schuyler himself almost disregards the line break
but then turns back to it, pours his thought over its topiary hedge, and
this experience of "pour" (for reader and writer) is like having sex after
you'd sworn it off, or like having poetry after aesthetic abstinence, or
like visiting the country after years cooped up in the city. The line flow
weds blank-verse monumentality and gossip's languid shuffle, an oscil-
lation between public and private, an alternation of roles (Big/Little)
like a springy mattress to be enjoyed, not obeyed:

> There are not many islands I really
> Like, the ones where the rocks are slithery under the
>   thick seaweed when the tide is out, where the
> Heart of the island beneath tall trees is all overgrown with ferns
>   and moss begemmed with fog and is silent, spongy

To walk on: on other days, a scented springy mattress to stretch
out on.

Hear the all-important "is": "Heart of the island beneath tall trees *is* all
overgrown with ferns / and moss begemmed with fog and *is* silent." The
"is" functions as a mystical aporia: Where a reader wants or expects an
action verb, a development, a motion, instead Schuyler delivers a fey
equivalence, a swish.

. . . .

In "The Morning of the Poem," the short lines get longer as the poem
progresses, so that by the end they are almost as long as the long; while
toward the poem's beginning (he couldn't have foreseen the poem's
eventual massiveness), the short lines are nicely brief:

> . . . the day when I arose
> Seemed lost and trash-picking for a meatless morsel,
>   a stinking
> Bone, such as in this green unlovely village
>   one need never
> Seek or fear and you descend to your studio
>   leaving on your roof
> The exhalation of Baudelaire's image of
>   terror which is
> Not terror but the artist's (your) determination
>   to be strong
> To see things as they are too fierce and yet
>   not too much: in
> Western New York, why Baudelaire? In Chelsea,
>   why not?

Explanation: Darragh Park, the poem's dedicatee, is painting in Chelsea;
Schuyler is writing in western New York. The poet in the country needs
the idea of a painter in the city, just as art needs faraway referents in the
real, and just as, in a poetry of systolic-diastolic movement, of expansion
and contraction, long lines need short. (The long lines recall blank
verse—Stevens—while the short recall Williams, and a certain "femi-

nine" Imagism.) Flamboyance needs the closet. Expenditure needs thrift. A writing life needs silence. Not-understanding needs display as painter needs poet, as realism needs the real, as city needs country, as Mme. de Sévigné needs her daughter, as Keats needs the Nectarine, as Schuyler needs Ashbery and Ashbery Schuyler, as long lines need short, as short poems need long, as morning needs poems, and as poems need death (a poem rushes toward monumentality—or toward acute brevity—only because death supplies the parenthesis).

. . . .

His last long poem, "A Few Days," ends with the death of his mother: "Margaret Daisy Conner Schuyler Ridenour, / rest well, / the weary journey done." The weary journey of poem-making? The weary journey of pretending that love existed where it was absent.

> And so I won't be
> there to see my Maney
> enearthed beside
> my stepfather:
> once when I was
> home a while ago
> I said I realized
> that in his way he
> loved me. 'He did
> not,' my mother said.
> 'Burton hated you.'
> The old truth-teller!

Of James the son we might say the same: truth-teller! Truth the mother tells is truth the son is unafraid to include in the poem: *Burton hated you.* Some of the many truths that Schuyler told: I am lazy, I enjoy cigarettes and Guerlain's Imperiale, taxi-rides and lists, gifts and letters, quotations and flowers, names and fantasies, houses and boredom. I like to read but also to half-read: "Riding along in the beautiful day (there go two / blue enamel silos), half-reading about marvelous / Chamfort. . . ." Reading Schuyler I'm also half-reading him: noticing inattention's radiance.

. . . .

All the poems James Schuyler never planted: Past is past. Each poem marks the place where there might also have been others, but these shadow poems live inside the ones that remain, making the *Collected* a set of epitaphs for undisplayed sentiments. Displayed poem stands in for the veiled experience, as a named rose placemarks the real rose and eventually replaces it. Schuyler loves words and therefore he often forgets and must search for them—the process of retrieval is the unfolding of "poem":

> But oh dear: I forgot the five Old China Monthly
> roses, and I always wish I'd planted Félicité
> et Perpétue—it's their names I like. And
> Climbing Lady Hillington.

And—line break—Climbing Lady Hillington is not a rose but a name. Schuyler salutes roses, but also rose books, the veritable flower buried in its epitaph, and he shows no remorse that fossil memorabilia conceal the tangible petal: "I didn't plant / a winter garden, but the book led on to his / rose books: 'The Old Shrub Roses,' 'Shrub Roses / of Today,' and the one about climbers and ramblers." Old rambler, old truthteller!

. . . .

Another "is," from an early poem, "Fabergé," to prove that the climactic Schuyler act is to espouse an equivalence, to correct a perception, and to reclaim the beauty of the prior misapprehension: "Here, just for you, is a rose made out of a real rose and the dewdrop nestled in a rosy petal that has the delicate five-o'clock-shadow fuzz—blue—is not a tear." That was a prose sentence. Studying Schuyler, one reconsiders the difference between poetry and prose, revisits the line break and asks what it hosts.

. . . .

Words in his short lines float, stressed, atop the line's surface, bubbles or corks sometimes bumping against each other, more buoyant than most poets' solo syllables. Now as I search through the *Collected* for an example of syllable flotation, I am surprised to note that many of his feet *are* iambic ("the other dark") so what explains the not-rising not-falling weightlessness of the opening of, say, "Korean Mums"—

> beside me in this garden
> are huge and daisy-like
> (why not? are not
> oxeye daises a chrysanthemum?),
> shrubby and thick-stalked,
> the leaves pointing up
> the stems from which
> the flowers burst in
> sunbursts. I love
> this garden in all its moods . . .

His trick is parenthesis; he performs an act of metaphor (this is this, this is not this) which gets interrupted or reversed, so the simple act of identification (Korean mums are Korean mums—but this tautology climbs no ladder of definition) turns into a mis-identification, a voyage away from the readily nameable. Korean mums turn daisy-like, "in" bumps into its across-the-linebreak cousin "sunbursts." "Beside me": The poet writes with one hand, holds a figurative Nectarine in the other hand, and admits the fruity distraction into the poem. (Stein's credo: *Use everything*.) He allows the stuttering "why not? are not?" to suffice as a line, and shoves the meatier words "oxeye daisies" and "chrysanthemum" into a separate line, thus segregating flat stammer syllables ("why not? are not") from gorgeous flower names nearly composing an iambic pentameter line: "oxeye daisies a chrysanthemum?"

. . . .

Schuyler's poems exemplify. They are salesman samples, shopwindow displays of what is possible in poetry and what is not feasible in life, or what miraculous acts quicken in the actual because he found a way to break them down into lines. Here, in "Growing Dark," simple syllables in a short line glow because metaphor or misidentification has happened—nature displaying itself but also seeming not to mean what it says. "The grass shakes. / Smoke streaks, no, / cloud strokes. / The dogs are fed." Shakes, strokes, streaks: The words sound alike but aren't; and yet the words exist in relation. They have experienced lovely nepotism. The incest of assonance. Endogamous consonance.

· · · · · · · · · · · · · · · · · · ·

One of the only Schuyler poems in numbered parts is the great "Dining Out with Doug and Frank." I don't want to force him into "great" even though I think he deserves that designation, more often reserved for writers with occluded, unchatty vision; instead, Schuyler loves the marmoreal possibilities of the instantaneous, the slow duration of the nothing-in-particular. The poet tells us that J.A. once asked him: " 'I don't think James Joyce is any good. Do you?' " Schuyler remembers: "Think, what did I think! I / didn't know you were *allowed* not to like James / Joyce. The book I suppose is a masterpiece: freedom of choice / is better." (Consensual reading: consensual sex. Freedom to espouse.) Like Schuyler's simplest sentences, "Dining Out with Doug and Frank" is devoted to postponement. It begins with a gesture of turning away from the act of exposition or narration. *Soon I'll tell you about dining out with Doug and Frank, but not yet. Let me digress, first, to ephemera, queers, and soap.* "Not quite yet. First, / around the corner for a visit / to the Bella Landauer Collection / of printed ephemera: / luscious lithos and why did / Fairy Soap vanish and / Crouch and Fitzgerald survive? / Fairy Soap was once a / household word!" Rule of thumb: Before the poet writes, he or she must say, "Not quite yet," and go around the corner to visit a collection that will always remain marginal (yet connected) to the poem; a realm (like Keats's Nectarine) that the poem gestures toward, but that can only enter language through hesitations, detours, self-cancellations, and self-chastisements. ("*Write* it!")

· · · · · · · · · · · · · · · · · · ·

Will Schuyler—his poems—survive only as printed ephemera? On the survival of his cakes of line-broken fairy soap rests the life or death of poetry. To say it melodramatically: In order to write poetry, one must cultivate belief in the continued life offered by the line's end. One must imagine that there are readers eager for the silence it proposes. One must turn away from a busy, beguiling, media-rich world that does not revere or notice or propose a use for our Cain mark, the line break. To read Schuyler is to envision its death, if only because his are so deft and neurasthenically self-conscious—aware, in their delicacy, of the indifference and scorn surrounding all hypermodulated, hypernuanced sensation and utterance. The death of the line break: "Millay wrote a lovely poem about / it all. I cannot accept their / death, or any other death." Or: "Why is this poem / so long? And full of death?" One feels sorry for the line break, as if it were a dying heroine, or consumptive Keats, spitting blood in Rome. "Millay wrote a lovely poem about / it all"; poems are about "it all." After the "about," what comes but an empty gesture, "it all," signifying the things that neither Millay nor Schuyler, who accepts his Millay-like "minor" status, has the mastery to put into words?

. . . .

Secret stoicism of Schuyler's keenly observant eye: In "The Payne Whitney Poems," he admits enough details of the context—nervous breakdown, time in mental hospitals—for the reader to gather how much is left out of the other poems, despite their apparent intimacy and casualness. (Recall those famous 1950s and 1960s poetries of breakdown, and observe Schuyler's difference; with Bishop he stands apart from the "confessional"—though what poet has *not* broken down, what poetry worthy of the name has *not* originated in an experience of break down, if only indirectly echoed in the line break's swan's down?) From "February 13, 1975": "Some- / one is watching morning / TV. I'm not reduced to that / yet. I wish one could press / snowflakes in a book like flowers." Pronoun is broken down: "Some- / one." One can't preserve real snowflakes in a book, and can't include, in a poem, the Nectarine. Hear the sound of the ward in these lines from "What": "What's in these pills? / After lunch and I can / hardly keep my eyes / open. Oh, for someone to / talk small talk with. / Even a dog would do." Not melo-dramatic, not hysterical. "Talk" and "talk" monotonously cohabit one line: "talk small talk with." The first "talk" is a verb, the second, a noun. On its measly mental-institution day, "talk" performs two separate tasks. Dreadfulness of the inner life leads him to ask, in a beautiful, if fragile, poem, "What is a / poem, anyway." Contemplate the line broken between the article "a" and the noun "poem": Poems can't be so important, if the word "poem" isn't allowed to embrace its petty indirect article in the self-same line. Probe the meaning of "anyway," the throwaway word. The poem's earlier question: "And what / is that generator whose / fierce hum comes in / the window?" The generator outside the window, fiercely humming, is the force that through the sick mind drives the flower. As Dickinson would say, "*that* is poetry."

. . . .

I slept two hours and woke up thinking, "My aesthetic health depends on describing accurately what is remarkable about James Schuyler's poetry." But I wonder if aesthetic health is an imaginary, repressive category, serving to divide unfit from able specimens. Reliable witnesses attest that Schuyler was mentally ill. But he was the picture of poetic wellbeing: pink and prime. Maybe my constitution depends on not describing, on letting the object of pleasure remain unexplained. Does Schuyler require the sanction of explication? Wanting, like a plaque, to announce a location on 23rd Street where Schuyler, and poetry, once lived, I open (more or less at random) to the following line from the *Collected Poems:* "I pick up a loaded pen and twiddle it." How to avoid twiddling? How to explain the contiguity of poetry and twiddle, and Schuyler's deep affirmation of indecision, error, and illness?

. . . .

An early line from Schuyler: "Then the moon goes crocus." He coldly yet exultantly notes the moment of metamorphosis: the moon turning crocus. Crocus is a flower, not a color. I salute the long "o" of "goes" and "crocus," words to sit on. "Then the moon goes crocus" is the last line. How do you know when to end a poem? When the poem goes crocus, it's time to stop.

. . . .

"All things are real / no one a symbol." Schuyler must have known leaden hours when the soul is not present to itself, and he must have been grateful for moments when sensation, through poetry, returns, when reality pours its warm oil back into the seeing "I," and when one becomes nominal—a citizen, a voter, a head of a household; when one (I, Schuyler) matters; when oddball, loner, bachelor, fag, or fatty deserves to observe the snow, figures highly enough in the Family of Man to ask "Who is Nancy Daum?" Take the poem "April and Its Forsythia." In it, observe that for Schuyler and reader, the barest retinal moment (*I see snow*) counts, makes the seeing "I" count. Observe with what alacrity Schuyler's democracy grants citizenship. The census taker describes Schuyler (authorizes him as a citizen, head of a household) only after Schuyler, first, notices her. Schuyler as census taker affirms you, reader, authorizing your residency in the crowded republic:

> It's snowing on the unpedimented lions. On ventilator hoods
> white triangles. It evens up wrinkled tar roofs,
> smooths out rough concrete coping, showing the shape
> of a wall side between coping and roof. The census
> taker was just here. She had on transparent overshoes, coat and
> hat: are clothes less secret? Less snowlike?
> Snow isn't secret, showing further aspects, how small
> cast lions would look if they grew maned, tame yet whitely
> fierce; how the center of the sidewalk is always a path
> steps tend to, as across a plain, through a wood; how cars
> swing out heavily and big at a corner, turning voluminously
> as a fleshy dancer. That census taker. I'm the head of a household.
> I am also my household. Not bad.

It's snowing. Schuyler is writing a poem. The census taker comes. He notices her transparent clothes. He thinks about secrets. He has many. His homosexuality, so-called, isn't a secret, yet it grows more important to his work as the decade progresses. And the census taker must take note of his singularity, his voluminous bachelorhood. Also she must see (so must we) his not-badness, his O.K. aspects, and we must observe the census taker's interruption of the poem's time: The lines conceal her visit inside their purse. The poem, snow, evens up wrinkled surfaces and hides age. In the poem it continues to snow and Schuyler continues to be head ("not bad") of his household.

. . . .

As I write these words, I am living on 23rd Street right next to James Schuyler's Chelsea Hotel and the plaque honoring him. From evidence in the poems, I've reconstructed that his apartment looked northward, toward 23rd, while mine faces south, toward 22nd. (This may be untrue.) The light in my room, when I have the energy to notice it, is not damned. I think of it as Schuyler's light. "What can one write / between the lines? Not one damn thing."

. . . .

Schuyler light: noticed and therefore put into poems, even as it—the light—goes:

> This beauty that I see
> —the sun going down
> scours the entangled
> and lightly henna
> withies and the wind
> whips them as it
> would ship a cloud—
> is passing so swiftly
> into night.

What are withies? Willows with flexible branches. The keynote of a withy is its willingness to be whipped. Beauty enters the room, the self, the poem, only to scour the surface: to punish it. He writes "it goes, it goes." What goes? Beauty. This beauty that I see, goes. This poem is called "Poem," and it dwells in a section of *Hymn to Life* entitled

"Elsewhere." Schuyler's beauty has now gone elsewhere: onto the inanimate, withy-invoking page. Into the mind of a reader flexible enough to be entangled by the nearly obvious. Schuyler was "just able" to collect, into lines, what he saw.

> . . . This
> beauty that collects
> dry leaves in pools
> and pockets and goes
> freezingly, just able
> still to swiftly flow
> it goes, it goes.

So it goes, into the uncollectable. Reading Schuyler's *Collected,* one hears and admires—one loves—the "just able," the almost not able: a poetics on the verge of not emerging; a poetry on the verge of not being able to exist.

. . . .

A more complete quotation from the Lord Byron letter excerpted at this essay's beginning: "So you and Mr. Foscolo &c. want me to undertake what you call a 'great work' an Epic poem I suppose or some such pyramid. —I'll try no such thing—I hate tasks—and then 'seven or eight years!' "

. . . .

Writers depend on what other writers have thought but not transcribed; writers depend on between-the-lines ecstasies and fears of other writers. Rapport between a dead and living scribbler is not agon but identification, a sequence of heady questions: All I want from Schuyler's poems is that they speak, even if I can't quite identify the nature of this speaker, so profuse in what he espouses, so diffuse in what he displays. From Schuyler's "Amy Lowell Thoughts":

Draped one,
speak.
Are you a larch?

Schuyler depends on Amy Lowell having had Amy-Lowell-type
thoughts: inscrutable, unstudied, unsaluted. Draped poet, I want to
know what you were thinking on a certain silent afternoon, a nothing
day. I want to hear the gnomic thoughts that passed and dispersed before
poetry, the enemy of loss, found the means to incorporate them.

. . . .

Many, some, or a couple of his poems end with the word "goodbye."

WAYNE KOESTENBAUM

MICHAEL VITTI
Brooklyn Gothic, Summer 1995

Fireflies in a Jar

Guy Davenport. *7 Greeks: Translations. Archilochos Sappho Alkman Anakreon Herakleitos Diogenes Herondas.* New Directions 1995. 241 pp. $16.95

Jim Powell. *Sappho: A Garland. The Poems and Fragments of Sappho Translated.* Farrar, Straus & Giroux 1993. 65 pp. $15.00

Let us begin with a cliché, and compare the remains of classical Greek literature with the ruins of classical Greek cities. Search for the cities of ancient Greece and you will find a few intact or almost intact structures and a good many piles of bewildering rubble; most of what once stood is simply gone. Turn to the literature: For every complete or nearly complete work, there are scores of fragments. An astonishing number of authors have simply vanished, and only their names cited in later writers' works testify that they ever lived. Pythagoras, Solon, Agathon exist only in shards; Arion and Thespis are mere names—the melancholy list stretches on. Sometimes a lost papyrus treasure rises from an Egyptian scrap heap or the wrappings of a mummy; in the past forty years an almost complete play by Menander and our longest fragment of Archilochus have reappeared after centuries of silence. Lovers of Greek poetry live in the hope of more to come, but such resurrections are rare, the gaps to be filled vast.

Where does Sappho fall in this line between survival and oblivion? In the middle, but slanting toward oblivion; the shattered remnants of her poems equal perhaps one-twelfth of her body of work. We have one complete poem (often called the "Hymn to Aphrodite"); the first three stanzas of another poem, with a garbled opening line of a fourth stanza ("That man appears the equal of the gods"); some fifteen or twenty badly damaged partial poems (the count depends on how one divides the manuscript lines); one verse of what is perhaps a folk song; and nearly two hundred fragments, some preserving a scatter of random words from several continuous lines, some only a word or two long. Yet even in ruins, Sappho teases the imagination. Her delicate, sensual, piercing words cry out to any classicist with the slightest pretensions to poetic ability. The yearning to reproduce them, to carry them across (the literal meaning of translate) into modern, spoken language, is almost irresistible. I know the works of other classical poets more intimately. I have taught Homer many times, both in Greek and in translation; I can recite long passages of Catullus from memory. But I have never felt a compulsion to re-create Homer or Catullus in English; ever since I first read a few lines of Sappho I wanted to translate her.

To read Sappho is to confront a series of mysteries and conundrums, eternally insoluble. In her voice and that of her contemporary Alcaeus, personal lyric springs full grown and shining from the void left by the decline of the epic. Without antecedent or rival, she stands alone—a woman in a fiercely patriarchal society, whose poetry was extravagantly praised even in fifth-century Athens, a bastion of male dominance if ever there was one, as among the greatest ever written in Greek. One of the most recognized figures from the ancient world (people who have never read a word of any classical author will often know that Socrates was executed, that Julius Caesar was murdered on the Ides of March, and that Sappho was a "Lesbian"), she retains among classicists an ability to inflame passions and to attract fanatical devotion, although we know almost nothing of her life. True, we have only a passing acquaintance with most ancient authors' lives, since biographies, when they were written at all, tended to be brief and stereotyped. But the details of Sappho's life are unusually opaque, and the little we think we know is continually disputed. Most books about her disguise how scanty our information is by including a brief summary along these lines: Sappho lived on the island of Lesbos, in the late seventh and early sixth centuries B.C.E. She was married to a man named Kerkylas, from Andros; she spent some time in exile in Sicily; she had a brother, Kharaxos, and a daughter, Kleïs; she ran some sort of school or ritual circle for young girls and wrote erotic poetry for some of them. Small, dark, and plain, she may have committed suicide by jumping from a cliff after an unhappy love affair with a man called Phaon.

Unfortunately, such a summary is based on thin air and wishful thinking, and almost every detail (including her sexual orientation) has been challenged. Sappho was from Lesbos and did live in the seventh-sixth century; that much we know. The rest of her biography depends on bits and pieces culled from various ancient authors (none of them her contemporaries), and mainly on the *Suda,* a Byzantine encyclopedia from the tenth century A.D.—sixteen centuries after Sappho's lifetime. The *Suda,* a compilation drawn from miscellaneous earlier sources, preserves traditions that probably date from Sappho's own day; but unfortunately, most of what it tells us about her is clearly gleaned from the poems themselves, and some details may well derive from Attic comedies in which Sappho was a character. (The supposed name of her husband, for instance, seems to be a bawdy pun.)* Because Sappho's surviving poems evoke personal experience with painfully intimate directness, we are easily seduced into embellishing the scraps of fact we own and reconstructing her life from her lyrics. This endeavor, however tempting, is dangerous at best and absurdly misleading at worst (fantastic images spring to mind of future biographers assembling the life of Tennyson from the first-person monologue "Ulysses").

We can recoil in despair from the impossible task of attempting a biography of Sappho; we can even assert that the details of her life have little or nothing to do with our appreciation of her poetry. But like the facts of Sappho's life, the poems rebuff our first eager approach, their damaged words reminding us how distant Sappho's Lesbos is. We can never hear these words and feel their power as a native speaker would. Still, Sappho's music echoes in other ancient authors' lavish praise: Socrates called her *kale,* "beautiful"; since tradition recorded that she was, in fact, plain, Maximius of Tyre hastens to add that the epithet reflects her poetry, not her person. Plato hailed her as "the tenth Muse," an accolade repeated like a mantra by other authors.

---

*The name "Kerkylas" appears nowhere else, and seems to be a made-up name based on *kerkos,* "penis"; Andros is a legitimate place name, but also means "of man." In short, we are asked to believe that the famous Lesbian poet was married to a man named, in Holt N. Parker's paraphrase, "Dick Allcock from the Isle of Man" ("Sappho Schoolmistress," *Transactions of the American Philological Association* 123 [1993]: 309).

Modern readers of classical Greek echo these judgments. In Sappho's language we encounter a blinding brightness that resists translation; her poems shimmer with newly forged compounds, agile and evocative words that dance lightly in Greek but stumble and turn clumsy in English (Aphrodite is *poikilothronos,* "on a many-colored throne"; Eros is *glukupikros,* "sweet-bitter/piercing"). Yet for the most part her vocabulary is simple. So is her subject matter: apples, groves, springs of clear water, altars, incense, garlands, roses, stars, lying alone at night, memories of absent loves. Hackneyed in English, these familiar topics are somehow lucent, magical, new, and unsentimental in Sappho's Greek. Trying to describe the quality of her language, translators fall back on comparable phrases. Jim Powell comments on "the spare, limpid, embarrassing directness of her sentences . . . the delightful music of her Greek . . . and the vivid tones of her poetic voice."* Mary Barnard cites "the music of her poetry . . . [and] the fresh colloquial directness of her speech"; Guy Davenport says she "spoke with Euclidean terseness and authority. . . . Her words are simple and piercing in their sincerity, her lines melodically keen, a music for girls' voices and dancing."** Music and plainness; directness and melody. All archaic lyric was written to be sung—or at least chanted—to the accompaniment of the lyre (hence "lyric"), but translators and critics do not consistently analyze the poetry of Alcaeus, for instance, in musical terms. It is Sappho's diction that inspires the metaphor of music, and here we touch the essence of her style. The words are plain, the concepts familiar; greatness lies in this poetry's "how," not in its "what." Take that "how" away, change the tongue, and what is left? Translating Sappho is like catching fireflies in a jar; once brought into the house, under the commonplace glare of electric light, their radiance fades and they quickly die.

At the heart of the translator's craft lies an enigma, an internal paradox. Translation's job is to bridge the gap between one language and another, but the greater the distance between languages, the more

---

*Powell, p. 41.

**Mary Barnard, *Sappho: A New Translation* (University of California Press, 1958), p. 102; Davenport, p. 5.

difficult translation becomes. An inflected language with extremely flexible word order, Greek is also highly economic; it may take an entire English phrase to convey the sense of a single Greek participle. If this distinction plagues even the translator of prose, imagine what a Promethean task it is to ignite English words with stolen sparks of Sappho's Greek fire.

If words are Sappho's fire, meter is their fuel. Greek meter is quantitative, not stress-based, but because ancient Greek had pitch accent as well as quantitative rhythm, the poetry involves a complex counterpoint of length-based meter and pitch-accent "melody" in which the accented syllables may be either long or short. English speakers find such an interplay of length and pitch notoriously difficult to reproduce in speech (as anyone who has ever struggled to learn to read Greek aloud can attest), although we manage the same thing in music with little difficulty.

Sappho controls these highly structured and complex meters, foreign in every sense of the word to English poetry, with such flawless skill that words and meter seem to flow inevitably into and from one another. She wrote in various meters; the most characteristic of these—the one that came to be called "Sapphic"—molds the "Hymn to Aphrodite," her sole complete poem. This meter consists of a basic stanza, made up of three long lines and one short one. The pattern is this (– indicates a long syllable, ◡ indicates a short syllable, and × indicates an anceps, a syllable that can be either long or short):

$$- \, ◡ \, - \, × \, - \, ◡ \, ◡ \, - \, ◡ \, - \, - \quad \text{(repeated three times)}$$
$$- \, ◡ \, ◡ \, - \, -$$

The basic unit of this meter, the sound chime around which the lines are built, is the choriamb, a trochee followed by an iamb: $- \, ◡ \, ◡ \, -$. The natural pitch accent of the words forms the melody against the rhythmic background of long and short syllables. Let's try reading the first stanza of the "Hymn to Aphrodite" aloud in the following transliteration. Long syllables are underlined, accented syllables indicated with an acute accent. Read this as though it were music. Give each long syllable two beats, each short syllable one beat, and pronounce each stressed syllable at a pitch one-third above the unstressed syllables. Vowels can be pronounced more or less as in Spanish or Italian.

> P<u>oi</u>- ki- <u>ló</u>- thron' <u>a</u>- tha- nát' <u>A</u>- phró- <u>di</u>- ta
> P<u>aí</u> dí- <u>os</u> do- <u>ló</u>- plo- ke, l<u>ís</u>- so- <u>maí</u> <u>se</u>
> mé m'á- <u>sai</u>- si <u>med</u>' o- ní- <u>ai</u>- si <u>dám</u>- na
> <u>pót</u>- ni- a, <u>thú</u>- mon

Even so crude a demonstration as this illustrates some of the thorny problems in Sapphic meter and Sapphic style. The pitch accent is clearly not the same thing as the length-based meter; the accent moves about in the line, counterpointing and playing against the meter. Quite aside from the music of interlacing length and stress, the stanza is filled with alliteration and assonance—look at the p's/ph's, the t's/th's,* the l's, the d's, the m's, the a's. A translator cannot catch half of these elements and still retain anything of the sense. Yet here sound and sense are linked so strongly that to omit either is to falsify the translation.

Before looking at four different translations of this poem, I offer a purely literal, prose rendering of its content:

> Immortal Aphrodite on a many-colored throne, child of Zeus, weaver of tricks, I pray you; don't burden my spirit, powerful lady, with troubles or sorrows, but come here, if ever before you heard my cries and listened from afar, and having left your father's golden house you yoked your (golden) chariot and came, and beautiful swift sparrows led you over the black earth beating their thick wings from the sky through the middle of the air, and suddenly they arrived; and you, oh holy one, smiled with your immortal face and asked what I suffered this time, and why I called this time, and what, in my maddened mind, I most wanted to happen for me: "Whom should I persuade to lead you back into her love this time? Who is treating you unfairly, Sappho? For even if she flees, she will quickly pursue; if she doesn't accept gifts, yet she'll give them; and

---

*Aeolic—the dialect in which Sappho wrote—did not distinguish in pronunciation between aspirated (ph, th) and unaspirated (p, t) consonants.

if she doesn't love, she will quickly love even though unwilling." Come to me even now, and free me from this bitter yearning, and whatever my heart wants accomplished, accomplish it; and you yourself be my fellow fighter.

Although very literal, this translation begs many questions. For example, the Greek leaves ambiguous whether the adjective "golden" modifies Zeus's palace or Aphrodite's chariot; the line "Whom indeed should I persuade to lead you back into her love?" is corrupt, and may refer to the personified goddess Persuasion; and in a subtle effect that cannot be captured in English, the sex of the beloved is indicated only once in the Greek, in the participle *etheloisa*, "willing," that ends Aphrodite's speech. (Some nineteenth-century editors, uncomfortable with the implication that Sappho was yearning for the love of another woman, suggested emending the participle to read *etheloisan*, which would then modify Sappho as the understood object of the verb: The beloved will soon love you even if you are unwilling.)

The poem is seven stanzas long—twenty-eight lines. Perhaps the most stunning thing about it is how it leaps off the page at the reader, pulled along by its own syntax and rhythms as swiftly as Aphrodite's chariot by her sparrows. The first six stanzas are, in fact, one long sentence, incorporating a direct quote of the goddess Aphrodite's words to Sappho; the final stanza, which resumes Sappho's prayer, is a separate sentence. Any attempt to preserve the word order of this poem in English disintegrates into gibberish. The actual order of words in the last stanza, for instance, is "Come to me even now, bitter and free from yearning, whatever and for me to accomplish heart wants, accomplish; you and yourself fellow fighter be."

Drawing attention to the word order here is not mere pedantry; it was particularly noted by Dionysius of Halicarnassus, who rescued the "Hymn to Aphrodite" from oblivion by quoting it in his essay "Literary Composition" as an example of "polished, brilliant" style. "The verbal beauty and charm of this passage," Dionysius said, "come about from the continuity and smoothness of the joinings. For the words follow upon one another and are interwoven according to certain natural affinities and groupings of the letters."

So much for mechanical details. No less difficult to keep alive in translation is the tone of the poem. In Aphrodite's epiphany, the divinity's own lighthearted, companionable banter counterpoints the worshiper's awe of and reverence for the goddess' power. Sappho's Aphrodite is both a terrifying, powerful force that rushes down from Olympus at dizzying speed and an amused, teasing goddess who laughs at her devotee's frequent love affairs. This blend of piety and playfulness appears in other Greek poetry (for instance, in the "Homeric Hymn to Aphrodite"), but nowhere are the two so marked and so inextricably linked as in this poem.

The ideal translator, then, would juggle meaning and metrics, sound and sense, to produce an English poem with something of the original's speed, lightness, aura, and beauty. Sacrifice any one of these elements, and you lose Sappho's poem; poetry you may still have, but it will not be Sappho's. The intractable nature of these problems becomes obvious when we compare translations of this poem. The translator must first decide whether to approximate the original meter. There are probably as many views about how to handle meter in translation as there are living translators; the choices range from ignoring the meter entirely to trying to reproduce it exactly. To translate Sappho into prose is a counsel of despair, and no serious poet would resort to it, but what type of English verse might serve? The Sapphic meter presents a stumbling block*; some translators opt for a more natural English rhythm, rather than forcing our language into a pattern that can sound jingly. Taken to its extreme, this approach yields:

> Dapple-throned Aphrodite,
> eternal daughter of God,
> snare-knitter! Don't, I beg you,
>
> cow my heart with grief! Come,
> as once when you heard my far-
> off cry and, listening, stepped

---

*As I can attest from personal experience, having once done a metrical translation of this poem.

from your father's house to your
gold car, to yoke the pair whose
beautiful thick-feathered wings

oaring down from mid-air from heaven
carried you to light swiftly
on dark earth; then, blissful one,

smiling your immortal smile
you asked, What ailed me now that
made me call you again? What

was it that my distracted
heart most wanted? "Whom has
Persuasion to bring round now

"to your love? Who, Sappho, is
unfair to you? For, let her
run, she will soon run after;

"if she won't accept gifts, she
will one day give them; and if
she won't love you—she soon will
"love, although unwillingly . . ."
If ever—come now! Relieve
this intolerable pain!

What my heart most hopes will
happen, make happen; you yourself join forces on my side!

(Mary Barnard)*

*Barnard, n.p. no. 38.

To adapt Bentley's famous criticism of Pope's *Iliad,* "It is a very pretty poem, but you must not call it Sappho." Barnard keeps Sappho's simplicity of diction, but when the poem is stripped of her characteristic meter, the shape of her stanzas, her alliteration and assonance, what remains is an impression or a paraphrase of content, with no trace of Sappho's unique style. And Sappho's poetry does not consist (*pace* Dudley Fitts in his introduction to Barnard's translation) only in spare, plain words, "stripped and hard, awkward with the fine awkwardness of truth."* To translate her in such a manner is as deceptive as to drown her in Victorian sweetness. The essential Sapphic combination of sharp-edged, jewel-like words and intricate rhythmic patterns is missing; Barnard's stanzas, with their three repetitive lines of seven syllables and three or four stresses, are completely misleading. The successful translator must somehow yoke together a plain diction and an instinct for the *mot juste* to rival Frost's with meters as exact and complicated as Swinburne's. An impossible task? It may well be, but the attempt can be made:

> Rich-throned immortal Aphrodite,
> scheming daughter of Zeus, I pray you
> with pain and sickness, Queen, crush not my heart,
>
> but come, if ever in the past you
> heard my voice from afar and hearkened,
> and left your father's hall and came, with gold
>
> chariot yoked; and pretty sparrows
> brought you swiftly across the dark earth
> fluttering wings from heaven through the air.
>
> Soon they were here, and you, Blest Goddess,
> smiling with your immortal features,
> asked why I'd called, what was the matter now,

---

*Barnard, p. ix.

what was my heart insanely craving:
"Who is it this time I must cozen
to love you, Sappho? Who's unfair to you?

For though she flee, soon she'll be chasing;
though she refuse gifts, she'll be giving;
though she love not, she'll love despite herself."

Yes, come once more, from sore obsession
free me; all that my heart desires
fulfilled, fulfil—help me to victory!

(M. L. West)*

Clearly, this is not Sapphic meter. But it manages to retain some sense of the choriamb as the underlying unit of the verse; such phrases as "voíce from afár" and "thoúgh she refúse" successfully transpose Sappho's meter into English stress patterns. The three-line stanza, with the third line proportionately longer, reflects scholars' uncertainty about how Sappho actually divided the lines of her stanza; she may have originally conceived them as two repetitions of the basic line followed by a third line with an additional – ‿ ‿ – – grafted onto it. West does not ignore the Sapphic meter, nor does he try to reproduce it exactly in English. His is the middle way.

Next, Guy Davenport:

Aphródita dressed in an embroidery of flowers
Never to die, the daughter of God,
Untangle from longing and perplexities,
O Lady, my heart.

But come down to me, as you came before,
For if ever I cried, and you heard and came,

---

*M. L. West, *Greek Lyric Poetry* (Clarendon Press, 1993), p. 36.

Come now, of all times, leaving
Your father's golden house

In that chariot pulled by sparrows reined and bitted,
Swift in their flying, a quick blur aquiver,
Beautiful, high. They drew you across steep air
Down to the black earth;

Fast they came, and you behind them, O
Hilarious heart, your face all laughter,
Asking, What troubles you this time, why again
Do you call me down?

Asking, In your wild heart, who now
Must you have? Who is she that persuasion
Fetch her, enlist her, and put her into bounden love?
Sappho, who does you wrong?

If she balks, I promise, soon she'll chase,
If she's turned from gifts, now she'll give them.
And if she does not love you, she will love,
Helpless, she will love.
Come then, loose me from cruelties.
Give my tethered heart its full desire.
Fulfill, and come, lock your shield with mine
Throughout the siege.*

This meter is far less regular than West's; the numbers of syllables and stresses per line vary, and the patterns change constantly. But although Davenport misses the uniformity of the Sapphic meter, he does reproduce its complexity. He also excels at approximating the *sounds* of Sappho's poem. If his patterns of alliteration do not match Sappho's exactly, they echo them clearly; examples are the f and d sounds of "Aphródita dressed in an embroidery of flowers / Never to die, the

---

*Davenport, pp. 69–70.

daughter of God," and later the fine "quick blur aquiver" to render the "beating thick wings" of Aphrodite's sparrows. Though much less literal than West in expressing the poem's content, Davenport brilliantly conveys the feel of the Greek. Some word choices, however, grate on my ear. "God," in line two, although useful for its final d, is unfortunate as a translation of Zeus. The capitalized word "God" suggests, unwisely, monotheism, completely misplaced in this poem. In stanza four, "hilarious" does not perform its job because for us it means "extremely funny, laughable," where what is needed is a word to indicate that *Aphrodite* is laughing (or actually, smiling). Davenport picks up this idea in his excellent next phrase, "your face all laughter." Why, then, does he add a heart that is "hilarious," and omit that the face is deathless? Elsewhere, too, he neglects crucial words and inserts others not in the Greek. In the first two lines, for instance, the epithet *doloploke,* "wile-weaver," is missing. Though this word chimes in "untangle," in line three, still I feel a loss. We need to know that because Aphrodite is the goddess who weaves schemes and entangles her devotees in plots, Sappho is asking her not to do so this time; we should not think that Sappho has gotten herself enmeshed and is asking the goddess to extricate her.

These reservations aside, Davenport has a rare gift for filling out a single Greek word into an English phrase and thereby glossing the meaning of the Greek. Consider the last two lines of the poem. The Greek says, "you yourself be my *summachos,*" a word that means "fellow fighter," "comrade-in-arms." Davenport expands this simple phrase into "lock your shield with mine / throughout the siege," and opens up to the Greekless reader the whole image (implicit in *summachos*) of the phalanx, the battle formation in which comrades stood shoulder to shoulder and shield to shield. This is nonliteral translation at its best.

Finally, Jim Powell confronts head-on the Herculean task of preserving the meter, and grapples with it valiantly. Realizing that the Greek interplay of length and stress is impossible to mimic, he substitutes English stress for Greek length:

> Artfully adorned Aphrodite, deathless
> child of Zeus and weaver of wiles, I beg you
> please don't hurt me, don't overcome my spirit,
>   goddess, with longing,

but come here, if ever at other moments
hearing these my words from afar you listened
and responded: leaving your father's house, all
    golden, you came then,

hitching up your chariot: lovely sparrows
drew you quickly over the dark earth, whirling
on fine beating wings from the heights of heaven
    down through the sky and

instantly arrived—and then O my blessed
goddess with a smile on your deathless face you
asked me what the matter was *this* time, what I
    called you for this time,

what I now most wanted to happen in my
raving heart: "Whom *this* time should I persuade to
lead you back again to her love? Who now, oh
    Sappho, who wrongs you?

If she flees you now, she will soon pursue you;
if she won't accept what you give, she'll give it;
if she doesn't love you, she'll love you soon now,
    even unwilling."

Come to me again, and release me from this
want past bearing. All that my heart desires to
happen—make it happen. And stand beside me,
    goddess, my ally.*

In meter, sound, and meaning, this is a remarkably faithful translation. The punctuation reflects the syntax of the original (the first six stanzas are again all one sentence); Powell adds little "padding"; and his choice of words is mostly felicitous. Only occasionally do the difficulties

---

*Powell, pp. 3–4.

involved in matching English words to Sapphic meter intrude, as in the awkward, archaic phrase "these my words," in the second line of the second stanza. Overall, however, Powell's translation balances fidelity to the original meter, words, and style with natural-sounding English.

Which of these styles of translation succeeds best as a poem *in English* is finally a matter of personal taste. Had I no knowledge at all of Sappho or of Greek lyric meter, I would prefer Davenport's translation to the other three. But a large part of the translator's art lies in remembering that these are not original poems, free to reflect the translator's own style and preferences. Translation's priority is to convey the flavor of the original's style to those who cannot directly taste it. This Powell has done more successfully than Davenport, West, and Barnard. I prefer Davenport as a poet; I prefer Powell as a translator.*

If the problems of translation are frustrating in the complete and nearly complete poems, they cause despair when one turns to the fragments. Some true fragments are scraps of papyrus that yield only a few random words. Many others survived because grammarians and lexicographers quoted them as interesting items of vocabulary. Tantalizing in the true sense of that word, they brush across the consciousness like the fruit trees over Tantalus' head and then flit away before they can be grasped, phantom images of a beauty that spans twenty-five hundred years yet is irrevocably lost. Davenport has set out to translate *all* the fragments, and his renditions are painfully faithful. Look, for instance, at a relatively lengthy fragment—

>]above[
>]you shall remember[
>]in our girlhood[
>]we made[
>]for and[
>]the town-[
> [*several lines gone*]

---

*Occasionally Davenport includes two very different translations of the same poem; they are such fascinating commentaries on the difficulties and treacheries of the translator's art that I would have liked more of them.

```
]facing[
[                    ]
]endurance[
        ]man[
[                    ]
    ]all[*
```

—which bears an almost uncanny resemblance to certain kinds of modern poetry. Pound's "Papyrus," for instance, plays on this similarity:

```
Spring . . . . . .
Too late . . . . . .
Gongula . . . . . .**
```

More recently, Olga Broumas and T Begley have designed their poems to mimic Sapphic fragments. In their lack of punctuation and their spatial arrangements, poems such as

> within two days walk to flower
> alone wash off his blood wash off his young
> leaf spray

or

> Desert silence
> who must constantly beat her wings***

look strikingly Sapphic. Other poetic traditions also recall the fragments; a graduate student remarked to me that they "read like haiku." False

---

*Davenport, p. 110.

**Ezra Pound, *Personae: The Collected Shorter Poems of Ezra Pound* (New Directions, 1971), p. 112. This famous little poem is, in fact, probably a *mis*translation of three lines from Sappho (fragment Diehl 97).

***Olga Broumas and T Begley, *Sappho's Gymnasium* (Copper Canyon Press, 1994), pp. 29, 72.

likenesses, dangerous analogies: Sappho did not place these ambiguous words in ragged lines. Chance or time or fate did that; the fragments are not the poems. But they are what we have, and at least in the fragment cited above, we can grasp some lingering residue of the poem's overall subject: a lament for lost girlhood, perhaps a regret (reading more into the meager words) that girls must submit to husbands, that marriage must be endured. If these words have not withstood erosion, neither have they disappeared.

But what are we to make, in translation, of such fragments as "Of the Muses," Davenport's translation of the single Greek word *Moisaon*.* The word has reached us only because an anonymous grammarian once picked it to illustrate noun formation in Aeolic, the dialect of Sappho's poetry. This is slight material even for the Greek scholar, but at least when I glance at such Sapphic words in Greek, my eye and mind are caught momentarily by their difference from the familiar forms of the more common dialects, and I can for an instant sense the strangeness, the distance, of Lesbos and of Sappho. The single word, like an image seen through the wrong end of a telescope, is bright and clear-cut, but utterly remote. How convey such remoteness in translation? In so short a fragment, the only way would be through differences of spelling, and of pronunciation if the words are read aloud. Any difference of spelling, however, will look bogus and creaky (Of ye Muses), while any attempt to reflect the Lesbian spelling results in incomprehensibility (Of the Moisas).

Davenport very wisely makes no attempt to preserve the dialect difference. But without it, why include the word at all? It is a fragment of Sappho, true; yet it tells us little. Some one-word fragments give us our only hint of lost poems; the name "Medeia," in its stark solitude, witnesses that Sappho once told Medea's story, a thought that fires the imagination. But "Of the Muses" adds nothing to our knowledge of Sappho's subject matter, since we already know from other poems that she wrote about the Muses (it would be extraordinary for a seventh-century B.C.E. Greek poet never to mention them). We have no sword to

---

*Davenport, p. 109.

cut this Gordian knot. Any translator of Sappho who ventures beyond the "Hymn to Aphrodite" must grapple with fragmentary material. Most choose to ignore the smallest fragments; Powell, according to the dust-jacket blurb, translates all the "poems and fragments that make consecutive sense" and "arranges them into a collage or mosaic, allowing the briefer fragments to create contexts for each other." Undoubtedly this contributes to the readability of the English poetry; it is delusive, though, since it imposes a unity not present in the shards of Sappho's work. The fragments' challenge yields no easy victory. To translate all or to pick and choose among them—either course distorts. The smallest fragments remain, in a fundamentally implacable sense, opaque to another language. They beguile like music from a farther room; open the door and they fade into silence.

Still, it is exactly this aspect of Sappho's work, the fragments speaking from a void of irrecoverable loss, that seduces so many readers. In ruins, Sappho's work provides a Rorschach test for the reader, particularly for the Greekless reader. Who knows what these poems originally said? Each reader can fill in almost anything and claim that it "is" Sappho. Shattered by the passage of time, Sappho's fragments not only allow but almost require the individual reader to repair them.

And so we end with the same paradoxes with which we began: lost works that still compel; silences that speak across the centuries; a small, plain woman from an obscure island who is hailed as the beautiful one, the tenth Muse. No thread of Ariadne leads us out of this labyrinth. Our only clues are the remaining words themselves, *glukupikron* in a sense that Sappho could never have foreseen.

> Some say thronging cavalry, some say foot soldiers,
> others call a fleet the most beautiful of
>
> sights the dark earth offers, but I say it's what-
> ever you love best.*

ELIZABETH VANDIVER

---

*Powell, p. 28.

In a Greek Village a Blood-Spotted Sheet

In a Greek village a blood-spotted sheet
hanging from a newlyweds' window
proclaims a ruptured hymen, though
often it's only a splash of red wine.

That's all right. The real task is to subvert
the hypocrisy of a place and time (Me,
I had to give up being a glutton
of glossy pages that reeked of cologne

to discover the moles and yum-yum odors
of my beloved). Years from now, you newlyweds
may look closely at your ballyhooed stain
and so transform its meaning. Let it be

the crucial mark on a treasure map:
the spot where you became conspirators,
buddies in falsehood, so happy you could burst.
Look. Truth is small and between two people.

ROGER FANNING

One Hand Clapping

Blaise Cendrars. *Complete Poems.* Translated by Ron Padgett. University of California Press 1992. 422 pp. $45.00

After you have taken in the battered old boxer's mug and the inevitable Gauloise glued to the lower lip, the thing you most notice about Blaise Cendrars in the old photos is his missing hand. The left hand writes, smokes, drinks, eats; but from above the elbow down, the right arm just hangs there, all sleeve.

Cendrars lost his right hand to a mortar shell at the Ferme Navarin in 1915. As he would later describe it, part of him lay there by his side, "planted in the grass like a great spreading flower, a red lily, a human arm streaming with blood, a right arm severed above the elbow, its hand, still alive, digging its fingers into the soil as if to take root."[1] From the killing fields of the Marne, the hand then rose up into the sky to become the constellation Orion:

> It's my star
> It's in the form of a hand
> It's my hand gone up into the sky
> During the entire war I saw Orion through a lookout slit
> When the zeppelins came to bomb Paris they always came from
> Orion
> I have it above my head today
> The main mast pierces the palm of that hand which must hurt
> As my amputated hand hurts me pierced as it is by a continual
> stabbing pain

This is one of the *Travel Notes* Cendrars jotted down as he crossed the Equator en route to São Paulo in 1924—and it reads just as flatly in the original French as it does in Ron Padgett's English. The zeppelins over Paris and the dazed camera eye of the *poilu* looking out of the aperture of his loophole are, by the early twenties, fairly standard-issue modernism. But the mythopoeia at work in these lines might be Dante's: A pilgrim poet looks to the heavens and sees the entire cosmos transformed into a vast projection of the martyred body of Jesus. The vision telescopes the carnage of war, the mast-pierced palm of the warrior Orion, and his own missing hand, a sidereal Christ nailed to the firmament like a pulse-star of pain.

In an uncanny coincidence, Cendrars' hand was blown off the very day Remy de Gourmont died. Influential editor of the *Mercure de France,* polymath novelist, poet, and critic, Gourmont was the Roland Barthes of the prewar avant-garde, a figure whom Cendrars so idolized that he actually signed some of his own early manuscripts with the master's name. With his spiritual father now gone, Cendrars-the-son, orphaned, maimed to the core, also undergoes a symbolic death. Switching from the right hand to the left, having literally to learn to write all over again, he will compose almost no more poetry after 1915—indeed, if we are to believe his own carefully forged hagiography, he will abandon Literature altogether, choosing instead the career of a latter-day Rimbaud or Dada saint. Though he will continue to publish enormously over the following half century (his collected works come to eight hefty tomes in the standard French edition), what he writes with his left hand no longer strictly matters: After the mortar shell, all his works are posthumous, ghostwritten by a phantom limb. One of his last poems runs: "Je suis l'homme qui n'a plus de passé. —Seul mon moignon me fait mal." I'm the man who no longer has a past. Only my stump aches.

The ache is already there in Cendrars' very first poem, *Les Pâques à New-York,* published in 1912—the same year as Apollinaire's *Zone.* Compared to Apollinaire's exuberant, kaleidoscopic collage of modernity, Cendrars' poem, inspired by the incantatory cadences of Gourmont's *Latin mystique,* scans more like the coarse gougings of a medieval woodcut, its blocky alexandrines thudding down the page. Padgett's translation catches the rhythm beautifully:

> The apartment windows are filled with blood
> And the women behind them are like flowers of blood,
>
> Orchids, strange, bad, withered blooms,
> Chalices inverted underneath your wounds.

> They never drank of your blood collected there.
> They have red on their lips, and lacy underwear.

The violent juxtaposition of the Savior's sacrificial blood with the menstrual effluvia of the modern world is typical of the poem's rather lurid expressionistic effects. Whereas *Zone* is closer to the futurist experiments of a Boccioni, Severini, or Balla, Cendrars' agonistic litany of Easter in New York—down to the very frontispiece he designed for it, which depicts a man bent over, holding his crotch—is pure Kollwitz, Kokoschka, or Schiele.

Cendrars' residences in Russia and his bilingual Bernese background make him one of the few intermediaries between the modernisms of Mitteleuropa (notably, the Blaue Reiter school) and the Parisian avant-garde; *Easter in New York,* significantly enough, was first published in a Franco-German anarchist review printed in Paris. He is, for example, probably the only French poet of his period to know all of Rilke's work by heart in the original. A key image from the latter's *Malte Laurids Brigge,* published in 1911, is adapted by Cendrars to express the utter facelessness of New York:

> Lord, make my face, buried in my hands,
> Leave there its agonizing mask.
>
> Lord, don't let my two hands, pressed here
> Against my lips, lick the foam of wild despair.

In an inspired feat of translation, Padgett manages to capture Cendrars' expressionistic *Menschheitsdämmerung* by transposing it into the more familiar idiom of the early Eliot:

> In the night the street is like a gash
> Filled with gold and blood, fire and trash.

Or this couplet, which reads like something Pound might have slashed from the manuscript of *The Waste Land:*

Lord, the humble women who were with you at Golgotha
Are hidden, in filthy backrooms, on obscene sofas.

Unreal city, indeed.

Easter in New York was the *Howl* of its generation. Written while Cendrars was down and out in New York, living the life of a dharma bum, its hallucinatory catalogue of Lower East Side immigrants, skid row drunks, and assorted spiritual and sexual cripples is one slow scream of pain. The theology of the poem (a further link to the German expressionists and the American Beats) is darkly gnostic, dismissing as it does the entire incarnate world as an obscene, female simulacrum of the Creation. If there is redemption, it lies only in the suffering body of the crucified Christ—a body, however, that is no longer (or not yet) ready to rise:

Lord, cold as a shroud the dawn slipped away
And left the skyscapers naked in the day.

Easter in New York concludes with a vision of failed resurrection in the New World; the harrowing night of the soul it records, however, at least allowed its author to be reborn. Sloughing off his previous identity as the Swiss Freddy Sauser, the poet for the first time signs his work "Blaise Cendrars"—a man on fire (*braise*), determined to reduce the world to cinders (*cendres*) through the flame of his art (*ars*).

Nineteen thirteen is Cendrars' *annus mirabilis*. Returning to Paris, he is quickly caught up in the vortex of the avant-garde. He meets Apollinaire and Jacob, but his closest imaginative commerce is with painters: Léger, Chagall, Modigliani, Soutine, Robert and Sonia Delaunay. With the last, he collaborates on his first great *simultanéiste* work, *Prose du Transsibérien*, an object half-painting, half-book: Cendrars' poem runs down the right hand of the two-meter sheet, while Sonia Delaunay's swirls of color occupy the left, now and then spilling over into the typographical indentions of the text. One hundred and fifty copies were printed; folded like a pleated map, the sheets came to the size of an average paperback—stood end to end, however, they equaled the height of the Eiffel Tower. Modern editions of the text, of course, cannot convey the full optic and semiotic complexity of this publishing event.[2] Following in the footsteps of Mallarmés' "Un coup de dés" and anticipating the experiments of Apollinaire's *Calligrammes,* Cendrars scores the page, using a range of typefaces and blocks of print to syncopate his epic (and purely imaginary) journey through Russia on the Transsiberian Express. A similar attention to the graphic lie of print on page informs his other great poem of 1913, *Panama* (not published until 1918). Designed by Cendrars and executed by Raoul Dufy, the book's folded format imitates a steamship schedule or railway timetable, its cover emblazoned with a logo that parodies the trademark emblem of the Union Pacific Railroad. The stanza breaks within the body of the poem are in turn filled with maps of train routes in the American West—vectors of verse visually rhymed with the branching trunk lines of modern transportation.

Despite their cinematographic appeal to the reader's eye, these are also very much poems about new ways of hearing. Nineteen thirteen is, after all, the year of Stravinsky's *Rite of Spring* and *The Prose of the Transsiberian* is accordingly "dedicated to musicians" (later, in the early twenties, Cendrars will work with Darius Milhaud on his jazzy *Création du monde*). The very "Prose" of the title gestures toward music—specifically the Latin *prosa* of medieval Gregorian chant that Cendrars (like Pound) discovered in the elastic rhythmic units of Gourmont's *Latin mystique,* a prose both colloquial and liturgical, a cadence to be at once spoken and droned.[3] This particular fusion of the hieratic and the vernacular is perhaps the most difficult thing to translate—and for the most part it eludes Padgett's ear, attuned as it is to the deadpan diction of the New York School. Here are the opening lines of his *Prose of the Transsiberian:*

> Back then I was still young
> I was barely sixteen but my childhood memories were gone
> I was 48,000 miles away from where I was born

Compare Dos Passos' version: "I was a youngster in those days," where, right off the bat, we feel ourselves in the presence of a great spinner of yarns; "Hardly sixteen and already I couldn't remember my childhood," which retains the original's clunky copula, smoothed out by Padgett's adversative "but," and "I was sixteen thousand leagues away from the place I was born," whose register is appropriately epic, involving distances measured in mythical leagues, not in Padgett's American miles.

Translating the *Transsibérian* and *Panama* in 1931, Dos Passos of course came to his task with certain advantages: Cendrars was a personal acquaintance whose poetics of montage had already influenced the jump cuts of his own *Orient Express* and the "Newsreel" and "Camera Eye" sections of *The 42nd Parallel*.[4] Although his versions are often slapdash and their slang now somewhat dated—their lexicon includes words like "flappers," "hornswaggled," "jack" (for money), and "on the bum"— they at least manage to register something of Cendrars' characteristic voice: "J'ai été libertin et je me suis permis toutes les privautés avec le monde." With his trained novelist's ear, Dos Passos catches the precise inflection of wounded swagger: "I've done what I damn pleased I've taken all sorts of liberties with the world." Padgett, by contrast, chooses to remain more literal, but in the process misreads the French "libertin" as a false friend of the English "libertine," producing the awkward repetition of "I've been a libertine and have taken every liberty with the world"—a line one cannot imagine anyone possibly *saying*. Or take this famous phrase from *Panama:* "Je tourne dans la cage des méridiens comme un écureuil dans la sienne"—where the subtle internal off-rhyme established at the median caesura ("méridiens" / "sienne") reproduces the futile rotation of a mind trapped on its own treadmill. Padgett merely sight-reads the original, giving us the stunted line: "I go round in the cage of meridians like a squirrel in his," whereas Dos Passos conveys the frenzy of immobility: "I go round and round inside the meridians like a squirrel in a squirrelcage."

If Dos Passos' ear is almost always superior to Padgett's, it is because he has actually experienced the acoustic universe of the great international express trains:

> Women brushing past
> Hiss of steam
> And the eternal rack of crazy wheels in the ruts of the sky.

Padgett is more bloated:

> Swishing of women
> And the whistle blowing
> And the eternal sound of wheels wildly rolling along ruts in the sky.

A veteran of the Great War like Cendrars, Dos Passos also knows the precise shadings of military jargon. His Captain Dreyfus, for example, is "reduced to the ranks before the army," whereas Padgett's, "stripped in front of the army," is actually forced to publicly unclothe. Furthermore, Dos Passos has lived through the dawn of aviation: When, toward the end of *Panama,* Cendrars dreams of participating in a "rallye aérien," he perfectly renders the period feel with "Air Circus" (as opposed to Padgett's blander "airplane races"). The original French is deceptively simple:

> La voie lactée autour du cou
> Les deux hémisphères sur les yeux
> A toute vitesse
> Il n'y a plus de pannes

Padgett's version is entirely correct, but, as usual, overcautious:

> The Milky Way around my neck
> The two hemispheres on my eyes
> At top speed
> There are no more breakdowns

Dos Passos gives the last two lines as "Full speed ahead / Never stall again," at least capturing something about the flight of early airplanes. And his first two lines miraculously improve upon the original, sharpening the image of the pilot as an astral Icarus, transmogrified by ascension:

> With the Milky Way around my neck
> And the two hemispheres for goggles

The Prose of the Transsibérian is a narrative about the distintegration of narratives, a modernist *Childe Harold's Pilgrimage* whose fast-forward imagery culminates in a vision of holocaust at Port Arthur before looping back (somewhat cornily) to the Eiffel Tower and the arms of Jeanne, the brave little Paris whore. *Panama, or The Adventures of My Seven Uncles* in turn deploys a dazzling array of plots and location shots—less to map the modern world in all its photogenic variety than to erase it, to denounce it as a Big Lie. (Despite his advanced poetic techniques, Cendrars remains very much the fin-de-siècle student of Schopenhauer, Nietzsche, and Mallarmé.) Leaving these experiments with cinematographic epic behind, he now turns, in late 1913 and 1914, to the dismantling of lyric in a series of texts later collected as *19 Elastic Poems.*

Padgett on the whole does very well with this collection, perhaps because it so explicitly anticipates the repertoire of the New York School, particularly the knowing in-jokes about the art world ("The Weather Bureau is forecasting bad weather / There is no futurism"; "Art criticism is as idiotic as Esperanto"; "Simultaneism is old hat"). The language of these texts, originally published in such avant-garde magazines as *Les Soirées de Paris, Der Sturm, De Stijl, Cabaret Voltaire,* and *Littérature,* reads like a cross between the culled snippets of Apollinaire's "conversation poems" and the cut-ups of Tzara. Cendrars himself referred to them as "poèmes de circonstance," underscoring the deliberate casualness of their occasion—browsing through a newspaper, having a drink in a café, chatting with a fellow poet, looking out a window, having one's portrait painted. Their idiom is supple enough to explore the smallest, most prosaic incidents of daily life and then to compact these anecdotes into a private, often gnomic shorthand.[5] Though they still gesture toward narrative, most of these poems take the form of lists—as in this stroboscopic record of a visit to Chagall's studio, dated October 1913:

> Cossacks Christ a shattered sun
> Roofs
> Sleepwalkers goats
> A lycanthrope
> Pétrus Borel
> Madness winter
> A genius split like a peach
> Lautréamont
> Chagall
> Poor kid next to my wife

> Morose delectation
> The shoes are down at heel
> An old jar full of chocolate
> A lamp that's split in two
> And my drunkenness when I go see him

The "I" who makes his appearance here is no longer, strictly speaking, a lyric subject. Recording his drunkenness as he would any other random stimulus or association, he has become an impersonal seismograph of the self (Rimbaud's "Je est un autre"). His job, in short, is no longer to express the world but merely to document it, to inventory it, to place it within quotations, as in the following "News Flash":

> OKLAHOMA, January 20, 1914
> Three convicts get hold of revolvers
> They kill their guard and grab the prison keys
> They come running out of their cells and kill four guards in the
>   yard
> Then they grab the young prison secretary
> And get into a carriage waiting for them at the gate
> They leave at top speed
> While guards fire their revolvers in the direction of the fugitives

This rapid-fire narrative reads like the shooting script for one of Mack Sennett's manic two-reelers. Cendrars copied it out of the morning newspaper. It is said to be the first found poem in French, the literary equivalent of the ready-mades Duchamp had exhibited at the Armory Show the previous year. Well before Dada, Cendrars is trying to find a way out of Poetry once and for all.

Although he continues to compose a few scattered poems after his amputation, the *Elastic Poems* of 1913–1914 announces Cendrars' crossover into left-handed prose, or a genre that might be best labeled anti- or post-poetry. After a hiatus of ten years, he returns to the lineations of verse in a series of texts jotted down over the course of 1924 and published in book form under the titles *Kodak* and *Feuilles de route;* under the threat of a trademark infringement suit from the Eastman Company, however, the title of the former was changed to *Documentaires.* This legal contretemps, coincidentally enough, underscores the (postmodernist) strategies of reappropriation at work throughout the volume. As its title suggests, *Kodak* displays the world in the age of mechanical reproduction as a snapshot album or a medley of souvenir postcards. As it moves out from Manhattan into the great American vastness, the camera pans down the Mississippi, up to Canada and Alaska, then across the Pacific into Asia and Africa—an entirely imaginary tracking shot, for Cendrars never visited any of the landscapes he photographically documents with such precision. Nor can he really be said to be the owner or originator of the texts gathered in the volume, for virtually every word has been cut and pasted from the adventure stories of the minor French popular novelist Gustave Le Rouge (bearing out T. S. Eliot's dictum that bad poets borrow but good poets steal). Cendrars' samplings from Le Rouge's novels are exactly contemporary with the archival montage techniques of Pound's "Malatesta Cantos," but whereas Pound, working as a historian, still believes in the recoverable truth inherent in fact, Cendrars' documentary footage functions more ironically, reminding us that the world is mere representation (Schopenhauer again), that all reality has now become as virtual as his missing hand.

Padgett's translations of *Kodak* and *Travel Notes* are among his finest achievements. Far more relaxed than Monique Chefdor's previous renderings of these same texts,[6] Padgett's versions actually manage to invent Cendrars as a plausible twentieth-century American poet. We hear hints of Hart Crane, for example, in this Florida landscape:

> On these stinking waters in the poisonous muck
> Flowers bloom with a stunning scent a heady and persistent smell
> Burst of blue and purple
> Chrome leaves
> Everywhere

Or this, a possible outtake from an early Williams poem, lensed through the precisionist eye of Charles Sheeler:

> A six-cylinder and two Fords out in the field
> All around and as far as you can see the slightly tilted sheaves form
>   a checkerboard of wavering rhomboids

Not a tree
From the north the chugging and clatter of the thresher and hay
    wagon
And from the south the twelve empty trains coming to load the
    wheat

Or this, from Gary Snyder's poems of the Northwest:

Strings of wood doves red-legged partridge
Wild peacock
Wild turkey
And even a big reddish-brown and white eagle brought down from
    the clouds

Or this, an objectivist Cid Corman noting the specifics of a Japanese
home:

Bamboo stalks
Thin boards
Paper stretched across frames
There is no real heating system

Kodak presents us with a world drained of all affect and exotic glamour.
Though he knows its landscapes to be mere simulacra, mere images,
mere quotations, Cendrars arrives at an almost Zen-like acceptance of
their lovely, illusory prose. He is, as he reports in his *Travel Notes,*
content to be simply here—that is, as always, elsewhere:

Today I am perhaps the happiest man in the world
I have everything I don't want

RICHARD SIEBURTH

Notes

1. *La Main coupé* (1946). Quoted in Miriam Cendrars' biography of her father, *Blaise Cendrars* (Paris: Balland, 1984), p. 289. My translation.
2. Portions of the original edition are reproduced in Marjorie Perloff's *The Futurist Moment* (University of Chicago Press, 1986), pp. 3–43. Her pages on Cendrars' visual poetics remain the finest to date.
3. For the impact of Gourmont's *Latin mystique* on Pound's prosody, see my *Instigations: Ezra Pound and Remy de Gourmont* (Harvard University Press, 1978), pp. 28–49.
4. Dos Passos' first translations of Cendrars appeared in the chapter of his *Orient Express* (1927) entitled "Homer of the Trans-siberian." A fuller selection of translations (including "Prosody of the Transsiberian," "Panama," and snippets from *Documentaires* and *Feuilles de route*), illustrated with Dos Passos' own watercolors, was published by Harper and Brothers in New York in 1931 under the title *Panama, or The Adventures of My Seven Uncles*. A bilingual edition of the Dos Passos translation, complete with the original illustrations, was reissued in 1994 as *Voyager avec Blaise Cendrars* under the Paris imprint of La Quinzaine Littéraire/Louis Vuitton.
5. See Jay Bochner, *Blaise Cendrars: Discovery and Re-Creation* (University of Toronto Press, 1978), pp. 126–131. Bochner's monograph is far and away the best study of Cendrars in English; I am indebted to it throughout.
6. Blaise Cendrars, *Complete Postcards from the Americas,* translated with an introduction by Monique Chefdor (University of California Press, 1976).

Richard Wilbur's Civil Tongue

Richard Wilbur. *New and Collected Poems.* Harcourt Brace Jovanovich 1988. 393 pp. $27.95

Richard Wilbur is too elegant to be good, and too good to be elegant. The complaints against his work are a litany of old virtue: its sweetness, and its polish, and its cordiality, and its complacence—you'd think he were a peaceable kingdom all to himself, a lamb that has devoured all the lions in sight. His critics have lived within the tensions of his poetry by an ignorant celebration of his faults or a gleeful damning of his perfections. His middle name might as well be Suckling, Lovelace, or Crashaw.

Poets of a silver age bear uneasy relation to the poets before them, though almost any age remembers poets just dead as giants. The critical affinities invented for Pound, or Eliot, or Stevens, or later poets like Lowell have made it that much harder to appreciate poets with a different bearing. Wilbur's complex relation to the moral world of Frost has made matters more, and not less, difficult. That Wilbur is most of the time a classical poet, a poet secure (some would say *ossified*) in the longer line of tradition and descent, has set him against the Romantic progress of our poetry.

Who but a poet confident in the artifice of tradition would talk so about the potato?

> Cut open raw, it looses a cool clean stench,
> Mineral acid seeping from pores of prest meal;
> It is like breaching a strangely refreshing tomb:
>
> Therein the taste of first stones, the hands of dead slaves,
> Waters men drank in the earliest frightful woods,
> Flint chips, and peat, and the cinders of buried camps.

Scrubbed under faucet water the planet skin
Polishes yellow, but tears to the plain insides;
Parching, the white's blue-hearted like hungry hands.

(from "Potato")

It takes smiling effrontery to treat vegetables like crown jewels. The subject troubles the high seriousness of the diction; and yet the fine physicality of the writing draws what might have been a Dutch still life, a varnished oil almost alive, almost dead, into the underground of fertility and death: All flesh is the flesh of the potato. A number of Wilbur's early poems make their peace in the aftermath of war, but only when speaking publicly do these lines go false: "Times being hard, the Sikh and the Senegalese, / Hobo and Okie, the body of Jesus the Jew, / Vestigial virtues, are eaten. . . ." His familiarity seems a form of contempt.

Robert Bly called Wilbur one of the "jolly intellectual dandies." Certainly other poems in his first book, *The Beautiful Changes* (1947), poems like "&" and "O" and "The Walgh-Vogel" and "The Melongène" ("Natural pomp! Excessive Nightshades' Prince! / Polished potato, you wear / An Egyptian rinse"), gave hostages to his critics. There is something rich and richly excessive, something beyond natural pomp, in such verses. They are too pleased with their own grotesqueness—a dandy dresses for his mirror as much as for his friends, but a poet has to go a long way to seem a greater dandy than Auden.

From the vantage of half a century, such coy irrelevance seems less playful and more to the purpose of postwar formalism. Lowell, Nemerov, Wilbur, Moss, Hecht, Simpson, Bowers, Justice, Merrill, Snodgrass, Merwin, Hollander, Howard—these poets with concerns variously classical and variantly formal took modernism at its word, the word wrenched from the terrors of its time. Poetry in the afterthought of war absorbed the relief of death averted and the sorrow of death observed. Many of these poets had a dilettantish, sweetly insouciant air taken from middle Auden. They were so much like boulevardiers you wouldn't have known who had fought overseas and who had been too young to serve—but then our best war poet, Jarrell, never saw combat. Preciousness and purpose often stood side by side, and for Wilbur in sharp conflict with each other. The writers of the Jazz Age were similarly afflicted: This was the source of a privileged torsion. Consider "First Snow in Alsace":

> The snow came down last night like moths
> Burned on the moon; it fell till dawn,
> Covered the town with simple cloths.
>
> Absolute snow lies rumpled on
> What shellbursts scattered and deranged,
> Entangled railings, crevassed lawn.
>
> As if it did not know they'd changed,
> Snow smoothly clasps the roofs of homes
> Fear-gutted, trustless and estranged.
>
> The ration stacks are milky domes;
> Across the ammunition pile
> The snow has climbed in sparkling combs.
>
> You think: beyond the town a mile
> Or two, this snowfall fills the eyes
> Of soldiers dead a little while.

The concealing snow returns the war to landscape, much as the gorgeous fluency of the terza rima conceals a tetrameter often rigid in design. The mood is vaguely troubling, as if the speaker a little too blissfully welcomed this prettied-up war; but the calmness of the arousing voice seems the proper medium of the voyeur—it convicts the visible. The cost in detachment, in lack of passion, in composure-in-the-face-of, would eat into the art if the camouflage of death, and hence emotion, were not itself the subject. Nature is the disinterested moral arbiter here, or the arbiter assuming a mask of ignorance ("As if it did not know they'd changed"). Beauty is a destruction of the pitiless, and nature effaces the evidence as it transforms the evidence. The cold ironies would scarcely exist without the sentimental touches ("And frost makes marvelous designs"), but the touches cannot subvert the grim tragedy beneath the snow. Eventually the snow will melt.

The subject here bears an assuming modesty—the small, bright transfigurations are what a soldier would notice (as if there were many soldiers with the eye of a Wilbur). Compare Lowell's bullying meter and bludgeoning certitudes among the shattered roofs of "The Exile's Return":

> There mounts in squalls a sort of rusty mire,
> Not ice, not snow, to leaguer the Hôtel
> De Ville, where braced pig-iron dragons grip
> The blizzard to their rigor mortis. A bell
> Grumbles when the reverberations strip
> The thatching from its spire,
> The search-guns click and spit and split up timber
> And nick the slate roofs on the Holstenwall
> Where torn-up tilestones crown the victor.

Lowell was a conscientious objector, but the roofs and the meter have been subject to violence still raw. Though *Lord Weary's Castle* was published in the same year as *The Beautiful Changes,* the difference in sensibility is more than a variance in title. If Wilbur's is the better poem, it is not because of the form; it's because the form has a more intimating plan. The plan allows for the excesses that in Lowell seem merely errors of tact (though elsewhere Lowell's tactlessness produced greater poems).

The dangerous insolence of Wilbur's verse courts and fends off such irrelevance. A poem could hardly begin less promisingly than "A Dutch Courtyard": "What wholly blameless fun / To stand and look at pictures" sounds like some undergraduate's effusion. What saves the poem from being merely another example of postwar ekphrasis (what might be called *ut pictura poesis* with a vengeance) is the dollying at the end out of the frame, out of context.

> What surprising strict
> Propriety! In despair,
>
> Consumed with greedy ire,
> Old Andrew Mellon glowered at this Dutch
> Courtyard, until it bothered him so much
> He bought the thing entire.

Beyond the frame, pictures are a part of commerce (and so they were for the Dutch, as Simon Schama reminds us in *The Embarrassment of Riches*); and yet they retain the capacity to shock the magnate a little, to turn him briefly from material ends, whatever his material means. The wit still lies coiled in wait, for Mellon has bought, not the courtyard itself, only the painted semblance. This semblance is what's disturbing: The courtyard would have been just another courtyard.

Such a slight poem (on a slight painting) is hardly worth lingering over, except for the way Wilbur darkens his concerns by a slight shadow of emphasis. Behind his artifice, when it is more than artifice, is something Greek and sacrificial. Unable to reach into the painting, to take the life while partaking of the likeness, the old banker rouses to a sudden greedy act of possession—he cannot live with the negative capability art requires. The art remains self-possessed, whoever possesses it.

That postwar fondness for the sealed world, a world beyond feeling, cannot conceal in aestheticism the aftershock of a Holocaust witnessed but unavenged. Ten years after the war, the antagonism felt by many poets toward the Beats was largely a recognition that the search for a language of feeling had been conducted in the wrong terms. Wilbur's rages are conducted with lecture-hall civility: Only in his best work do they threaten the placid comportment of his verse.

A poem like " 'A World without Objects Is a Sensible Emptiness' " (from his second book, *Ceremony* [1950]) is remarkable not in the haughty ripeness of technique or the studied texture of allusion—technique and allusion are the peace that never passeth understanding—but in the beautiful withholding of subject.

> The tall camels of the spirit
>   Steer for their deserts, passing the last groves loud
> With the sawmill shrill of the locust, to the whole honey of the arid
>   Sun. They are slow, proud,
>
> And move with a stilted stride
>   To the land of sheer horizon, hunting Traherne's
> *Sensible emptiness,* there where the brain's lantern-slide
>   Revels in vast returns.

> O connoisseurs of thirst,
> Beasts of my soul who long to learn to drink
> Of pure mirage, those prosperous islands are accurst
> That shimmer on the brink
>
> Of absence; auras, lustres,
> And all shinings need to be shaped and borne.

The caravan, leaving the last lush landscape of grove and locust (we are meant to cast our minds emptily back toward the camels and hard hopes of Eliot's "Journey of the Magi"), nearly refuses its function as metaphor (one almost as long as a caravan)—it is more alive than what it represents. The mind is in search of its mirages, in search of an emptiness sensible in Traherne's sense—an emptiness less empty, because a matrix of sensation. What are the sensations of the poem but a commentary on the physical world, the sensory employment, of verse itself? The long shimmering of sentences, the tender acoustic variations (how often Wilbur is our poet of timbre), the delicately muted rhymes. Rhyme and syntax cooperate in the small dramas of the quatrain, unshowy in all sorts of showy ways. This is a model of how a poem of great intellectual energy can also be a poem of tact.

Here is the most exacting statement of the rupture between pure philosophy and the duty the poet feels toward the world (Wilbur would rather be a Stevens than a Frost, though he often sounds like Frost). The argument of the poem runs precisely counter to the force of its feeling: Light must have something to illuminate. And yet how attractive, how delightful, the imagination has made those camels. The languorous metaphor is the imagination's counterargument: Imagination can create its own world, a world often more tactile and less remote than the world outside our windows. However much the poet admonishes his instinct, the "trees arrayed / In bursts of glare," the "country creeks, and the hills' bracken tiaras" have little of the sensuous immediacy of those camels. They live in the action of metaphor; the objects of the world are a still life in comparison.

The poem ends with a vision of the birth of Christ:

> Wisely watch for the sight
> Of the supernova burgeoning over the barn,
> Lampshine blurred in the stream of beasts, the spirit's right
> Oasis, light incarnate.

Light made incarnate might be called the terminal case of illumination. Poets of light tend to be religious and classical—the Romantics were haunted by the moon far more than by the sun. (Electric illumination has forever altered the imaginative tension between them.) Wilbur's moral sunniness is one of his least attractive qualities; but it *is* a quality, and qualities are edged by their opposites. His most striking images are sunlit: "morning's cannonades of brightness," "That lavished sunlight," "Lucent as shallows slowed by wading sun," "This chamber furnished only with the sun," "the noon's perfected brilliance." In "After the Last Bulletins," night is the world of trash, unruliness, vandalism, death, and anarchy, while at dawn the words are whole again and the birds sing. Lowell and Wilbur form a naked and correlative pair: the one, emotion reaching upward toward philosophy; the other, philosophy reaching back toward emotion. They are opposed gods. Wilbur understands the tragic—his most luminous poems are shot through with tragic apprehension, but he is no Pluto. He will only visit the nether regions, like Persephone. (His attempts to write like Pluto sound like playacting, as if he were a boy in a costume beard.)

It is the condition of most poets to write in terms only partly flattering to their talent: Much poetry is written against the grain of an author's gifts. In the greatest poets, either the gifts rise to meet the crisis of expectation, or failure brings compression and control, a narrowing of the enterprise with a gain of intensity (neither Hardy nor Merrill will be remembered for his epic, but the ambition driven to epic permitted the fluency of poems less ambitious and more lasting). Wilbur's gifts were perfected so early, it is good to remember where they have betrayed, in their very fluency, a poetry that could succeed only despite fluency. His early poems subside eagerly into the merely pictorial, into the plain skin of the writing—he becomes a scene painter paid for every inch of canvas. Jarrell was right to ridicule the ending of "The Death of a Toad," saying, "You think with a surge of irritation and dismay, 'So it was all only an excuse for some Poetry'."

> He lies
> As still as if he would return to stone,
> And soundlessly attending, dies
> Toward some deep monotone,
>
> Toward misted and ebullient seas
> And cooling shores, toward lost Amphibia's emperies.
> Day dwindles, drowning, and at length is gone
> In the wide and antique eyes, which still appear
> To watch, across the castrate lawn,
> The haggard daylight steer.

The lines are excruciating, even if posed in greater exaction than Jarrell was willing to admit (excruciating, and yet forlorn and lovely). In irony such talent reaches its greatest excess.

Lines only a little less gilded and inlaid, however, force the beauties to become a moral boundary. Here is "Marché aux Oiseaux":

> Hundreds of birds are singing in the square.
> Their minor voices fountaining in air
> And constant as a fountain, lightly loud,
> Do not drown out the burden of the crowd.
>
> Far from his gold Sudan, the travailleur
> Lends to the noise an intermittent chirr
> Which to his hearers seems more joy than rage.
> He batters softly at his wooden cage.
>
> Here are the silver-bill, the orange-cheek,
> The perroquet, the dainty coral-beak
> Stacked in their cages; and around them move
> The buyers in their termless hunt for love.
>
> Here are the old, the ill, the imperial child;
> The lonely people, desperate and mild;

> The ugly; past these faces one can read
> The tyranny of one outrageous need.
>
> We love the small, said Burke. And if the small
> Be not yet small enough, why then by Hell
> We'll cramp it till it knows but how to feed,
> And we'll provide the water and the seed.

This descends into its knowledge of Hell: Wilbur can be as merciless as Hecht, while seducing the reader with intimations of the beautiful. It isn't merely that culture here is the perversion of nature (the birds present a civil contrast, in their innocence and vain singing, to citizens desperate in their unloveliness for love), but that the moral pollution is only gradually evident beneath the gorgeous vision of the birds. This city square encloses a pastoral of Edenic forest, where Blake's rhyme of "rage" and "cage" (this square is a kind of Heaven) introduces the prison house. In each stanza the last line is the caution or condition of the next. It makes matters worse that the birds don't quite understand their circumstance—their songs are made in dumb pleasure.

The neatness of the rhymed couplets contributes to the daintiness of spirit, a daintiness the images gradually corrupt. The one tainted moment of rhyme, where "small" rhymes with "Hell," is also the moment of greatest passion and violation. The poem is merciless toward that need for love and that entrapment by love (it isn't difficult to read the moral for marriage here), while not failing to implicate the poet in this human failure. How tempting it would have been to write:

> We love the small, said Burke. And if the small
> Be not yet small enough for them, by Hell
> They'll cramp it till it knows but how to feed,
> And they'll provide the water and the seed.

Though dark and chilling, such lines would remove the poet from the precincts of the human. The final line in Wilbur is an act of recognition: A more cynical reading might note that this as cleverly evades judgment, that so human an admission makes the inhuman more inevitable. But in a poet often felt to be impersonal—to be a renderer of surface and a maker of isolated and stylized structures (almost inhuman, however much the talk is of morals and the human)—this embrace of the evil within, this refusal to escape damnation, is as humbling as it is unnerving.

Such attention to the small is the inheritance from Herbert that makes the best of Wilbur's work almost religious. Where Elizabeth Bishop turns that inheritance into clever pathos (thereby risking a glibness only her emotional conflicts avert), Wilbur burns for the philosophy at the heart of example; and in the best poems it is usually a moral, afflicting example. For all their different weights and measures, Wilbur's polished veneer and Bishop's coy reserve, both poets find solace in the trivial and the ordinary. When Wilbur flinches from the mortality of the moral, he collapses into academic draftsmanship, where craft lies short of genius—you feel his ambition is to be a Gray or a Goldsmith. His rhymes seem to tidy matters up (Bishop's poems live in a blur of untidiness, the messy mortality of the world), succumbing to what he calls "a coating of quietudes." (Those rhymes are often dutiful and time-serving—you don't feel he ever sat back in surprise and said, "Now *there's* a rhyme!")

These quietudes, however, are embraced in a different spirit. Wilbur's poetry was the far example of formal elegance much admired in the fifties, and much loathed. The arguments have moved to other quarters, but at this reach the quarrel over rhetoric has been altered by our own expectations—the earlier achievements of line were undermined by *Howl.* Consider the following passage:

> At Colonus Oedipus complained;
> Antigone attended him. He thought
> the sun too hot, she shielded him;
> his enemies too strong, she fought
> for him; his life bitter, she soothed him;
> and hope gone, like all things.
> His blinded eyes pained him, she bathed them. . . .

In 1956 a critic called this "a flat near-prose." The poem was by David Ignatow, and the critic, James Dickey, continued: "Aside from the flatness, which is only in a very rudimentary sense a technique, Ignatow does almost completely without the traditional skills of English versification. He makes no effort to assure his lines rhetorical effectiveness; the import of each poem is thus far too dependent upon *what* is said."

The parallelism, the balanced phrasings, the internal rhymes, the persistent iambs: We'd call this a highly measured rhetoric now, but then English poetry has gone much further toward prose in forty years. This ought to leave Wilbur a hideous Louis Quatorze antique, beyond the rescue of taste. The movement away from formal ornament and classical decoration has instead made him part of the exemplary perfection of another era. The craft, so easily managed and so willfully mannered, that once set him apart now looks ripe for revival, as fresh as a Chippendale pattern book.

Nineteen fifty-six was the date of publication of Wilbur's third book, *Things of This World,* a book ordered between, or disordered by, the world of transcendence and the world of the human. In the title poem, "Love Calls Us to the Things of This World," it is the other world that remains unsoiled:

> The eyes open to a cry of pulleys,
> And spirited from sleep, the astounded soul
> Hangs for a moment bodiless and simple
> As false dawn.
> > Outside the open window
> The morning air is all awash with angels.
>
> Some are in bed-sheets, some are in blouses,
> Some are in smocks: but truly there they are.
> Now they are rising together in calm swells
> Of halcyon feeling, filling whatever they wear
> With the deep joy of their impersonal breathing. . . .

The language is full of sly entanglement: the soul "spirited" from sleep (as if a spirit could be bundled off, like laundry) and hanging bodiless (later the clotheslines will be called a gallows), the stinging ambiguity of "simple" (lured from the phrase "simple souls"), the "false dawn" within this real one, the ebullient pun of "awash." A transcendence in meaning prepares the transcendent vision of the angels. The angels are incarnated by their clothes: bed-sheets, blouses, smocks (they are su-perbly unfashionable). If the laundry were *itself* mistaken for angels (the way sheets are ghosts at Halloween), they would be merely a myopia. Freed from the physical, the soul "shrinks / / From all that it is about to remember, / From the punctual rape of every blessèd day." The dark irreligion of the puns (days are "blessèd" more in anger than adoration) suspends the poem between the pure immaterial and the compromised physical world. But in a week the clothes will be dirty again.

The poem never admits that these angels are half-sleepy imaginings. Visionaries must be allowed their visions, however tainted by the temporal: Otherwise the soul too might be an airy nothing. Only when the soul cannot remember the murderous physics of this world do such visions open themselves. But Wilbur refuses to end there, and the poem inverts itself. The vision of supernal order is not an invitation: It is a reminder that love must first be achieved among fallen objects (the title is a line from Augustine). The soul accepts the waking body (surely this is an aspect of love), and the body is "changed" by what it has seen.

> "Bring them down from their ruddy gallows;
> Let there be clean linen for the backs of thieves;
> Let lovers go fresh and sweet to be undone,
> And the heaviest nuns walk in a pure floating
> Of dark habits,
> keeping their difficult balance."

The clothing is called down from the gallows, as Christ was taken down from the cross. The Gospels have Christ's clothes gambled away—the magic of clothing touched by death extends from the shirt of Nessus through the shroud of Turin.* Thieves, lovers (undone by their love or undone in their clothing), and nuns represent three private societies: crime, eros, and religion, or, more abasingly, evil, sin, and faith. Even the thieves are to be given the dress of angels, while the nuns (how their heaviness seems both a gravity and a susceptibility to gravity!) walk on

---

*Or the papyri of Oxyrhynchus: Those grave wrappings are the real books of the dead.

in their "dark habits": The wit infringes on organized religion for the sake of the spiritual. It is exactly that difficult balance between the everyday and the unworldly that the poem means to compromise, and keep in compromise. In the misperception of one world the other world is allowed to enter.

It is not just the expectations of line that distance Wilbur's poetry, but what might be called the expectations of spirit. The high formality of his rhetoric serves the stately withdrawing of personality. Cool, almost brittle, the formal intelligence preserves its manners with its mannerisms, behind cracked glaze. The being who suffers is rarely present within the being who sees—that is why it is scarcely believable that the man mowing the lawn in "The Death of a Toad" is Wilbur *in propria persona.* But contemplation is, after all, one of the important modes of art. We do not look at paintings to be lectured about the world; we go to be moved by their removals, by their abstract operations upon feeling. We learn of the world through the infidelity of its art. To ask for warmth from poets like Wilbur is a mistake in category. The high logic of his poetry takes place almost entirely within the contemplative. When he asks less of himself, as his later poems make clear, there is almost nothing to give.

For a poet secure in the self, the authorial "I" can be an intrusion, an unforgivable impersonation. The "I" is what lies behind the words, not in front of them: For such a poet, the personality is incarnate in language, in the intimate operation of the words, not insinuated as a dramatic character. We are still writing largely within the shadow of postwar poetry, and the difference in assumptions across half a century is nothing like the change from 1775 to 1825 or 1890 to 1940 (or roughly from the death of Goldsmith to the death of Byron or the death of Whitman to the death of Yeats). We understand the authorial withdrawal in Wilbur in part by the common reaction still in place against it.

His argument for the baroque proceeds by meticulous examination of its virtues. In "A Baroque Wall-Fountain in the Villa Sciarra" (the subject itself announces certain removed and special aesthetic concerns—there is no exemption for privilege), the water

spills
In threads then from the scalloped rim, and makes

> A scrim or summery tent
> For a faun-ménage and their familiar goose.
>   Happy in all that ragged, loose
> Collapse of water, its effortless descent
>
>   And flatteries of spray,
> The stocky god upholds the shell with ease,
>   Watching, about his shaggy knees,
> The goatish innocence of his babes at play;
>
>   His fauness all the while
> Leans forward, slightly, into a clambering mesh
>   Of water-lights, her sparkling flesh
> In a saecular ecstasy, her blinded smile
>
>   Bent on the sand floor
> Of the trefoil pool, where ripple-shadows come
>   And go in swift reticulum,
> More addling to the eye than wine, and more
>
>   Interminable to thought
> Than pleasure's calculus.

This tender description, spilling from stanza to stanza, is undone by the severe, spiritual abstraction of the fountains before St. Peter's. And yet, the poem argues, the fauns of this bizarre fountain "are at rest in fulness of desire / For what is given, . . . / Reproving our disgust and our ennui / With humble insatiety." The crammed-together, sweatshop artifice is a fulfillment of the urge to life: The elaborated ground of Wilbur's verse requires an ars poetica of the spirit. The poem ends with an invocation of St. Francis:

> Francis, perhaps, who lay in sister snow
>
>   Before the wealthy gate
> Freezing and praising, might have seen in this
>   No trifle, but a shade of bliss—
> That land of tolerable flowers, that state

>   As near and far as grass
>   Where eyes become the sunlight, and the hand
>   Is worthy of water: the dreamt land
>   Toward which all hungers leap, all pleasures pass.

The fine trembling of the unexpected adjective "tolerable" takes root in the Latin of "bearing." The language is part of the learning—a parade of classical, religious, and literary figures crowds the last stanzas of Wilbur's poems to salvage or secure the moral example.

Classical poets draw strength from influence. Influence is not merely an aversion. The moral realm so strongly implicated in Wilbur's verse lives with its debts to the physical constructions of Frost. A poet may absorb an influence, but also be divided against it. In that resistance some of Wilbur's feelings reach the greatest force of authenticity. "Sonnet" is a little cast-iron Frost piece about a farmer and a scarecrow:

>   The winter deepening, the hay all in,
>   The barn fat with cattle, the apple-crop
>   Conveyed to market or the fragrant bin,
>   He thinks the time has come to make a stop,
>
>   And sinks half-grudging in his firelit seat,
>   Though with his heavy body's full consent,
>   In what would be the posture of defeat,
>   But for that look of rigorous content.
>
>   Outside, the night dives down like one great crow
>   Against his cast-off clothing where it stands
>   Up to the knees in miles of hustled snow,
>
>   Flapping and jumping like a kind of fire,
>   And floating skyward its abandoned hands
>   In gestures of invincible desire.

This is one of Wilbur's many poems about the division of self (he has Cartesian dialogues between milkweed and stone, aspen and stream). His farmer is almost a harvest of himself. The crops are in; but that hard annual victory leaves him in "the posture of defeat," and the "rigorous content" meant to modify what only *seems* defeat bears against a notion of contentment *in* defeat. The clothing has been cast off in a contrary yet collaborative sense: A chrysalis is transforming, a shed skin only outgrown. Out in the snow, the scarecrow is a cold vision of desire, desire forlorn, panicky as a traveler freezing to death, yet "invincible." It is a haunting statement of loss, and of private costs.

Wilbur is tough and unsentimental about the soul (even while romantically indulgent in describing the harvest—he's like Keats when he gets a chance to describe nature). He wears Frost's old clothing here, and through the classical realm his poems inhabit—the infusions of Greek and Latin and European literature—lie these strange American pastorals. Wilbur can hardly write about nature or compose in quatrains without becoming a version of Frost—the moral strain of his being has been purchased secondhand from our moral New England farmer. His certainties come as Frost's do, from trust in the ordered operations of the universe (though Frost is a cynic surprised into gruff serenity and Wilbur an optimist with a dark and troubling stain).

The Frost in Wilbur rescues him from dandified Gongorism—his poems were loaded with words like "retractility," "periploi," "areté," "rachitic," "bombination," "phlebolith," "informous," "fovea," "noyade," "râle," or phrases like "the ping-pong's optative bop" and "A bell diphthonging in an atmosphere" and "habitude, if not pure / / Hebetude" and "Now all this proud royaume / Is Veniced." This division is shaped beneath the level of style, since style, if it doesn't accord with division, at least makes certain assumptions about accord. A poet who dissolves himself in influences so little in relation to one another can seem a disjoint presence: not a multiple personality, but a personality that never coheres beneath the ease of style. There is a difference between a classical culture lived (the Horace in Frost) and a classical culture worked from books.

In *Advice to a Prophet* (1961), how oddly the precious Cartesian dialogues, an allegory about puppets in love, poems titled "Gemini," "Ballade for the Duke of Orléans," "To Ishtar," "Pangloss's Song," and "Eight Riddles from Symphosius," plus translations from Guillén, Quasimodo, de Nerval, and Molière sit next to homely old American subjects like "A Hole in the Floor," "A Fire-Truck," "A Grasshopper," and "In the Smoking-Car." This may suggest the problematic attention of a dandy cum democrat, an arch and academic temper darkened by moral, mortal nature. Those sudden declensions into skepticism and mistrust in poems that begin like bright still lifes mark a distinguishing unease. Wilbur's most beautifully unstable poems are problems of identity.

Saying through others what the self has no language for might be called the state of influence. It seems surprising that Wilbur has not been driven to dramatic monologue, that uneasy formal disguise of the self—but then one realizes that in middle career he was driven to, and finally absorbed by, translation instead.

Any critic of Wilbur must face the decline in his original work after about 1960. The variety and intensity of a loyalty to translation comment uneasily on a poet's organization of feeling and display of the substance of feeling. Translation is a tricky medium. It is easy to give up higher imaginative satisfactions for the pleasures of setting right the negotiation between one language and another. A translator becomes the medium or permeable membrane at the cost of his sovereignty. Poets like Lowell or Pound could never fully submit to such a regime: They could translate only by eminent domain. But submission too can be a form of genius. It is to Wilbur's more governed character that we owe his remarkable renderings of Molière and Racine, among the finest translations of our period. Here the formal brilliance, accommodated in the masters because approved by them, becomes a tour de force of faith in and sympathy toward a literature otherwise dead, instead of a force used without sympathy for, because radically unfaithful to, contemporary life. The formality of the plays is no different from the formality that drew criticism to the poems.

Translation provides a pure and alternate world, the raw matter and ready emotion the imagination longs for. Some poets say their piece and retire to gunrunning, and surely gunrunning is better than publishing increasingly indecipherable Xeroxes of earlier work. The slight snobbery many writers feel toward translation is not misplaced, if we value the writer over anything he might have translated. We would not have had a Molière or a Racine worthy of their art; but there is about Wilbur's career a sense of incompleteness, of great talent willingly abandoned.

Wilbur's later poems are increasingly occasional. The poems of *Walking to Sleep* (1969) and *The Mind-Reader* (1976) and the new poems collected here are the work of a man whose mind is on other matters, often on the matter of translations with which the books are interlarded (so that they seem books by Brodsky, Villon, du Bellay, Voltaire, Borges, and Akhmatova, as much as by Wilbur). Only Auden, among recent poets, was a genius of the occasional: It fired the frivolousness of his imagination. Eliot's occasional verse (not his comic verse) was embarrassing. To take the depths of a writer's imagination, an action usually has to fall on prepared ground. Otherwise a poem is a whim. Wilbur's translations are great monuments to sympathetic imagination—he has made numerous foreign poets as grave and sweet and witty as, well, as Richard Wilbur. His pride in them would be a measure of what he has had to surrender.

Even in elegy, the later poems fall into postures, where the earlier often *were* brilliant postures. Wilbur has lost not just the careless ease, but even the studied ease that made him more Montaigne than Malvolio. In their perfunctory ends, poems like "On Having Mis-identified a Wild Flower" or "Wyeth's Milk Cans" or "Flippancies" or "A Riddle" or "Two Riddles from Aldheim" or "For the Student Strikers" are starved of substance, unpleasant in their self-satisfactions. Wilbur can be as coquettish as Updike ("*Rillons, Rilletes,* they taste the same, / And would by any other name, / And are, if I may risk a joke, / Alike as two pigs in a poke"), and any poems short of a sonnet have been refined past some necessary coarseness: Elegance has become a frozen, plump composure. Auden and Merrill were also trivial in their later work: A poet of great instincts in language often becomes a mere collection of instincts. The public voice of Wilbur's cantata, "On Freedom's Ground," shows how far he has strayed from his demons:

> Now in our lady's honor
> Come dance on freedom's ground,
> And do the waltz or polka,
> Whatever spins around,
>
> Or let it be the raspa,
> The jig or Lindy hop,
> Or else the tarantella,
> Whatever doesn't stop,

> The Highland fling, the hornpipe,
> The schottische or the break,
> Or, if you like, the cakewalk,
> Whatever takes the cake. . . .

This poem on "a national occasion" (the centenary of the Statue of Liberty) reminds us how poets suffer when they speak not for themselves but for a country. Taste is the enemy of patriotic sentiment—we would not have to appoint a poet laureate otherwise.

For all their classical proportion and design, Wilbur's best poems move into uncharted territory. Their ends are not a consequence of their beginnings. We are always at the mercy of our personalities, but at best we become simply the mercy of them. The scholar-farmer, fussily constructed professional verse had a density, a scalding extremity as rich as a revenge play (something clotted and magisterial by Webster). The glittering surfaces concealed a dangerous undertow: Critics rarely recognized that Wilbur's work was more bitter, more severe, more darkly demanded than mere ornament. Even in late poems there are moments of intensity and superb moral resonance:

> The horse beneath me seemed
> To know what course to steer
> Through the horror of snow I dreamed,
> And so I had no fear,
>
> Nor was I chilled to death
> By the wind's white shudders, thanks
> To the veils of his patient breath
> And the mist of sweat from his flanks.
>
> It seemed that all night through,
> Within my hand no rein
> And nothing in my view
> But the pillar of his mane,
>
> I rode with magic ease
> At a quick, unstumbling trot

Through shattering vacancies
On into what was not,

Till the weave of the storm grew thin,
With a threading of cedar-smoke,
And the ice-blind pane of an inn
Shimmered, and I awoke.

How shall I now get back
To the inn-yard where he stands,
Burdened with every lack,
And waken the stable-hands

To give him, before I think
That there was no horse at all,
Some hay, some water to drink,
A blanket and a stall?

("The Ride")

There is almost nothing here not available in Frost. Frost is not so much a particular influence as a sufficient one: a consequence and not a cause of divided nature. To write in Frost's voice is no different from writing in Molière's or Racine's: The echoes of "Stopping by Woods on a Snowy Evening" and "The Draft Horse" are not just beneath the horizon of style, they are mute within the style itself. And yet the unappeasable despair of this sleeper (recall the waking man in "Love Calls Us to the Things of This World") is not for his own loss—his bereavement from dream—but for that horse left unwatered and unfed. Dream, the blind form of memory, is drawn to matters unfinished or acts regretted (as the shades in Homer are drawn to blood)—and yet how selfless and generous this consideration is. When Paradise was lost, Adam didn't worry about feeding the animals. And neither would that farmer-ego Frost. We want our dreams restored for other reasons.

In poetry, the surplus value is whatever is created beyond the direct or intimate need of the poem. This is not merely where the incidental or the incidence of art exceeds the virtue of language, but where something not quite predicted, not quite planned, overtakes the prepared form. The fatal condition of our poetry is that we value authenticity only when it is spelled out or noisily claimed, not where it is implicit in the craft. We have settled for the authentic, but our authentic is a surface value only.

The most obvious (and least oblivious) cast of Wilbur's talent takes seriously the subject—call it broadly the moral function of the visible—that most severely tests the form. The order of form finally has no moral value, though it may have moral suasion (we are all emotion susceptible to rhetoric). Wilbur's poetry must be seen as not just a radical exposition of style, but an uneasy indictment of the limits of style. That his early work had a richness beyond the coy or beautiful exchanges reminds us how impoverished our poems now often are. If the world were an abstraction, Wallace Stevens would have written its theology and Richard Wilbur its poetry.

WILLIAM LOGAN

Taxonomy

Language is only an instrument for the attainment of science
Jefferson wrote Marbois
among the columns of names—
Senna, snake-root, lupine, Cherokee plum
At Poplar Forest he planted rows of scaly bark hickory,
measured fisted buds of poke.

*

Random strokes and knots, scribbles
of hair on the crushed, sweat-drenched linen
of his wife's pillow as she lay dying.
Present occupations disable me from completing
the Notes, he wrote. His fine fingers
brushed ordered corners of coffin—
his infant daughter's. Outside,
jasmine and wethawk in the marbled cold
of spring sky.
              Royston crow, towhee,
and the sting of Tarleton in the wide, shallow mouths
of common salt near Monticello.

*

Nights he walked ragged, trampled rows
of cabbage to the line of small shacks, yellow oil
lamplight, a neighborhood of slaves.
The spirit of the master is abating.

*

You can stand on a cliff before the heave and tear
in Jefferson's mountains, in the sublime,

and not escape the awe. You can kneel above the abyss,
two hundred and seventy feet
of gouged rock and silver threads of stream, your back
to silver grilles of cars parked row on row in searing sun.
Here the eye ultimately composes itself
Jefferson added later, much later—looking away to the plain,
away from the arch that sprung
as it were, up to heaven.

JOY KATZ

Lasting Words

Peter Viereck. *Tide and Continuities: Last and First Poems, 1995–1938.* University of Arkansas Press 1995. 320 pp. $36.00 $20.00 (paper)

Theodore Weiss. *From Princeton One Autumn Afternoon: Collected Poems of Theodore Weiss, 1950–1986.* Macmillan 1987. 436 pp. $27.50

Theodore Weiss. *Selected Poems.* TriQuarterly Books/Northwestern University Press 1995. 330 pp. $49.95 $15.95 (paper)

Theodore Weiss. *A Sum of Destructions.* Louisiana State University Press 1994. 99 pp. $19.95 $9.95 (paper)

I wish I could call this essay "Death and the Poet," but Thomas M. Disch has conscripted that title in his collection *The Castle of Indolence: On Poetry, Poets, and Poetasters.* There Disch notes:

> Alas, for most poets . . . immortality is usually a delusory hope. Most will be unread within their lifetimes, their books either unpublished or unsold; the happier few who secure some readership while they are alive will soon thereafter join the moiety, as their Selecteds and Collecteds are elbowed off the shelves of bookstores and libraries by younger, living aspirants, to be deaccessioned into Dumpsters or retired into the cryogenic twilight of the library's deepest stacks.

Peter Viereck and Theodore Weiss are among Disch's "happier few." Both are much published and much honored: Viereck has won the Pulitzer and two Guggenheims, and Weiss has won a Guggenheim and the Poetry Society of America's Shelley Memorial Award. With their latest publications, both are clearly signaling that they are putting their poetic affairs in order. At the same time, they would be less than human if they did not hope to colonize as much of the bookshelf as they can with work so formidable that younger, living aspirants will be stopped dead in their deaccessioning tracks.

Laurels notwithstanding, neither poet has the name recognition that, say, Creeley or Levine has, in part because Viereck and Weiss are more "elitist" than those poets—than almost any poet, actually. Each is the kind of old-boy writer your average performance poet or radical feminist would shove cheerfully into the wood chipper. No Nuyorican poet is going to find a word, possibly even a mark of punctuation, to revere in the works of these elderly male Caucasians who have written poems like "Dionysus in Old Age," "Love Song to Eohippus," and "Paysage Moralisé" (Viereck) and "Sonata Pathétique," "To Yeats in Rapallo," and "Paradis Perdu" (Weiss). By their titles ye shall know them: You don't need a Ph.D. in African-American or Women's Studies to see, even from across a street teeming with people of every race, ethnicity, and gender, that sooner or later these two poets are going to be Dead White Males.

Since Viereck and Weiss know it as well, the only question is how to position themselves now that the Great Transformation is nigh. When one poet issues a 320-page collection subtitled *Last and First Poems* and the other publishes first a *Collected Poems* and then a *Selected* that is little more than a refinement of the former, one sees about the whole enterprise an aura of self-conscious finality. And one hears a voice saying, "Remember me this way, for this is me at my best."

In the last years of his life, my father commissioned a portrait of himself that he hung across from the entrance to our house so that it was the first thing a visitor saw. Literally larger than life, the man in the picture looked crafty and hawklike, more like a *condottiere* preparing to take someone's castle than the gentle man whose idea of a high time was to read to his children at night and then sip a single weak highball as he sorted nails in his workshop. Many of my father's friends did something similar, and one went a step further by placing the current *Who's Who* on a stand beneath his portrait, opening it to his own name, and illuminating the entry with a spotlight.

In midlife, it is easy to pooh-pooh this gerontological vanity, but who is to say that we, too, will not give in to it when our time comes? Shelley died young, so he wouldn't have known, but there is an Ozymandias in each of us. It isn't a question of whether our big egos will appear at the last, only how they will look. And if we are poets, chances are our last ego-manifestations will run to 300 or 400 pages and say either *Selected* or *Collected* (or some witty variation such as *First and Last*) on their jackets and spines. The question is, should they? The answer is a yes, I think, if a highly qualified one.

Tides and Continuities ("my last because of age and illness," Viereck writes) consists of either three or six parts, depending on how you read a preface that is as full of paradox, irony, and downright contradiction as the poems themselves. The first part consists of new poems written mainly in hospitals; the second comprises four sections of selected poems composed over a sixty-year period; and the third is devoted to long poems that tie the first two parts together.

The book's thematic leitmotifs are as ambitious as its formal architecture. They are, as Viereck sees them, "the seesaw of ambivalence between Persephone and Dionysus; the merging of Dionysus with Jesus, the Son of Man; and, thirdly, ageing and its doomed last venture." Of these three, the first is the most insistent—so insistent that one wishes the poet had appointed a handful of poems on this theme to represent the many included here. Viereck is fond of multiple roles for his characters (name tags like "Eve-Aphrodite" and "God-Mephisto" recur in these poems), and his gods take all too human form at times:

> *"Are we slumming Olympians, earth our importer?*
> *Or, second choice, each a sleazy imposter,*
> *The 'traveling salesman' (of firewater)*
> *With the porn-joke 'farmer's daughter'?*
> *Or, third, Viereck's puppets, his strings our halter?*
> *Check one of three."*

Even if "we" are slumming, this is a project of Olympian proportions, though shot through with foolishness, self-mockery, and a wit so acid I was relieved to read in the front matter that the book will be printed on "alk. paper."

The following poem gives something of the flavor of the poems overall, from the ponderous title to the list of dramatis personae (it is hard to imagine a Viereck poem without one) to the relentless *sui generis* formalism:

Now That Holocaust and Crucifixion Are Coffee-Table Books

The two speakers are Christ and modern man, the latter voice always in
quotes and italics.

> Waiting for dying? Tell me how
> It feels to grow up mortal?— *"Ow."*
> So long since I did dying on my own.
> How did you manage it?— *"Alone."*
> I mean, what does it feel like?— *"Cold."*
> Resist! Young rebels how do *they* end?— *"Old."*
> But ethics—brothers all—. *"Like Cain."*
> Asylums needed!— *"For the sane."*
> Man's load, I'll share it.— *"No such luck."*
> I sold for thirty—. *"Lambchops for a buck."*
> From me they made Wafers.— *"From later Jews, soap."*
> But Christians, being Christians, saved us.— *"Nope."*
> But I'm Mr. Christian in person, not solely a Jew.
> *"Sure. By the way, Mr. Eichmann is looking for you."*
> Six million! Where can I find the memorial booth
> For their lost golden dreams?— *"In a German gold tooth."*
>
> . . . .
>
> Unique: I rose.— *"Some lambs escape the stew."*
> At least my Stages went unshared by you:
> I lugged a cross uphill once; say
> If you have.— *"Nine-to-five each day."*
> Who else blooms Easter back with April showers?
> *"All funeral parlors 'say it with flowers.'"*
> My parents didn't help.— *"Whose really do?"*
> My lonely hour both copped out on.— *"Who?"*
> My father wouldn't stop the spear.— *"Same here."*
> O mother, I'd hoped it wouldn't hurt.— *"Me too."*

In the course of this clipped call-and-response dialogue, two speakers
with very different attitudes become more and more like-minded, yet
the One who changes is not the one who would be expected to change:
Instead of modern man being redeemed, it is Christ who is corrupted,
his naïveté and good cheer eroded by the man's dour outlook; the latter

speaks in fragments and monosyllables, as though too discouraged to say more, and his simple end rhymes chip away at his would-be Redeemer's confidence. Not all of Viereck's poems are this tightly wrapped, though even the more loosely constructed ones would appear extremely formal by anyone else's standards.

Poets use as much or as little form as they need, and it is easy to say that form fits content ideally here, that so arch a scold has to anneal his pronouncements lest they collapse into mere whiny rancor. Viereck himself would not hold with such relativism, for form is such an absolute to him that he devotes almost half of his preface to a rather touchy apologia:

> Imagine you're drowning. The water swallows you. Suddenly an arm tugs you to shore. A lifeguard revives your heart and your lungs, breathing into your mouth once for every five heart messages, as he or she has been taught. Five ta-TUMS per line of breath. Your life has just been saved by an old "outdated" iambic pentameter. How Elizabethan of nature! Both life and poetry depend on such body rhythms. Would you trust your life to a free-verse lifeguard?

Um, an *exclusively* free-verse lifeguard, no, though I would hope my savior had lots of instruction and experience in all the life saving techniques and could improvise if he had to.

Viereck is not the only one who wants to put all the free-versifiers in a weighted sack, drop them over the side, and rub his hands with glee as they caterwaul unrhythmically to the bottom. But in keeping with his cranky nature, he has a similar fate in mind for the neoformalists. "Form's living metronome of walking, breathing, feeling is replaced by a dead mechanical metronome," he writes, and the result is "the net without the tennis." So instead of "full-throated song," the reader gets "a bloodless correctness, a thin-lipped disapproval."

No one would accuse as feisty a Jeremiah as Viereck of being either bloodless or thin-lipped. And regardless of how one plays tennis, one has to admire Viereck's constant fidgeting with received forms and invention of new ones. To wit, crisscross rhymes:

> Image of ambush,
> Hushingly dim:

> Gold-bellied hornet
> Hanging from ceiling.
> Torment is dangling
> Feelers at man.

So "Im-" rhymes with "dim" in the line below, as "-bush" does with "Hush-"; "hornet" and "torment" make crisscross half-rhymes, as do "hanging" and "dangling," with "cei-" and "fee-" as a kind of true-rhyme sandwich in the middle. In a note, Viereck explains that he also moves "rhythm forward to first syllable, overthrowing the tyranny of over-accenting the rhymed last syllable of lines." Fine, but this is a fifty-line poem, and it never becomes any more engaging than this.

Viereck does better with his "uncouplets," by means of which he proposes "a kind of coitus interruptus to frustrate the ear's expectancy of cliché rhymes." Thus:

> I remember, I remember
> Love's leaf fell in July.
> I desire, I desire
> To live forever; in the end I flame like ash.

and

> Now when your sky-queen eyes of blue
> Swear to be false,
>
> At least I'll go down without blah or blink: my dove
> Coos hate.

Now these are formal experiments to be excited about, to show to one's bedmate or party guests or students. The fun here is contagious; a fine line separates the identification of the expected rhymes ("September," "fire," "true," and "love") and the composition of one's own uncouplets. What makes this exercise successful is that substitution of un-rhymes for the expected clichés compels one to rethink not only how poetry operates but the heart as well. Viereck spoils the effect somewhat with a the-formalist-doth-protest-too-much headnote declaring that "the aim of the poem is not these mere formalist gimmicks but a protest against the sentimental cult of nature and earth-mother." Yes, yes. Any reader who finds himself on page 170 of a collected works knows how to read poetry without over-the-shoulder advice, but then no amount of ham-fisted authorial intervention can truly ruin a poem one admires.

Viereck's best formal work seems unstudied, if that adjective is at all applicable to so self-conscious a poet as he. Couplets like this one flash wittily without calling too much attention to the technical aspirations that underlie them:

> In the month of March the snails climb tender trees
> To be nearer the Pleiades.

As with the uncouplets, the comic unexpectedness of the second line whisks the reader away from any ponderous consideration of form; one is too busy appreciating the effect to analyze its cause.

Viereck is often cynical to the point of bitterness, as a poem like "Now That Holocaust and Crucifixion Are Coffee-Table Books" illustrates. Wisely, he offers the candy of humor fairly often. Yet he is at his most appealing when being frank about the difficult struggle of writing and even living. The alternation between Dionysian scattering and Persephonean restoration is the major theme, played out in the alternation between the two kinds of writing that Viereck practices. The first, represented by the excerpts quoted above, is seemingly casual, and appears to come to the surface of the page as smoothly as Persephone on the up-escalator out of Hell. The second kind is the foredoomed yet nobly persevering verse that strives to bring great fragments of the psyche together, as though Dionysus might have tried to reassemble himself unaided. In a long poem called "At My Hospital Window," he writes:

> Nothing shaped. Once a bore came to abort
> (*Flagrante delicto*) doped Coleridge's hug of the muse.
> Pain-killer-drugged, I, too, have Xanadus,
> My promised ode being daily cut short
> By some goody-bore's "HAVE A GOOD DAY."
> Well, back to work; now I'll finish—
> What was it I promised her I'd finish?
> And who was "her"? And why of the sea? And where did I lay
> My glasses? Memories shed.

> (We differently-abled golden agers
> Are mnemonically-challenged underachievers.)
>   Tomorrow I'll shape, not shed. The best is ahead.

A line later, Viereck writes, "Days passed. Nothing shaped." This frank admission is more endearing than any of the technical wizardry of the other poems. The most touching poetry is not the most finished; it is the poetry that we finish ourselves.

Of course, one way to be perfect is by letting the rest of us know that we are im-. (Another is by spelling words as they once were but no longer are, though I have to admit a soft spot for a poet who writes "rôle" and "haemophilia.") Parodies are often good-natured, and the best reveal the parodist as at least half in love with that which is being spoofed. But there is something condescending about such a "blues" as the one entitled "To Helen (of Troy, N.Y.)":

> I sit here with the wind is in my hair;
> I huddle like the sun is in my eyes;
> I am (I wished you'd contact me) alone.
>
> A fat lot you'd wear crape if I was dead.
> It figures, who I heard there when I phoned you;
> It figures, when I came there, who has went.
>
> Dogs laugh at me, folk bark at me since then;
> "She is," they say, "no better than she ought to";
> I love you irregardless how they talk.
>
> You should have done it (which it is no crime)
> With me you should of done it, what they say.
> I sit here with the wind is in my hair.

Mr. or Ms. Copy Editor, don't touch a single solecism; the poor grammar and seeming typos are all too deliberate. The faux blue-collar phrasings seem to say, "That's how the uneducated do it, folks—just in case you didn't know." But we do, and we know how an educated person does it as well. And while we like much of what he has done, we wish he had been a little choosier about what he has included here. So much of what Viereck has written is the very best of its kind; poems from the "Mostly Hospital and Old Age" section (Part I of *Tide and Continuities*) echo and extend the legacy of Johnson, Swift, and especially Pope. But after a while, later poems begin to recall things done slightly differently in earlier poems rather than striking the reader as fresh and original. Viereck is a needler, and a little needling goes a long way.

If Viereck is Prospero, choleric and imperious, Weiss is Lear: earnest, tragic, chastened by experience. Viereck likes to remind the reader of his poetic and intellectual gifts; Weiss takes the opposite tack, denying ego and even decrying it. The first piece in his *Collected Poems* is the book's title poem, "From Princeton one autumn afternoon, 1986." (Interestingly, this is the work chosen to close the *Selected Poems* published eight years later, but more of that in time.) Here Weiss addresses Zbigniew Herbert in the epistolary manner (right down to the signature at the end), invoking Herbert's poem "The Old Masters" and those artists of yore who, because "they never thought / to autograph their work," are urged to "make the serpent scales of pride / fall from me / / let me be deaf / to the siren calls of fame." Besides,

> . . . as the newest
> critics tell us, it's a mistake,
> if not a downright fake, to think
> a work, whether it be painting,
> poem, or song, belongs to anyone.
> By godly language alone it's done.
>
> And anyway would a rose or one
> of those accomplished leaves be rosier
> were it, beyond its own intricacy,
> like a curled-up scroll, a painting,
> proudly, plainly signed by its maker?
>
> In any case, I judge the Old Masters
> lucky because they knew the only
> certain fame wholehearted striding—
> sumac-, maple-, sycamore-wise—
> barefoot into glory,

> instantly
> immortal, in their name-free works.
> Yours,
> Theodore Weiss

The signing of a letter in praise of anonymity is both ironic and welcome, since too much ego-quashing can be a way of saying, Look, Everybody, It's Overly Modest Me! Would that subsequent poems showed the same sense of humor. If Viereck's collected poems present an embarrassment of riches, like those meals at pricey restaurants in which the waiter brings a tray of little tarts and cookies after you have already spooned down the last of a dessert you could barely finish, then Weiss's push humility on the reader with an almost saintly arrogance. Again, it is less a question of the worth of individual poems than of the inclusion of too many good poems that say the same thing.

But they are good poems, worthy of notice both for their particular charms and for what they tell us of Weiss's overall program. For example, the preface to an early collection (*Outlanders*, 1960) parallels the cock-eyed optimism of the much-married skating champ Sonja Henie to the travails of a poet who carries on despite his dissatisfactions:

> *And Sonja Henie,*
> *the star, the thin-ice skater,*
> *after many tries, tries once more.*
>
> "The poem's not right. I know,
> though I worked at it again and again. . . .
> I'm not satisfied, but I'm not done
> with it yet."

This is a recurrent idea in Weiss: that while we may not reach our destination, how better spend our lives than by pressing toward it relentlessly?

"The Fire at Alexandria" rephrases and extends this idea of ego-less devotion to a perfection that will, in all probability, never be achieved. The poem begins with a précis of the works lost to posterity when the greatest collection of manuscripts in antiquity (more than 400,000) went up in smoke:

> Imagine it, a Sophocles complete,
> the lost epic of Homer, including no doubt
> his notes, his journals, and his observations
> on blindness. But what occupies me most,
> with the greatest hurt of grandeur, are those
> magnificent authors, kept in scholarly rows,
> whose names we have no passing record of:
> scrolls unrolling Aphrodite like Cleopatra
> bundled in a rug, the spoils of love.

Subsequent stanzas go back to the beginning: A wharf fire spreads to the library, where one burning book seems to inspire another, "to remind it of the flame enclosed / within its papyrus like a drowsy torch." The spectacle is "awesome" ("The Fire at Alexandria" is also from the 1960 collection, when "awesome" applied to phenomena other than pizza), but the poem's real awe is reserved for the fire that lights the best writing from within, the ardor that transcends time, place, maybe even catastrophe. That, at least, is still around:

> Now whenever I look into a flame,
> I try to catch a single countenance:
> Cleopatra, winking out from every spark;
> Tiresias eye to eye; a magnitude, long lost,
> restored to the sky and the stars he once
> struck unsuspected parts of into words.
> Fire, and I see them resurrected,
> madly cracking perfect birds, the world
> lit up as by a golden school, the flashings
> of the fathoms of set eyes.

Weiss takes a king-size risk with his metaphor here. Imagine telling a friend that the loss of his clothes, paintings, and family photographs is somehow redeemed by the fact that the vanished beauty lives on elsewhere. But what else should poetry do? And what other choice do we have than to make the best of the lousy hand that chance—in this case, an inadequate fire code—has dealt us? Weiss never quite comes across as a card-carrying Platonist, but it is clear that perfection and permanence are not as interesting to him as one's attempts to achieve them, attempts so intense and so intensely personal that ego itself becomes just one more stick of kindling in the "witty conflagration." Some joke! Some magic trick, rather: The self disappears into the fire of great art, which just burns higher.

A handful of poems celebrating the death of ego amounts to no more than that; 400 pages of such poetry announce a different program altogether. Naturally, certain poems step forward to spell things out. One such is "Robes of the Gods," arguably the most beautiful in the book, which contends, in effect, that our quotidian moves, however careless, are reflections of godlike behavior, and that our human forms are simply costumes the gods slip in and out of in their waggish Olympian manner.

> Still, sly
> as they are, loving to lie low, showing
> off—a few of us their special finery—when
> it suits them, they put on the mob
> for daily wear:
> jeans, worsteds,
> uniforms. But changes they propose here
> too, from shrill mad children, newly dipped,
> skipping in and out, designs-not-yet,
> to sots, hags, beggars,
> patches
> stitched into a motley. And the fitting
> wardrobe inbetween, when, stript to nothing
> but a skein, hooks-&-eyes the network
> of taut veins,
> lovers set off Mars
> and Venus, wrapt in another's arms;
> like a battlefield, in the rough and tumble
> of a naked bed, the lightning flashes
> then, rain shuddering.

If sots and hags are a definite possibility, so are more glamorous roles; it is good to know that even if one wakes up a caterpillar, there is always a chance of metamorphosing into Venus somewhere around the cocktail hour. To maintain such an attitude requires a Sonja Henie-style confidence that, sooner or later, one's luck is going to improve. Nor would it hurt to have the same powers of interpretation that allow the speaker in "The Fire at Alexandria" to find something of value in what anyone else would consider an unmitigated catastrophe. Interestingly, Weiss uses fire imagery to similar effect in this poem as well. The last stanzas read:

> Even as gods, riot-
> hearted, drag us, muck their highway,
> into bedlam, its engrossing frolics enough
> to crack our seams, exultancy bursts
> forth that's nameless,
> whole, inexplicable.
> And as they shine through us, like rags,
> like blubbered stuff a fire, donning,
> flaunts, we shine; through tears
> and blood we, whirling, shine.

With this bravura ending, Weiss out-Paters Pater and his hard gemlike flame, which seems match-size when held up against the "exultancy" of spirit in this poem.

At the end, it is easy to be drawn into Weiss's tearful, bloody dance and to whirl and shine so much that we forget just how much he asks us to *think* in the first part of the poem. But since his ideas are never quite what readers expect, one has to do some retooling to get a fit between what a poem says and what one thinks already. The tongue-and-groove form of most of these poems suggests that process; it is as though the poet writes, halts, ponders a spell, and starts again at the point on the page to which his pencil has drifted.

Weiss's use of small-g "gods" reminds us that there is no God behind his Platonism, that he is, instead, for all things high and humanist, his oeuvre packed with allusions to everything from the Bible to Auden. For no reason that I can locate in a particular poem, he often sounds like a banished Stoic philosopher who has opened his veins in a bath and is singing the songs that got him in trouble in the first place, the ones that asked so much of the reader.

In his later collections, such as *The World Before Us* (1970) and *Fireweeds* (1976), Weiss comes across as more comfortable in his skin.

He still emphasizes the uncertainty and partialness of daily existence, but now he treats those qualities as ones to be embraced, even loved. The poem " 'Yes, But . . . ' " and inscribed "for WCW again" opposes Williams' instructive self-doubt to the complacency of Frost. Laureled yet feeble, Williams astonishes by asking his host for reassurance:

> There he was—having spent
> the night with us, the first
> time away from home alone,
> terribly frail for another stroke,
> his dreams still shaking him—
> his fame steadily leaping ahead,
>
> and he complaining to me,
> struggling just to be somebody,
> expecting me to comfort him!
>
> Manfully, if with a bitter sense
> of injustice, I did my best:
> "Why, Bill, you've left a good
> green swath of writing behind you."
>
> And he, in a low voice,
> most mournfully, "Yes, but
> is it poetry?"

The speaker confesses that it took years for him to realize that a life he describes as open and honest is going to be plagued by doubts, and then he thinks of the other poet:

> (Some months
> later Frost would visit,
> older, sturdy as an ancient oak,
> unlike Williams, who could not read
> to the end of a verse,
> intoning
> his poems well over an hour
> with tremendous relish, then
> standing on his solid stumps

another hour batting it out
with students,
                no doubts shaking
him and few new leaves breaking
out of him.)

An older man himself now, the speaker too feels "the doubts accumu-
lating" and describes himself as "grateful to Bill / for his uncertainty."
In a new twist on his now familiar Platonism, Weiss seems to admire
Williams' insecurity more than his actual poetic achievements (". . . I
lean / on it, lean more than on all / his accomplishments, those greeny
/ asphodel triumphs").

    More and more, the candid yet anxious tactic figures as a way of life
in these later poems. The older Weiss writes a number of epistolary
poems to poets of earlier generations, coming to terms with his poetic
fathers. "As You Like It," a letter of sorts to Auden, argues that ordinary
people are not oblivious to the great scenes around them, the case in
point being that of Mrs. Gudgeon, a London charwoman,

                          listening
to the wireless, a most impressive array
of "the best minds"
                    engaged in difficult,
arduous talk, and she intent on it,
to her husband's
                "What're you listening for?
You don't understand a word they say,"
rejoining,
            "O I enjoy it, just the sound
of it, so musical. And anyway I take
from it whatever I like,
                then make of it,
in my own mind, whatever I will. . . ."

So it is with the rest of us, who "bear off those bits / that we can use."
For each is a "mouse at the Feast / of the Gods, one crumb doing for it
/ what heaped-up platters cannot do for Them." This notion, that our
smallness and our fragility are really advantages, has changed from what

one encounters in earlier poems. What is different is the tone: The speaker in these later poems is less ponderous, more humorous and appreciative of others.

He can even afford to set his homegrown Platonism aside from time to time and celebrate life's juicy particulars, as in the aptly named "Pleasure, Pleasure" (a response to Frost's "Provide, Provide"?), which exalts a cat, a wife's violin practice, the light and color of a winter afternoon, even the snow descending in an "ecstacy of windy cold." There is also a jubilant "Your Father's Sunday Baths":

> What you remember best
> about him, your father,
> was his smell. Always,
> despite the nasty little
> black cigars forever puffing
> billows around him, he smelled
> nice and clean.
>
> . . . . . .
>
>   You'd go in
> after he was done, the whole
> bathroom swimming, lost
> in smoke. And now you think
> of him, a full-dress admiral
> in the flagship, smoke
> its standard,
>   leading
> a mighty fleet on a Sunday
> up the Amazon or the Zambezi,
> repeating words unheard of
> he had read that morning.
> And your mother thought
> he was a stay-at-home!

Writing about another poet once, I referred to what I called his "earned conventionalism," a late-career savoring of home truths justified in light of the rigorous explorations that came earlier (as opposed to the inherited conventionalism that many poets begin with and never depart from). The contrast is not so stark in Weiss, but there is something right about the realization that after the blazing fires of philosophy, it is okay to contemplate the coal of one's own stogie.

C'est tout, then, *fini.* As with Viereck, a formidable achievement—too much of an achievement, really, in that the great poems are insulated by the near-great, like the packing around a fragile treasure. But as the shadows lengthen, it is in the nature of poets to collect their poems; it is the final privilege of poetic license.

Why, then, is the *Collected Poems* of 1987 followed by the shorter *Selected Poems* of 1995? To be able to answer that question, let us compare the two.

	Collected	*Selected*
1.	Begins with the long poem "From Princeton one autumn afternoon, 1986."	Ends with a selection from the same poem.
2.	Includes ten poems from *The Catch* (1951).	Includes five poems from *The Catch.*
3.	Continuing in this way, the number of poems from each book . . .	. . . are roughly halved in the *Selected Poems.*
4.	The long poems *Gunsight* (1962) and *Recoveries* (1982) . . .	. . . are reproduced intact in both.
5.	But missing from the *Collected Poems* is . . .	. . . the 26-page *Pasternak and Ivanov,* included here.

It is hard to see the *Selected Poems* as anything other than an improvement on the *Collected.* It is not only more compact but also handsomer in terms of page design. And the decision to close with the shorter version of "From Princeton one autumn afternoon, 1986" is judicious; the 4-page abbreviation says just as much as the 19-page original, and the prideful signing of a manifesto against pride contributes a note of humor, a quality never out of place in good writing and especially welcome at the end. The *Selected* is evidently Weiss's absolutely final gathering and should be taken as such by readers.

For literary historians, though, the matter is complicated somewhat by the appearance in 1994 of *A Sum of Destructions,* a splendid collection issued after the *Collected* and before the *Selected* but excerpted in neither. Or at least, not exactly: There is a poem in both called

"A Sum of Destructions" that originally appeared in *The Catch* (1951) and which appears here in slightly different form. Although the more recent version is half as long as the earlier, both have a *Götterdämmerung* quality suggested by the discovery that the earth is "a terrible good." Indeed, the entire book is suffused with the sense of someone saying that it has been a great ride, but it's almost over. Not quite, though, because there is a never-say-die attitude in this book, invigorating the tombstone carving of the supposedly definitive "final" collections. In "The Answer," for example, a character describes himself as being like a graffiti-ridden church wall and searches for a spot for his "latest scrawl." This awareness of life's layered meanings figures as well in "A Place to Visit," in which the speaker tries to peer into the now overrun hamlets of his youth to see the bucolic original behind the condominia and malls.

Here (and elsewhere in *A Sum of Destructions*) the speaker is able to laugh at impermanence, whereas poems in Weiss's other books approach the same subject grimly. An essential poem in this respect is "A Summer Drive," in which a boy sleeps between his grandparents and dreams of buxom shopgirls until the car runs out of gas and his father makes him get out and push "into the vast, / uncharted dark" where everything (and nothing) awaits him. What lies ahead could be terrible or wonderful; mainly, though, it is invisible.

The full weight of these four books is too much for anyone to lift more than twice, though I am certain I will be rereading individual poems by both poets—fashioning my own micro-*Selected* from their macro versions, as it were. In the end, I am glad I spent as much time as I did in the presence of Viereck and Weiss. We chatted, we quarreled, we shared a laugh or two; I may have dozed off from time to time, but I came away better for the exchange. Saul Bellow once wrote that you can save an awful lot on your psychiatry bills if you have a smart neighbor, and these two distinguished poets are nothing if not smart. Still, I can't imagine choosing to live next door to someone as acid-tongued as Viereck. And while I'd rather have Weiss on the other side of the fence, I can see myself edging away from him, too, backing into the nasturtiums as he goes on and on, his gaze fixed on the vast, uncharted dark.

DAVID KIRBY

A London View of Light

John Gross. *The Oxford Book of Comic Verse.* Oxford University Press 1994.
512 pp. $25.00

Light verse is poetry's poor cousin, and poets who write it must seem triflers in the eyes of their serious-minded peers. It's true that one respectable prize for light verse, the Michael Braude (rhymes with "rowdy") Award, is now given out every other year by the American Academy and Institute of Arts and Letters to someone who writes in English, at last report Turner Cassity. And yet trying to print light verse in this country nowadays is like trying to peddle mink coats at a convention of militant ecologists. John Mella's ambitious quarterly *Light* is the lone magazine that welcomes the stuff in quantity. From 1984 through 1989, Robert Wallace's hardcover annual *Light Year* struggled along bravely, but could not break even. And as a rule, people who write book-length collections of light verse must either disguise their wares as children's books or else be their own publishers.

Yet paradoxically, when an anthology of light verse finds a trade publisher, it seems to find readers. Or so I assume from the apparent success of Russell Baker's *The Norton Book of Light Verse;* and from the news that, currently, Louis Phillips is editing a comparable volume for Random House. Now, Oxford, a champion of light verse in the past, gives us a solid new anthology with a historical sweep that extends from Chaucer to Glyn Maxwell. John Gross, theater critic, author of *The Rise and Fall of the Man of Letters,* and former editor of the *Times Literary Supplement,* seems a man well qualified to do the sweeping. As you might expect, his view is London-centered, for light verse has long held an accepted place in British poetry. After all, two of the very best English poets of the century, Larkin and Betjeman, wrote much that is light; and there remains an astoundingly large audience for light verse in the U.K., where Wendy Cope's *Making Cocoa for Kingsley Amis* and the unintentionally comic *Poetic Gems* of Victorian Scotsman William McGonigall have proved best-sellers.

Perhaps this volume was given its title to avoid confusion with Auden's classic *The Oxford Book of Light Verse,* Kingsley Amis' *The New Oxford Book of English Light Verse,* or William Harmon's *The Oxford Book of American Light Verse.* At any rate, by dubbing his book *Comic,* Gross sidesteps the problem of defining light verse and is able to include true poems that make us laugh. One such is James Joyce's "Post Ulixem Scriptum"—the tribute to Molly Bloom which ends not hilariously but touchingly,

> May you live, may you love like this gaily spinning earth of ours,
> And every morn a gallant sun awake you to a new wealth of gold
> But if I cling like a child to the clouds that are your petticoats
>   O Molly, handsome Molly, sure you won't let me die!

Because this vein of heavier poetry is lightly represented, Gross might have done more with Thomas Hardy—surely "The Ruined Maid" and certain of the "Satires of Circumstance" are both comedy and poetry—and Eliot, whose early "Sweeney Erect," "A Cooking Egg," "Hysteria," and "The Hippopotamus" are funnier, I think, than anything in the heavy-handed *Practical Cats.* But Gross sets forth his principles in an introduction so carefully worded that it is hard to quarrel with him. "Comic verse," he declares, "is verse that is designed to amuse." This policy, while it assumes that the editor knows the poets' intentions, leaves up to him the job of deciding which verse is comic.

Gross is generously inclusive. His widespread net takes in limericks, epigrams, double dactyls, ballads, song lyrics, advertising jingles. There are fine parodies, well-known ones like Henry Reed's takeoff on Eliot and William Empson's on Auden, also less familiar plums: Clive James's blast at Robert Lowell's *Notebook* sonnets and A. E. Housman's deft torpedoing of Longfellow's "Excelsior," which begins,

> The shades of night were falling fast,
>   And the rain was falling faster,
> When through an Alpine village passed
>   An Alpine village pastor. . . .

Gross even wedges in an ample slice of Joseph Moncure March's *The Wild Party*. However, he excludes anything from two likely sources: savage satire (although he does include a few vicious insults) and blue and bawdy humor, which he thinks more effective when heard aloud and covertly sniggered over. I ought to confess myself biased in favor of any anthologist who includes anything by me. So let me just note that Gross's inclusion of two of my opera proves him an editor of high good taste and rare discernment—may he live with sound digestion to happy old age!—and get on with the task of being hard on him.

Jingoists may ask, How well is America represented? I count 42 of our compatriots out of 290—a pretty fair showing in an English-made anthology of light verse. Most of the talents I'd think essential are indeed here: Bret Harte and Oliver Wendell Holmes (but not Ambrose Bierce or Ben King); and, earlier in our own century, Morris Bishop, Arthur Guiterman, Samuel Hoffenstein, Don Marquis, David McCord, Ogden Nash, and Dorothy Parker. Contemporary light verse masters are represented as well: John Updike, Tom Disch, William Cole, George Starbuck, Shel Silverstein. "Casey at the Bat" makes the cut, as does "The Cremation of Sam McGee." Gross includes several poets acclaimed for seriousness who have digressed into comedy: Eliot and Pound, Frost, Cummings, Roethke, Berryman, Nemerov, A. R. Ammons, Anthony Hecht, Donald Hall, Richard Wilbur, even Emily Dickinson (for "I'm Nobody! Who are you?"—hardly a rib-tickler, but then Gross disavows any wish to limit the book to "uninterrupted merriment"). To his everlasting glory, he includes Phyllis McGinley's "Squeeze Play"—

> Jackson Pollock had a quaint
> Way of saying to his Sibyl,
> "Shall I dribble?
> Should I paint?"
> And with never an instant's quibble,
> Sibyl always answered,
> "Dribble."

—and Edward Gorey's splendid, sadistic limerick:

> To his club-footed child said Lord Stipple,
> As he poured his post-prandial tipple:
>   "Your mother's behavior
>   Gave pain to Our Savior
> And that's why He made you a cripple."

As those samples might suggest, comic verse when tightly rhymed and metrical tends to be funnier than comic verse left free to sprawl. This point invites debate, but I think strict form can throw odd words into positions of great emphasis, and enables a poet to set up (as Gorey does) a ludicrous contrast between grim matter and sprightly, hippetty-hopping melody.

Arranged chronologically, this book in its first third does look a bit *Norton Anthology*-ish. It takes Gross 200 pages to get to the twentieth century, at which moment the party livens considerably. Reaching back to Chaucer somehow makes for a certain historical earnestness, and of course attention must be paid to Skelton, Shakespeare, Rochester, Dryden, Pope, Swift, Prior, Burns, Byron, Hood, Lear and Carroll, and a host of lesser lights. Familiarity dogs these pages. As Gross in his introduction seems well aware, many of the selections are like jokes that we have heard before. More bothersome is the fact that from this book, you'd think light verse or comic poetry mainly a white man's game. I don't want to insist that a light verse anthology ought to be politically correct, but it seems a missed opportunity that a scant 16 of these 290 contributors are women. Some, it is true, are major light versifiers: Stevie Smith, Wendy Cope, Dorothy Parker. But I can't help wondering: Didn't Gross consider Lady Mary Wortley Montague, Mary Alcock, Christina Rossetti, or Frances Cornford? On this side of the Big Drink he might have pondered work by Carolyn Kizer, Felicia Lamport, Marianne Moore, Katherine McAlpine, Janet Lewis, Eve Merriam, Judith Viorst, classic blues singers, and a whole host more. And as in so many poetry anthologies (serious ones) of times gone by, Langston Hughes is the token black.

Whatever his omissions, Gross has discovered troves of good stuff I hadn't known. Among his finds are Tom Moore's rhymed proposal for a company to accelerate the production and consumption of literature, and Edmund Wilson's lines on would-be poet Struthers Burt, which conclude,

> Burt sometimes goes to stay with God for weeks
> And utters fierce shrill Philadelphian squeaks.

Then there's a fine thing by film comedienne Joyce Grenfell, about the horrors of a dance where there are no gentlemen to dance with and the ladies all have big busts, and Paul Dehn's condensed version of Shakespeare,

> The devil damn thee black, thou cream faced loon—
> Whom we invite to see us crowned at Scone.

(Quintessentially dry British humor, that.) Fresh and choice, too, are "Born Too Soon" by John Fuller and James Fenton, and Edward Field's "Lower East Side: The George Bernstein Story." Bravely, Gross ventures into popular music and picks some fine items, such as Noël Coward's "The Stately Homes of England" and the British music hall monologues "The Spaniard That Blighted My Life" and "Burlington Bertie from Bow." The field of American pop songs supplies Cole Porter's "I'm a Gigolo" and "Brush Up Your Shakespeare," and songs by Gus Kahn, Irving Berlin, Johnny Mercer, Ira Gershwin, Lorenz Hart, and Dorothy Fields. The rich reservoir of Irish comic balladry seems barely represented, although we do get "The Ould Orange Flute," that raucous bit of antipapistry.

It is unfair to complain, as I have been doing, that Gross has left out my own favorites, although I must say he has shown rare skill at avoiding them. I looked in vain for (among other things) Joyce's "Gas from a Burner" and D. H. Lawrence's "Nottingham's New University." But, as a wise man said, one man's meat is another's anthology, and certainly Gross's selections supply ample protein and calories. His is a rich and nourishing book, one to crack open next to a fireplace on a winter's night, or to take along to the beach—fit reading for a moment when one's ambition to read more ambitious poetry hangs limp, like a pair of tired suspenders.

X. J. KENNEDY

Meditation: Exempla

The one lemon, restive, then settling to the bottom of its
porcelain bowl.

At the fence, where the ivy has admitted defeat, three
blueberries, missed, that were all summer long there waiting.

Later, the bird of no description alighting somewhere over
the building's bas-relief facing,

so that the griffins carved there, open-mouthed, seem most
to you like wanting the bird;

then the bird moves away—

and the griffins are that other thing, wanting with no
discernible object but more sky.

Meditation: Surrender

As when,
into the canyon that means,
whose name—translated—
means *Without Measure, Sorrow*

from the hand that,
for so long, has meant
give,
but now—broken—gives in,

is released
the garland   /swag   /bouquet
(that—look,
look again—means

only as much as what it is:
eucalyptus,
kangaroo's paw,
the grass called eel),

that he, impossibly, might catch it.

CARL PHILLIPS

Foot Soldier for Life

Louis Simpson. *Collected Poems*. Paragon House 1988. 385 pp. $12.95 (paper)

Louis Simpson. *Selected Prose*. Paragon House 1989. 516 pp. $24.95

Louis Simpson. *The King My Father's Wreck*. Story Line Press 1995. 202 pp. $24.95 $14.95 (paper)

Louis Simpson. *There You Are: Poems*. Story Line Press 1985. 102 pp. $16.95 $10.00 (paper)

With almost every volume of collected poems the question arises: Are we to read it from front to back or from back to front? That is, should the poet's completed opus be assessed from the perspective of its mature and final achievement or from the first careless rapture of its earliest aspiration? The *Collected Poems* of Louis Simpson, it can be safely said, are climactic. There are some indubitable successes scored in the quarter of a century between 1940 and 1963, but the volume gathers strength only in the quarter of a century that follows. The lyrical ballast is jettisoned; echo diminished; rhyme abandoned; a persona, and a personal poetics, developed. With impish detachment he salutes the presiding genius of the mid-century:

> O amiable prospect!
> O kingdom of heaven on earth!
> I saw Mr. Eliot leaning over a fence
> Like a cheerful embalmer,

while irrevocably drawn to Walt Whitman's omnivorous "stomach that can digest / Rubber, coal, uranium, moons, poems" without himself being absorbed.

A turning point was the celebrated and much anthologized "On the Lawn at the Villa":

> On the lawn at the villa—
> That's the way to start, eh, reader?
> We know where we stand—somewhere expensive—
> You and I *imperturbes,* as Walt would say,
> Before the diversions of wealth, you and I *engagés.*

> On the lawn at the villa
> Sat a manufacturer of explosives,
> His wife from Paris,
> And a young man named Bruno . . .

Here, in embryo, are many of Simpson's subsequent rhetorical tactics: the conversational address, as if at a public reading; the sly, personal disengagement; the mysterious drama (itself explosive, capable of infinite expansion) distilled to a vignette. The narrative theme would in time balloon beyond such précis, but the irony at the heart of the text ("Perhaps, after all, this is not the right subject for a poem") would continue to sound. What then is "the right subject"? That was the nagging question.

It may be that he first formulated this question—and this quest—in discovering his Russian-Jewish relations as an adolescent in New York. Growing up with his father in Jamaica, he had had no suspicion that he might be half-Jewish. It was his mother's reminiscences of Odessa and family talk of Meyer and Isidor, Adam Yankev and Baruch, and "Avram the cello-mender, / the only Jewish sergeant / in the army of the Tsar"— wholly wonderful and disorienting to an English, colonial lad—that must have first jogged him to an awareness of the disorienting otherness of his most familiar-seeming acquaintances. In literary terms, it was his discovery of Chekhov. Some fine poems, "Chocolates," for example, are wholly devoted to Chekhov. But his influence runs far deeper than that; he was to become the recurrent presence and inspiration of all Simpson's poetry in its humor and pathos, its circumstantial concision and narrative drive. As Simpson himself put it: "I have tried to bring into poetry the sense of life, the gestures that Chekhov got in prose. And I have tried to bring in humor. I do not believe that this is common; there is plenty of satire, but this is not what I mean by humor" ("Rolling Up", 1976). Chekhov remained the touchstone and the American became an apt mimic of his master's voice:

> They were lovers of reading in the family.
> For instance, Cousin Deborah
> who, they said, had read everything . . .
> The question was, which would she marry,
> Tolstoy or Lermontov or Pushkin?

His imagination had already been marked—or permanently branded, rather—by his experience of battling as an infantryman across France and Holland in the Second World War. That and the nervous breakdown, with attendant amnesia, which followed: "Before the war I had written a few poems and some prose. Now I found that poetry was the only kind of writing in which I could express my thoughts. Through poems I could release the irrational, grotesque images I had accumulated during the war; and imposing order on these images enabled me to recover my identity" ("Dogface Poetics," 1965). War poems surface throughout his working career. That ordeal was as decisive for Simpson, who survived his war, as for Wilfred Owen, who died in his. Not so much as a subject, primarily as an attitude to writing: "words to me were pale in comparison with experience," he recently wrote in *The King My Father's Wreck*, "mattered only in so far as they transmitted experience." That is why he has resolutely set his face against theorists who argue "that there is no direct connection between words and life." That, too, is why he nurses a grudge against W. H. Auden for pretending that poetry was "fundamentally frivolous." The frivolity of poetry, if that is the word, resides only in its ultimate helplessness in the face of horror. What the miracle of spontaneous life demands of poets is truth. Simpson articulated his ars poetica early on: "Ideas were only so many words, they had nothing to do with reality . . . a man spilling his intestines in the road." Or as he put it in his only novel, *Riverside Drive* (1962): "But I, by a quirk of chance, belong with those whose task it is to describe the surface of things, to record the gestures of men and women. If I must, then so be it—but I will speak only with reluctance. I will resist any expression that is not the truth. And, rather than say what is not true, I will be silent." His is a soldier's testament:

> That is why some men, when they think about war, fall silent. Language seems to falsify physical life and to betray those who have experienced it absolutely—the dead. As Hemingway remarked, to such men the names on a map are more significant than works of imagination . . .
>
> Like other men of the war generation, I began with middle age; youth came later. Nowadays in my poems I try to generate mystery and excitement: I have even dealt in general ideas. But I retain the dogface's suspicion of the officer class, with their abstract language and indifference to individual, human suffering. You might say that the war made me a footsoldier for the rest of my life.

Here is another reason perhaps for reading his *Collected Poems* backwards. Simpson concludes that testament, his contribution to *The Poetry of War* (ed. Ian Hamilton, 1965):

> Now I see that I was writing a memorial of those years for the men I had known, who were silent. I was trying to write poems that I would not be ashamed to have them read—poems that would be, in their laconic and simple manner, tolerable to men who had seen a good deal of combat and had no illusions.

Thus no magic, no suppressed secrets, no bardic intonations. No pathos, no attitudinizing, no heart-on-the-sleeve revelations. Only the barebones of daily existence, an anecdotal essence, are allowed to survive "a life beginning with 'Hi!' and ending with 'So long!'." The poetic ideals could be summed up as: a "Muse install'd amid the kitchenware" (Whitman); "The natural object is always the adequate symbol" (Pound); "those things which lie under the direct scrutiny of the senses" (Williams), blessed by that "saint of the quotidian / himself, Leopold Bloom." "To write poetry," he concluded, "one has to be at a distance from one's feelings and be able to play with the facts."

> The first step, therefore, was to get my controlling mind out of the poem and treat the subject impersonally. So I embodied my ideas

in a narrative—there would be a character to do the observing, and one or two others.

(from "The Terms of Life Itself: Writing 'Quiet Desperation'," 1985)

He adopted the pseudonym "Peter" as alter ego to detach the merely autobiographical, while remaining "both in and out of the game."

The problem of poetry, then, became the problem of narrative poetry in the most commonplace circumstances. "How to Live on Long Island," for example:

> There's no way out.
> You were born to waste your life.
> You were born to this middleclass life
>
> As others before you
> Were born to walk in procession
> To the temple, singing.

("In the Suburbs")

As if Louis Simpson had been called to become the poet of suburbia, or exurbia, at any rate small-town America where "lines of little colored flags" advertise "Foreign Motor Sales" and the shopping mall "is laid out like a cathedral":

> I am taking part in a great experiment—
> whether writers can live peacefully in the suburbs
> and not be bored to death.

Far from being bored to death, he has flourished on the Long Island shore among his querulous and quirky neighbours. The experiment consisted of seeing whether he could make them sing; or, if not sing exactly, at least resound without grace notes or frills, devoid of image or metaphor even. For where he lives "there are no legends, only gossip":

As I said, lots of stories,
and some strange ones. But few occasions
for song, as far as I know.

A transformation of some kind is what he seems ultimately to be after. But he knows there is no standing on tiptoe to grab it. It has to be patiently and unpretentiously and quizzically accumulated:

Wordsworth said that the passions
of people who live in the country
are incorporated with the beautiful
and permanent forms of nature.
In the suburbs they are incorporated
with the things you see from the train . . .

Methodically, then, without a hint of cuteness or nudging send-up, Simpson has turned himself into the pop laureate of commuterland. "An Affair in the Country" is a mature example:

As he lived on East 82nd Street
and she in Wappingers Falls
he saw more of the road than of her:

Kaufman Carpet
Outlook Realty
Scelfo Realty   Amoco   Color TV

Now and then there would be something out of the ordinary:
X-Rated Dancer
Fabric Gardens   Discount Dog Food

They would meet for a couple of hours
at the Holiday Inn. Then she would have to leave,
and he had to start back.

Speed Zone Ahead
Signal Ahead
Road Narrows

Bridge Out
Yield

This is like a revved up version of e. e. cummings, but without any of his tricks and trills. It is as if John Cheever or John Updike had been reduced to their ultimate essence. Or, better still, Raymond Carver recuperated for verse. The poetry is all in the concision, the antithetical swing of fragments. He risks verging on the commonplace, it strikes me, when the theme of adultery is extended, as in "The Previous Tenant," to a fourteen-page novelette. Whatever the length, however, Simpson has perfected the very style he had once mocked as that of Mr. Eliot the "cheerful embalmer":

> O City of God!
> Let us be thoroughly dry.
> Let us sing a new song unto the Lord,
> A song of exclusion.
> For it is not so much a matter of being chosen
> As of not being excluded.
> I will sing unto the Lord
> In a voice that is cheerfully dry.

It was T. E. Hulme who had prophesied that "the particular verse we are going to get will be cheerful, dry and sophisticated." Which Simpson turned into his own distinctive, acid-free type of dry-point engraving:

> What do definitions and divorce-court proceedings
> have to do with the breathless reality?
>
> O little lamp at the bedside
> with views of Venice and the Bay of Naples,
> you understood! *Lactona* toothbrush
> and suitcase bought in a hurry,
> you were the witnesses of the love
> we made in bed together.

Schrafft's Chocolate Cherries, surely you remember
when she said she'd be true forever,

and, watching "Dark Storm," we decided
there is something to be said, after all,
for soap opera, "if it makes people happy."

Born in the Caribbean, the product of a very British education, Simpson on Long Island still feels permanently estranged. "Sometimes when I look at Main Street," he recorded, "I feel like a stranger looking at the Via Aurelia, or the Pyramids" (1962). More recently: "to this day I have retained that sense of difference and excitement. I am still a stranger in America" (1995). But estrangement has not turned him into an exotic poet, a kind of British Martian. Since dropping the ballad form, decades ago, nothing British clings to him at all—not even when venturing on Larkin's territory, as in "The Boarder" say, or crossing Heaney's tracks, as in "The Peat-Bog Man." His life studies may suggest the example of Lowell, but all such comparisons are inept. He has become sui generis, moving gracefully from memoirs in prose to memorials in verse:

The poetry of life . . .
how impossible it seems!
Wouldn't it be nice to be mindless
and just write, like a "language poet."

Unlike such "mindless" poets, however, he welcomes "life." He welcomes the paradox that "the object of writing is to make words disappear." Or if not quite disappear, become fitfully transparent. His ideal is age-old as Chaucer (invoked in *There You Are*):

Speketh so pleyn at this time, we yow preye,
That we may understonde what ye seye.

HAROLD BEAVER

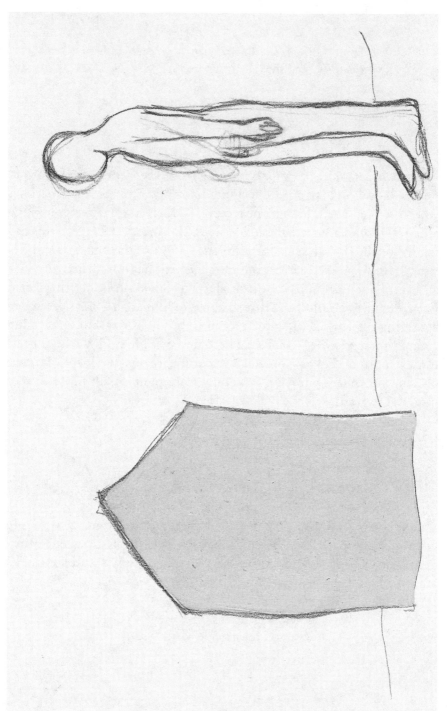

SALLY TITTMANN
Untitled

Just Looking

Charles Tomlinson. *Collected Poems.* Oxford University Press 1985. 351 pp. $29.95

Charles Tomlinson. *The Return.* Oxford University Press 1987. 51 pp. $8.95 (paper)

Charles Tomlinson. *Annunciations.* Oxford University Press 1989. 55 pp. $10.95 (paper)

Charles Tomlinson. *The Door in the Wall.* Oxford University Press 1992. 62 pp. $11.95 (paper)

Charles Tomlinson. *Jubilation.* Oxford University Press 1995. 63 pp. $11.95 (paper)

Sitting down with someone's *Collected Works* encourages thoughts of grading. We give a higher mark to the writer who changes noticeably over the years, taking risks and making radical ninety-degree turns, than to the one who remains at home in a poetic landscape that can easily seem spectral or monochromatic. But is consistency a flaw? Must the poet constantly reinvent himself? Think of painters: Matisse and Picasso offer one model—the more exciting one—for the modern artist; Mondrian, Morandi, and Rothko another, perhaps the more exacting one. Having found their vein, they mined it for all it was worth.

The British poet (and sometime painter) Charles Tomlinson fits comfortably in the second category. He has looked steadily at his subject for more than four decades and, having found a congenial style early on, stuck with it. Not for him a continual heroic quest for new techniques. Reading his books seriatim, one lands within a terrain where, as in Pope's "Windsor Forest," "though all things differ, all agree." His poetry examines the minutest fluctuations in the natural world, where difference and agreement go happily hand in hand. Constancy, in nature or in art, has a great deal to recommend it, especially when mitigated by its opposite; Tomlinson answers a question of Gerard Manley Hopkins ("What by your measure is the heaven of desire?") with his own paradoxical wisdom: "This inconstant constancy—earth, water, fire" ("Response to Hopkins," *The Door in the Wall*).

Tomlinson's habit of ignoring fashion and sticking to his guns may account for his relative obscurity. Ask any American to name the most important contemporary British poets, and the first choices would surely be Donald Davie, Seamus Heaney, Ted Hughes, and Philip Larkin. In the slightly older postwar generation, John Betjeman, Basil Bunting, David Jones, C. Day Lewis, and Dylan Thomas would spring to mind; and in the slightly younger one, James Fenton and Craig Raine have the widest readership in the States. Auden and Thom Gunn qualify as semi-Americans. Tomlinson might not make the list, an omission that says more about the uncertainties of poetic reputation-building than it does about literary value.

Tomlinson began publishing in the fifties during the waning of High Modernism. His influences have included Americans (first Stevens, then Moore and Williams) in addition to British landscape topographers like Wordsworth, Hopkins, and Edward Thomas and, from the start, Blake and Lawrence, those two English eccentrics. He has dedicated poems in a single volume (*A Peopled Landscape,* 1963) to James Dickey *and* Marianne Moore. Although his inquisitive sensibility is rooted in the English habit of contemplation and reticence, and in characteristic British landscapes, Tomlinson seems equally at home elsewhere in the world. Like any sensible rain-soaked Englishman, he also values sunshine. A former resident in the States and a fan of the American Southwest, he has been hard to pin down, even though he is a poet of place, because he has ranged from Mexico (old and New) to upstate New York, Provence, northern Italy, and, most of all, his native Stoke-on-Trent and the Gloucestershire countryside where he has lived for most of his adult life.

Despite his protests of impersonality, we can locate Tomlinson's originality in the claim he makes in the preface to *Collected Poems:* He has striven for a poetry "where space represented possibility and where self would have to embrace that possibility somewhat self-forgetfully, putting aside the more possessive and violent claims of personality." "Self-forgetfully" sounds the note that we on this side of the Atlantic have come to associate with Elizabeth Bishop, another poet whose modest demur ("It's just description . . . they're all just description") also forces us to ask: Exactly what *is* description? And, can a poet display passion along with modesty?

Like Bishop, Tomlinson is nonmilitant but strong-willed in his efforts to escape ego obsessions; he prefers writing humbly about what Wordsworth called "the world of all of us." For all his constancy and impersonality, Tomlinson makes each poem different from the others: In some, description serves its own end; in others, it provokes questions about transcendence. Heeding Emerson's famous command, "Ask the fact for the form," Tomlinson never sounds impoverished, as some American poets (Merwin, for example) do. Rock, stone, and water are for Tomlinson elemental but never naked, always embellished by language, by light, by one another. George Oppen, whom Tomlinson quotes, once suggested: "Let's take out all the adjectives." But this has never been Tomlinson's strategy. He loves adjectives. His dignified diction doesn't shy away from ornate description, nor does it seek out filigree for its own sake. Likewise, his poetic technique favors a small number of fairly conventional poetic forms but a vocabulary loaded with precise, often Latinate terminology. I think of Eliot's formula from "Little Gidding": "The common word exact without vulgarity, / The formal word precise but not pedantic."

Such polite exactness—along with stylistic ravishments—began early for Tomlinson. In his first books there are few first-person experiences or even pronouns; the confessional, self-explorative, or (to use Auden's word in "The Horatians") *foudroyant* mode always left Tomlinson queasy. Yet we can piece together the data of his life from his poems: his wife, daughters, and grandchild, his love of music, his travels to Italy and the States, his friendships with Donald Davie (his Cambridge tutor), Octavio Paz, and the Italian poets Attilio Bertolucci and Paolo Bertolani. And in the latest book the easy flow of pentameter couplets celebrating birthdays and retirements (his own among them) sounds a note of jubilant release after years of scrutinizing practically everything but himself.

When Tomlinson met Marianne Moore they discussed their mutual, intense admiration of Ruskin. All three are ardent observers, sharing a patient willingness to look hard at the world and a belief that "description is revelation," as Wallace Stevens tersely proclaimed. The precision and abundance of his language are even more impressive if we consider what his poetry does without: self-analysis, deep or dream images, heavy-handed symbolism ("Visions are not my style," he admits in his latest book), exclamations or frequent apostrophes (and, by and large, questions), sexual passion, and most other forms of excessive outburst.

Tomlinson himself has written about the relationship between the supposed objectivity of nineteenth-century science, separating the observer from the observed, and the methods of Cézanne and post-Impressionist painting, "an outward gaze that would draw the sensuous world closer to the inner man and that would narrow the gap between abstraction and sensation, between intellect and things" ("The Poet as Painter"). As Hopkins observes in a journal entry: "What you look hard at seems to look hard at you." One comes to self-understanding by examining the surround, in all of its strange otherness. Tomlinson may be our most important phenomenological poet, forcing readers to reenact his own confrontation with an external scene by engaging them in his thickets of diction and syntax.

Description is sometimes an end in itself, sometimes an earnest of something to come. "Apples Painted" (*Annunciations*) may allude to Cézanne, but the unnamed subject becomes the emblem for Everyman-as-Artist, whether master or Sunday dabbler, and for the poet as well:

> He presses the brush-tip. What he wants
>   Is weight such as the blind might feel
> Cupping these roundnesses. The ooze
>   Takes a shapely turn as thought
> Steadies it into touch—touch
>   That is the mind moving, enlightened carnality.
> He must find them out anew, the shapes
>   And the spaces in between them—all that dropped from view
> As the bitten apple staled on unseen.
>   All this he must do with a brush? All this
> With a brush, a touch, a thought—
>   Till the time-filled forms are ripening in their places,

And he sees the painted fruit still loading the tree,
    And the gate stands open in complicity at his return
To a garden beneath the apple boughs' tremulous sway.

These pseudo-elegiac couplets depict depiction. Though not technically ekphrastic, the poem brings the apples into focus only at the end when we have moved backward from result (the apples *painted*) to source. We see the apples now for the first time, but at a double remove, not in the painting but in the garden. "Enlightened carnality"—the fleshly pleasures that appeal to touch and soul simultaneously—provokes the painter to duplicate his delight within his picture, then within his audience.

Tomlinson has disparagingly referred to his "bits of ivory" (a phrase that nods in the direction of Jane Austen, another writer who was supremely confident in her modesty); a more generous evaluation would include his remark, "It is the mind sees," since every creation of a bit of ivory demands an act of total, self-forgetful concentration, whether upon works of art or physical scenes, changes in the weather, or even history and politics, which make infrequent but important appearances in his work. He knows that place is an event in time as well as space, that even when "the place has changed, the image still remains. . . . For place is always an embodiment / And incarnation beyond argument, / Centre and source." He modulates delicately between such polysyllabic phrasing and the nobility of plain speech:

              . . . And now
    The summit gives us all that lies below,
    Shows us the islands slide into their places
    Beyond the shore and, when the lights come on,
    How all the other roads declare themselves
    Garlanding their gradients to the sea,
    How the road that brought us here has dropped away
    A half-lost contour on a chart of lights
    The waters ripple and spread across the bay.

              (from "The Return")

Some of the most powerful poems (e.g., "In Oklahoma," *The Return*) treat bizarre, unpromising, or unconventional landscapes. Here, near the 1864 Tonkawa Hills massacre, prairie flatness has "nothing to hide," so Tomlinson must look even harder to discover (or create) its surprising beauty:

> . . . Only the red
> Declared itself among the leeched-out shades,
> Rose into the buttes, seeped through the plain,
> And left, in standing pools, one wine-dark stain.
> The trees, with their survivors' look, the grasses
> Yellowing into March refused their space
> Those colours that would quicken to the ring
> Of the horizon each declivity
> And flood all in the sap and flare of spring.
> The wideness waited. Sun kept clouded back.
> An armadillo, crushed beside the road,
> Dried out to a plaque of faded blood.
> Here, fundamentalists have pitched their spires
> Lower than that arbiter of wrath to come—
> The tower of the tornado siren
> Latticed in iron against a doubtful sky.

The poem's loose iambic pentameter, its sturdy but irregularly located rhymes ("plain" / "stain," "ring" / "spring"), consonantal or half rhymes ("grasses" / "space," "road" / "blood"), alliterations ("flood" / "flare," "wideness" / "waited"), suit its subject. We hear lazy, almost random sounds approaching but never achieving predictability; likewise, we can locate depth, power, even horror within a seemingly infinite landscape, a desert in which the humanizing details—another legacy from Ruskin and his "pathetic fallacy"—bear witness to a poignant historical scene. Looking hard is equivalent to listening well.

Tomlinson traveled avidly before the humdrum days of easy transcontinental movement. It's a nice irony that his latest volume contains one poem entitled "Against Travel" ("These days are best when one goes nowhere," it begins), followed by two entire sequences about journeys to Portugal and Japan. The urge to move everywhere challenges the need to stay put. At an earlier stage, he is surprised when New Zealand shearsmen turn up in his Gloucestershire valley as migrant workers, only to realize that "Shearsmen and poets travel far these days," and, more important, that the very world is on the move:

> The field now is empty of sheep, the migrants gone.
> Homebound, they must circle the world again,
> Itself a traveller through space and season,
> Trailing the wool wisp vapour of their jetplane.

("From Gloucestershire," *The Door in the Wall*)

In the same volume, "Hartland Cliff" equates poetry with natural movement:

> only the turns of verse
> could contain and then let go
> the accumulation of that flow
> to the shift of light
>
> late afternoon brings
> —to the reshaping of the waters
> by a moon unseen,
> to the sheen and spread of wings.

Attending to a landscape demands patience and a good eye. But Tomlinson is also a watcher of the skies; tracking the weather requires quickness as well as depth of perception. "Weather releases him from the tyranny of rooms, / From the white finality of clapboard houses" ("Weatherman," *The Way of a World*)—so begins a poem set in New England, whose subject could as easily be Tomlinson himself as any Yankee. The noise of migrating geese drives "the eye / Of the mind the way they go, through the opal / Changes of dawn light on the light of snow." In early poems Tomlinson reproduces these quicksilver changes through complex syntax and opulent diction. In later work we find the kind of simplicity of which only a master distiller is capable, as in "Picking Mushrooms By Moonlight" (*The Door in the Wall*), a delicate sonnet in which the mushrooms resemble little moons, a scattered crop that

Answers to the urging of that O,
And so do we, exclaiming as we go,
With rounded lips translating shape to sound,
At finding so much treasure on the ground
Marked out by light. We stoop and gather there
These lunar fruits of the advancing year:
So late in time, yet timely at this date,
They show what forces linger and outwait
Each change of season, rhyme made visible
And felt on the fingertips at every pull.

The poem contains a haphazardly articulated echo of Dryden's great elegy to John Oldham, "Farewell, too little and too lately known." ("Gather," "fruits," "advancing," "time," "show," and "rhyme" are all borrowings from Dryden.) The gentleness of that allusion and the insistence on the relation between natural activity and poetic harvesting—the importunate "O" of wonder paralleling the shape of the moon and the mushroom circle; the effort to "translate" shape to sound; the visible "rhyme" as itself an implicit pun on *rime*-frost which is soon to come—prove how lightly Tomlinson wears his learning.

Whether formal or casual, rhyme can carry metaphysical weight, as Tomlinson suggests at the beginning of "The Chances of Rhyme" (*The Way of a World*), a poem that constitutes a chapter in his ongoing *ars poetica*:

The chances of rhyme are like the chances of meeting—
In the finding fortuitous, but once found, binding.

This is what James Merrill, quoting Keats, meant by "the magic hand of chance." Rhyme is as likely to arrive by accident as by intention, but once the poet has hit upon, or been struck with, the proper music, he has made an inevitable connection. Like marriage, rhyme yokes. Even in the absence of a regular scheme, repeated sounds call our attention to the subject at hand. A distant crane unloads boulders from a boat at the end of a harbor:

. . . The crash
of each stone

> brings a flash of white
> up out of the blue
> and a ripple that still has not ceased
> to spread before the next
> wedding of stone and water
> on a risen sea-bed.

(from "Sight and Sound," *The Door in the Wall*)

"Crash" / "flash," and "spread" / "[wed]" / "bed" are especially delicious in a poem that presents a picture of things inaudible to mortal hearing; everything described takes place out of earshot, but Tomlinson wants us to hear it.

The chances of rhyme and meeting unfold in a series of poems based on simple accidents of misreading. For example, the first and last stanzas of the three-stanza "Autumn Piece" (*Written on Water*):

> Baffled
> by the choreography of the season
> the eye could not
> with certainty see
> whether it was wind
> stripping the leaves or
> the leaves were struggling to be free:
> . . . .
> As the car resisted it [the force of the wind]
> you felt it in either hand
> commanding car, tree, sky,
> master of chances,
> and at a curve was a red
> board said "Danger":
> I thought it said dancer.

"Chances" features natural chaos, autumnal choreography, willful and hopeful misreadings, and, of course, the irregular but happy rhymes in "see" / "free," "hand" / "command," and "red" / "said," those stays against confusion. The implicit meaning of such visual mistakes, cognitive dissonances, and rhyming schemes sounds most exuberantly in the Hopkinsesque "Ritornello" (and Tomlinson is seldom a bravura poet), an eleven-line jeu d'esprit that begins and ends thus:

> Wrong has a twisty look like wrung misprinted
> Consider! and you con the stars for meanings
> Sublime comes climbing from beneath the threshold
> Experience? you win it out of peril
>
> . . . .
>
> Abstraction means something pulled away from
> Humus means earth place purchase and return

Witty sequences like this one cannot disguise Tomlinson's serious engagements with sound. They also may encourage us to classify his work within that species of poetry most hospitable to the wit of performance and nature description: the pastoral.

In William Empson's famous formula, pastoral filters the complex through the simple. Tomlinson has been obsessed not only with the green world but also with our mythic relations to it. His version of Adam has been dispossessed of Eden; only Arden can harbor him. We, his heirs, are in danger of losing even this subsidiary version of paradise:

> Arden is not Eden, but Eden's rhyme:
>   Time spent in Arden is time at risk
> And place, also: for Arden lies under threat:
>   Ownership will get what it can for Arden's trees:
> No acreage of green-belt complacencies
>   Can keep Macadam out: Eden lies guarded:
> Pardonable Adam, denied its gate,
>   Walks the grass in a less-than-Eden light
> And whiteness that shines from a stone burns with his fate:
> . . . .
> Adam in Arden tastes its replenishings:
>   Through its dense heats the depths of Arden's springs
> Convey echoic waters—voices
>   Of the place that rises through this place
> Overflowing, as it brims its surfaces
>   In runes and hidden rhymes, in chords and keys

> Where Adam, Eden, Arden run together
> And time itself must beat to the cadence of this river.

(from "In Arden," The Shaft)

We are all (as the poet describes himself elsewhere) "poised between paradise and history." The similar-sounding words echo the displacement from the Garden we have been trying to overcome since that first day. Adam is out, Macadam in: The satiric note does not lessen the deeper allegiance of Tomlinson's sense of exile and reintegration to Wallace Stevens' stoic aesthetics: "From this the poem springs: that we live in a place / That is not our own and, much more, not ourselves / And hard it is in spite of blazoned days."

Tomlinson's eagle eye and his musician's ear have allowed him to read some of the runes and to hear some of those "hidden rhymes" that course through our precariously habitable Arden-Eden. Both given and denied paradise, we live ambiguously in a middle sphere, neither belonging nor disenfranchised:

> ... There is no
> Bridge but the thread of patience, no way
> But the will to wish back Eden, this leaning
> To stand against the persuasions of a wind
> That rings with its meaninglessness where it sang its meaning.

(from "Eden," The Way of a World)

The bridge of rhyme underlies Tomlinson's technique and accounts for his generally moderate tones. In "Against Extremity" (*The Way of a World*), he prudently demands:

> Let there be treaties, bridges,
> Chords under the hands, to be spanned,
> Sustained: extremity hates a given good
> Or a good gained.

To an American ear, such diplomacy must sound a distinctly British note of compromise. The pleasures of Tomlinson's poetry depend on a willingness to appreciate, if not to share, these elegant formulations of pastoral conservatism.

A left-leaning reader might argue that Tomlinson everywhere betrays the too easy demeanor of the aesthete. In "The Garden" (*Annunciations*), he takes a straight shot at those Marxist critics who fail to see the transcendent value of pastoral:

> And now they say
> Gardens are merely the expression of a class
> Masterful enough to enamel away
> All signs of the labour that produced them.
> This crass reading forgets that imagination
> Outgoes itself, outgrows aim
> And origin; forgets that art
> Does not offer the sweat of parturition
> As proof of its sincerity.

So much for all those whom Harold Bloom dismisses as the Resentniks. But elsewhere Tomlinson admits to a change in his own point of view, late in coming: "It took time to convince me that I cared / For more than beauty: I write to rescue what is no longer there—absurd / A place should be more fragile than a book" ("Dates: Penkhull New Road," *The Way In* [1974]). He is right. Many of the early poems (especially in *The Necklace*, 1955) are as brittle and self-consciously arty as James Merrill's contemporaneous early work. The Mediterranean "bewilders with an excessive formality" and "Art exists at a remove," he announces in two characteristic, tasteful lyrics. Like Merrill, Tomlinson moved out from behind the protective cover of aestheticism without giving up his devotion to the things of this world and to the ardors of his own eye. The move from aesthete to elegist is perhaps an inevitable progress as one ages, especially for a poet whom we can now, through hindsight, place in the greater Romantic tradition of Wordsworth, Tennyson, Hardy, and Yeats—which asks us to look soberly at and to feel at home in this world, however tentative our hold on it.

Yet even this note sounded relatively early, in "On the Hall at Stowey" (*Seeing Is Believing*, 1958). The poem reads as though the Philip Larkin of "Church Going" were walking the countryside with the Wordsworth of "The Ruined Cottage," but Tomlinson refuses to preach or to stretch toward symbolism. What he sees on his excursion is a hall ruined by updating and supposed improvements ("Each hearth refitted / For a suburban whim") and then undone by abandonment, neglect, and natural decay. The end prepares us for Wordsworthian moralizing, but there is none, just a rare statement of clarified emotion:

> . . . Saddened,
> Yet angered beyond sadness, where the road
> Doubled upon itself I halted, for a moment
> Facing the empty house and its laden barns.

This is hardly the elegiac tone of a conventional aesthete. Instead, it reveals its author's working-class distaste for wastefulness, superficiality, pretension, arrogance, conspicuous consumption, and unmitigated human stupidity. In an early *ars poetica,* he refuses "nothing which is not elegant / And nothing which is if it is merely that." Between these two Stevensian nothings Tomlinson has amassed the substantial stones of his edifice.

The first poem of Tomlinson's that I fell in love with was "Swimming Chenango Lake" (*The Way of the World* [1969]). It opens with chilling meteorological certainty:

> Winter will bar the swimmer soon.
> He reads the water's autumnal hesitations
> A wealth of ways: it is jarred,
> It is astir already despite its steadiness,
> Where the first leaves at the first
> Tremor of the morning air have dropped
> Anticipating him, launching their imprints
> Outwards in eccentric, overlapping circles.

For the rest, Tomlinson construes the "geometry of water" as his swimmer moves "between grasp and grasping" with a delicate breast-stroke through a frigid baptism, yielding to a buoyancy that braces and sustains. When I met the poet, years after I had first read the poem, I came equipped with the assurance of a critic who had already figured things out. It struck me that only a person who understood the pleasures of New England lakes (especially in the fall) and who knew the sensation of working through, within, and on top of water could have written such a sympathetic rendition of a physical event. The poem, I thought, disguised an autobiographical experience. I observed with matter-of-fact confidence: "You must love swimming; you know how it feels."

"Oh, no," he replied, "I can't swim at all; I was just looking at that fellow. I watched very long and very hard." *Just looking.* As Elizabeth Bishop said with equal parts of self-deprecation and self-understanding, "It's just description." You suspect, however, that it's also something more.

WILLARD SPIEGELMAN

Kingsley Tufts. *After Images: The Collected Poems of Kingsley Tufts.* John Daniel and Company / Fithian Press 1994. 365 pp. $19.95

My poet friends are a dedicated, even ascetic lot. Yet a recent poll—limited and haphazard though it was—revealed a conventionally hedonistic streak, at least as regards what they'd choose to be doing at the moment of their deaths. Beaches, alcohol, meals in Paris and Rome, drugs, sex, and Mardi Gras were mentioned. One loftier soul answered, after a moment, "Listening to Mozart. No—Beethoven. Or maybe Nirvana?" Another pollee reverted to the fear- and incense-shrouded aura of her Catholic childhood and said she hoped she'd be at Mass after having had "a really good time" the night before. But none of my music-loving pals wanted to die in the sweetly befitting manner of Kingsley Tufts: while reading a recently finished poem to loved ones. Tufts was an author of popular magazine fiction in the 1950s, but his true vocation, he came to feel, was poetry. Indeed, he stopped writing stories for *Collier's* and *Ladies' Home Journal* to devote the last three decades of his life to versifying, and when he died, on Christmas Day 1991, he'd amassed a 350-page manuscript of poems. "I feel dizzy" were Tufts's last words, according to his wife, Kate Tufts, who endowed a lucrative award in his name, she freely admits, to bring greater attention to her husband's work.

Neither dizziness nor other nouns indicating vertigo or intoxication spring to mind while reading *After Images,* the recently published collection of Tufts's work. For he carefully navigates the paths of moderation and acceptance in the book, whether the emotions he steers through are joy, despair, regret, or even rage. The poems work best when that stoic equanimity is questioned, as in the Larkin-by-way-of-Hardy piece "Flood":

> Rain was like blood on the cables of empty bridges.
> And wind was a dirge above rivers heavy with clay.

Men stood in their wet boots on the high ridges;
    Saw cattle and tools, saw everything carried away.
"We've saved ourselves," one said, "but the land is gone."
    "My house was new," said another, and picked up a stone
And threw it. "By god, you'd think . . ., his lips were drawn
    Tight as a sewed sack, and he walked off alone.

"You men ought to dry out your clothes." The tone was sharp.
    A man offered matches. "I guess they got wet," he said.
A boy's cold thumb struck twice on a Jew's harp
    Pressed to his teeth. A man in the group turned his head.
"It's all right, son—if you want to, go on and play."
But the boy stood still, and he put the harp away.

While this poem's title hearkens back to biblical apocalypse, the poet brings a contemporary and tough-minded specificity to bear upon the anecdote he relates. The *mise-en-scène* details of the blood-like rain on the bridges' cables and the mournful sound of the wind are exact and resonant, and the images that follow embody the bitten-back sorrow these men feel. One's lips are "drawn / Tight as a sewed sack"; another offers matches, a demotic version of that traditional symbol for hope, a candle; and a boy's dimestore instrument becomes an image of the impossibility of song in the face of catastrophe. That catastrophe may be local, but it assumes a larger and more mythic importance, the quotations from wet-booted men standing on the ridges above the swollen river working like an appropriately twentieth-century version of a Greek chorus.

   "Flood" appears in the section of *After Images* called "Nature." The book is arranged thematically, not chronologically, its poems positioned according to whether their subject matter seems closest to "Love," "Poetry and the Arts," "Perspectives," "Anti-War Poems," "Stories," "Potpourri," "Life and Death," and the aforementioned "Nature." This greeting card concept of poetry also applies, unfortunately, to the great majority of the poems themselves. Tufts is often predictable, cloying, and guilty of representing the most generic observations about sublunary existence as poetry. "The Wild, Wild Flowers" seems an appropriate quotation here:

> What has become of the wild, wild flowers?
> My heart cries out to know.
> Where are they now, my wild, young flowers—
> And where did the glory go?
>
> Was the summer sun too much for you?
> Did you quickly burn away,
> Or last until fall when the deep, deep blue
> Of heaven turned ashen gray?
>
> It is winter now and the long, long hours
> Of remembrance rest like snow
> On the silent fields where the wild, wild flowers
> Were blooming long ago.

The rhymes here are utterly hackneyed, as opposed to the deft off-rhyming of "gone," "stone," and "drawn" in "Flood"; the meter veers from singsong regularity to inept looseness. "The Wild, Wild Flowers" was written as though the decrepit school of Georgian poets that Pound railed against for choking on their own "emotional slither" had somehow resurfaced in the latter half of our century, entirely unscathed by modernism. The phrase of Georgian verse—"dim fields of peace"—that Pound skewers in one of his manifestoes could be inserted in the last stanza of Tufts's poem with no alteration.

Tufts preferred to work in received forms and meters, and he is at his best in the epigrammatic genre, which almost requires a measure of salt, like the best desserts. When his poems are sufficiently terse and anchored in the nuttiness of contemporary life, Tufts restrains his lunges toward the sublime. For example, "Fifty Minute Hour," an examination of the twentieth century's secular religion, ends with two deftly amusing stanzas whose strong rhymes are appropriate to the humorous tone:

> Fifty minutes may be shocking,
> Couch-recumbent noggin-knocking—
> Fur and feathers, such as farce is—
> Past and present, sex and schlocking,
> Plot and play—but no catharsis.

> Still and all, beyond a dim doubt,
> Weaseling in and weaseling out,
>   Self is self's own remedy.
> Talk and tears, turned roundabout
> Shed insight spiked with comedy.

And the genuinely moving "If Death Should Come" eerily anticipates the manner of Tufts's death (he was holding his pipe when stricken by the fatal heart attack):

> If death should come, and hiding wait for me
> To choose his hour and take me unawares,
> He'll find me much as an old man, who, tired of smoking,
> Knocks out his pipe, and slowly climbs the stairs.

Tufts doubtless yearned to be remembered for his poetry. While he may be recalled more for his association with an award than his art, there is a dignity and pathos in such longing reflected in a poem like this, even though the reader may be unsure as to whether "If Death Should Come" fits best in "Perspectives," "Life and Death," or "Potpourri."

Anne Porter. *An Altogether Different Language: Poems 1934–1994*. Zoland Books 1994. 94 pp. $16.95

An Altogether Different Language collects poems spanning sixty years in the life of Anne Porter, wife of the renowned painter, Fairfield Porter, with whom she reared five children. The poet comes bearing laurels in the form of praise offered by John Ashbery, Amy Clampitt, and Barbara Guest, who speak both of Porter's religious vision and her more worldly one, which is often turned toward the natural and domestic realms. These domains are united for Porter by the figure of St. Francis, that long-popular paragon of gentleness toward animals whose *Little Flowers* preach the acceptance, even glorification, of humble daily chores. Porter's patron saint appears in several poems included here; unfortunately typical of these is "Song for the Town of Assisi," a poem of mostly nebulous longing and resignation:

> And I know now
> I'll never climb
> That high wooded mountain
> Where Francis had his cave
>
> On one September night
> Beside that very cave
> The five wounds of the Passion
> Pierced him through and through
>
> And even now
> His every wound is singing

Later in the poem, Porter looks forward to the time of death as an occasion of mixed blessings, represented by the image of the Jordan River. "The black the terrible / The blessed river," Porter calls it, in one of the too-rare but genuine, God-dazzled instances of awe that light *An Altogether Different Language.*

This awe arises from the consideration of mystery, whose gifts are nearly always paradoxical. For example, the central mysteries of Christianity—Incarnation, Crucifixion, and Resurrection—each contain an impossible blurring of borders between man and God, between dull earthly matter and pure fiery spirit. Sylvia Plath writes of the terror of religious experience in late poems like "Mystic," where she asks "Once one has seen God, what is the remedy?" In Porter's work, however, the possibilities for terror, even for tension, are often entirely ignored. The many poems set in gardens tend to present visions and visitations blandly, as hardly more astonishing than the appearance of earthworms or cabbage moths. Whereas Porter's discovery that lilies emit a "feral perfume" is interesting and original, "Listen to the rose / Be the voice of the rose" provokes disastrous comparisons with Eliot's *Burnt Norton.* It's not surprising that a life combining five children, rural landscape, and devout Anglo- or Roman Catholicism would result in poems in which the immanent and the transcendent nudge and jostle each other; but that they do so like the most benign of sibling rivals—"Easter is growing / In the paschal moon / like a child in its mother"—is a disappointment.

Porter is at her best in lapidary bits of description and in moments that admit complication. The former are found in poems like "Consider the Lilies of the Sea," which begins with a beautifully orchestrated stanza reminiscent of Bishop's early work.

> Their salt wet life erased, eroded, only
> The shells of snails lie on the sand,
> Their color darkens toward the whorl's conclusion,
> The center is nearly black. Even the fragments
> Faithfully observe their tribal custom
> Of involution; the motionless whirlpool
> Is clearly written on the broken shield.

The iambic backbeat here provides a frame for memorable music, the liquids combining with the soft vowels to echo the ocean's susurrus. This poem further distinguishes itself from "Song for the Town of

Assisi" and most others in the volume by the specificity of its details. To be pierced by the five wounds of the Passion is pretty generic stuff; to see the contours of a snail's shell as bearing an emblem of the "tribal custom / Of involution" is fresh and telling. "Consider the Lilies of the Sea" stands as an oblique but resonant statement about the tribal customs of women and the ways in which art can be written—even brokenly—out of the lives that make shields and evasions necessary.

In a busier, more complex mode, "A Child at the Circus" shows the influence of one of Porter's frequent houseguests, James Schuyler. Here we are presented with bright messy incongruities that she doesn't insist on watering down into paler harmonies.

> When you're a traveller and the evening air turns golden
> Every house you pass begins to look like home
> Because it's supper-time, it's time to be at home.
> But there's another stormier light that's golden-green
> With the chemical green beauty of the green beans cooked in soda
> Or the false gold light on the false green trees of the theater.

The breathy tone of celebration and the ease with repetitions— "golden," "home," "time," "light," and "green"—that would have sent prissier writers scuttling for their thesauri are pure Schuyler. Being married to a visual artist doubtless helped to shape Porter's eye; however, the painterly, slightly wacky comparison of storm-light to the color of "green beans cooked in soda" again seems a legacy from Schuyler, showing that Porter has assimilated the lessons of poems like "December" and "Quick, Henry, the Flit."

But "Consider the Lilies of the Sea" and "A Child at the Circus" are rare notable moments in Porter's collection. Appearing far more frequently in *An Altogether Different Language* are forgettable poems about gardens and religion. No doubt the teachings of the latter—acceptance, compassion, and equability were Saint Francis's special virtues, after all—have served Porter well in a life that's had its difficulties, one of which has surely been her marriage to a more famous artist. Are we truly to believe, nonetheless, that the greatest hardship her mentally-handicapped son Johnny presented was a penchant for puns his mother couldn't always find funny? While Porter's temperament and system of beliefs are not causes for justifiable complaint, the too-many bland or treacly poems in *An Altogether Different Language* are. In their midst, I wish that Porter had invoked, with St. Francis's gentle and loving vision, the harsh roiling ecstasies of St. Theresa, at least every once in a while.

DIANN BLAKELY SHOAF

Selecteds

ALICE AYCOCK
The Silent Speakers: Every Day I'm Born, Every Night I Die

Balanced on the Ledge above the Dark

Howard Nemerov. *Trying Conclusions: New and Selected Poems, 1961–1991.* University of Chicago Press 1991. 161 pp. $18.95

Not too long before his death in 1991, Howard Nemerov must have watched on television a series on American poets called *Voices and Visions,* for which I was a consultant. After he died, I read the wry poem ("Media") he wrote about it; he watched the series, one could say, pre-posthumously, to see what becomes of a poet after he or she has died. I saw the series through his eyes: how in the films the poems, each a kernel of something felt, registered, and formulated, became a few excerpted words, muddled into the life, glossed with a few conventional images, appraised by one of the living (though in the brief time between production and presentation, Basil Bunting, who commented on Pound, had died). All is indiscriminately absorbed into the equalizing maw of the camera:

> The TV has been showing movies of dead poets
> lately, they come on once a week or so,
> movies mostly of stills of the dead poets,
> the passport photographs, the family groups
> with the child poet circled in sepia ink.
>
> The black and white poets are read and discussed
> by poets in living color, though some have died since.
> The camera doesn't always know what to do
> while the poems are being read, but drifts
> across a crowd of faces or a rural scene
> or waves breaking in splash and spray
> against black rocks and leaving a shampoo of foam;
> sometimes referring to the words that are being said,
> oftener not, but always in images poetical

suggestive of the well-loved themes of poetry,
nature and innocence and cruel indifference,
sorrow, and memories cemetery-still,

while the living poets read and interrupt
the reading with reminiscences of praise
and remarks interpretive about the dead poets
whose transitive poems are being printed out
across the screen, across the crowd of faces,
and all is again as though it had never been.

It is a genially polite despair that is recorded here, but it is despair
nonetheless—an acknowledgment on the poet's part that what to him
is supreme, language in an enacting arrangement, gets lost in every
unspooling public *hommage.* Since what the public wants is commentary—biography, theme, praise, interpretation, illustration, generalization—everything in the TV program is given more weight than those
"transitive poems" that vanish so quickly from the screen. Shakespeare
might have felt the same watching Verdi's *Otello:* No translation of
language to another medium could satisfy a writer.

This late poem by Nemerov indicts all the "meta-men and para-
things" (Stevens) around poetry itself, insisting on the irreducibility and
untranslatability of the complex system of relations we call a poem.
Nemerov was a natural teacher in his poetry, and one of the things I
noticed most, rereading him for this review, was how often he thought
of metaphors for that system of relations and what it could offer us. My
favorite figure occurs in a poem called "A Christmas Storm," when he
sees the landscape after an ice storm. He writes of the "scintillant fans /
Of bush and tree turned emblems of themselves":

Where every twig is one and three, itself,
Its chrysalis in ice transparent, and last
Haloed in splintering light.

The Trinitarian perfection of a poem is that it contains the real world,
which is then glazed (as is Williams' wheelbarrow) with the transparent
chrysalis of language, which in its turn gives off the "splintering light"
of insight, hallowed (haloed) by its freight of emotion. The sacredness

of a verbal work of art, in this view, is inseparable from its language (the transparency that cooperates with the eye of the beholder to make being glitter). Nemerov's glumness as he watched *Voices and Visions* is a response any reader of poetry will share. And yet maybe the transitive poems found their way to some viewers through the waves and the passport pictures; one can only hope so.

A reviewer, too, is conscious of binding in swathes of alien language the finely perfected things that are the cause of the review. Any poem is oddly denatured by being inserted into a piece of prose instead of standing free as music to be heard in the ear as well as read on the page. "Ah, Howard," I want to say, "your poems can stand by themselves; and it's a way of doing you honor, that's all, to festoon them with critical language." He would have offered his morose smile and a quip in return.

So, with apologies, I go on to the posthumous *Selected Poems*. It's only the tip of an iceberg, of course—the fiction is elsewhere, the copious *Collected Poems* elsewhere, the essays elsewhere, and the letters as yet uncollected. Nemerov was unsparing with himself in winnowing his work: I miss many poems from the *Collected* to which I am attached (especially the nature poems). But I also like having mostly the mature Nemerov here: The young imitator of Yeats, Auden, and Frost has been quietly suppressed from these pages, and the independent master remains.

What was interesting in reading early Nemerov was to see him looking for his subject. He knew it had something to do with the social world (Yeats and Auden) and with the natural world (Frost). And yet he was not a hot-tempered poet like Yeats; or a boys'-band secret-society poet like Auden; or a subtly malicious poet like Frost. That is, there was something "wrong" about each of them, temperamentally, as models for Nemerov. He was more gloomy than Yeats, more solitary than Auden, more indulgent than Frost.

There was something else "wrong" about them, too. Yeats, though a poet of philosophical abstraction of the sort Nemerov would also turn out to be, was not primarily that. He was essentially a psychological poet, interested in exploring his personal feelings (witness all the poems to women, from Maud Gonne through Dorothy Wellesley, and all the political polemics). And Auden, though a socially aware poet of the sort Nemerov would also turn out to be, was more sociable than Nemerov, and less sociological. And Frost, though a nature poet of the sort Nemerov would also turn out to be, wanted to draw explicit ethical morals from his landscapes, while Nemerov was interested in the precession of the planets, not in "counter-love, original response."

It speaks well of Nemerov that he knew whither he was drawn, and how to escape from those very attractions. In the *Selected Poems,* he is mostly the accomplished writer who has found his own way. He had a sturdy sense of the whole scale of the universe, from the Pleiades down to the sidewalk, and for him the best poem incorporated that whole scale—implied, if not described. The first requirement, then, for the Nemerovian template is a cosmic/domestic scale. He was determined, too, to employ a linguistic range running from the refined to the coarse; this aspect Nemerov managed less well, though it is to his credit that he tried to include, in the lyric repertory, the male coarseness that refers to "tits" and "shit" and "piss." A third requirement for the Nemerovian poem was that behind every image should lie its law. A fourth requirement had to do with momentum: No poem was alive, for Nemerov, unless it replicated in its processes the inexorable, if serene, unfolding of the universe's natural physical motions.

What a strange set of necessities that was! And how daunting it must have seemed to the young Nemerov, as he discovered his own compulsions, to have to obey these laws! Of course, sometimes, and even sometimes in the *Selected,* he fails: The balance of coarse and fine isn't quite right, or the momentum becomes a tic, or the cosmic aspects overbalance the domestic, or the law is lost in the image. Nonetheless, when it all works, it produces the amalgam of personal style we call "Nemerov," a style inimitable and recognizably his.

Here is a relatively unfamiliar poem from 1984 which exhibits all these characteristics in small. "Reverie of the Termite Queen" concerns free will and determinism in human beings, though focused onto the blind force observable in insects, as the termite queen speaks:

> Sealed with my consort in the royal room
> Under the hill that I have never seen
> But made the makers of, I lie in state
> While minions ply me with both food and drink

To cosset Majesty while I factor forth
The hundred million children whom I must
Outlive a hundred times before I may
Collapse the shrivelled whistle of my womb

At last effete and do what distinguished thing
One does to die. My proles, my infantry,
Parade on their endless errands hither and yon
Above my mystery, the soul of state,

Where I lie pulsing full with the ignorant host
That I dismiss into the world without,
Concerning which I am both dark and blind
As to what it may be, and why it is.

Like all suggestive allegories, this can be taken several ways. Its Hardy-esque blind unconscious will ruling as "the soul of state" and commanding ignorant armies is nevertheless a Jamesian consciousness aware of the approach of the "distinguished thing" (as James denominated death). Its disgusting hill-enclosure is all it knows of the universe; its teeming surround is all it knows of action. Its exhaustion in breeding is both physical ("the shrivelled whistle of my womb"—the most inspired phrase in the poem) and mental ("children whom I must / Outlive a hundred times before I may / Collapse"). The queen is as intensely conscious of the law ("I must") and of its irrationality ("my mystery") as she is of her ignorance of the what and why of the world. Her single-sentence unstoppable reverie ranges in diction from "proles" to "Majesty," from "errands" to "effete." And she is finally a parody of Milton's God:

His state
Is kingly; thousands at his bidding speed
And post o'er land and ocean without rest.

"I lie in state / . . . My proles, my infantry, / Parade on their endless errands hither and yon." Such are the grim pleasures of reading Nemerov.

He tended, in his later poems, to avoid rhyme, substituting for it cunning arrangements of alliteration and syntax to bind words and lines together. He had published, in 1962, an early *ars poetica* called "Lion & Honeycomb" (see Yeats in "Vacillation": "The lion and the honeycomb, what has Scripture said?" alluding to Samson finding a honeycomb in a dead lion's jaw: "Out of strength came forth sweetness"). The sort of sweetness Nemerov was after was not sensuous but visual and geometrical, and that, he thought, would come forth from the strength of blank verse better than from the frivolity of rhyme:

> He didn't want to do it with skill,
> He's had enough of skill. If he never saw
> Another villanelle, it would be too soon;
> And the same went for sonnets. If it had been
> Hard work learning to rhyme it would be much
> Harder learning not to. The time came
> He had to ask himself, what did he want?
> What did he want when he began
> That idiot fiddling with the sounds of things?
>
> He asked himself, poor moron, because he had
> Nobody else to ask. The others went right on
> Talking about form, talking about myth
> And the (so help us) need for a modern idiom.
> The verseballs among them kept counting syllables.

(*Plus ça change* . . . Nemerov's satire would do these days to skewer the neoformalists.) He proceeds to hope that he can find "vowels like water, consonants like rock." No matter that "everybody kept discussing values and the need for values"; he would go on looking for "an integer / Fixed in the middle of the fall of things, / Perfected and casual as to a child's eye / Soap bubbles are, and skipping stones." If the architectonics and the alliteration were in place, who needed rhyme?

Nemerov had no use for moral cant; he had his far more remote Spinozan view of immovable Necessity. He pricked pompousness impishly, and enjoyed, as one title has it, "Answering Back," even if the person purveying cant at that moment was his beloved Yeats, who had asked, with rhetorical grandeur, "Does the imagination dwell the most

/ Upon a woman won or a woman lost?" Thereupon Nemerov answers back (in rhyme, in homage to Yeats):

> You silly Willie, on the woman lost.
> The woman won sits in the inglenook
> Across from you, knitting or reading a book
> Or come your teatime doing the toast and bacon;
> Whereas the woman lost is God knows where
> In the world, and with whom, if not by now a ghost
> Past yours or anyone's love, though still you care
> Lest she be by another bespoken or taken—
> For what's romantic love unless forsaken?

Yet in dismissing cant, Nemerov did not dismiss moral discourse. He admired it in Larkin, for instance, whose unblinking view of things came closest, among modern poets, to Nemerov's own. One of the best poems in Nemerov's last collection, *Trying Conclusions,* is an elegy for Larkin, representing him as "the master of a style / Able to see things as he saw through things":

> The penetrative emptiness of that gaze
> Kindly accusing none, forgiving none,
> Is just the look upon the face of truth,
> Mortality knowing itself as told to do.

The absence of illusion Nemerov admired in Larkin (and in Lucretius among classical poets) is his own claim on us. It is the basis of his light verse as of his serious verse, and of the many verses he made that are both light and serious at once, among them his imperturbable account—full of his unsparing momentum—of U.S. presidential electioneering. It is called "The Process," and shows, somewhat unusually for Nemerov, an anthropologist's-eye view of a sociological process that has become so routinized it takes on the inflexibility of a natural law:

> Every four years or every eight,
> A dozen gents and maybe a couple of dames
> Announce they have received the money and the Word
> That fits them for the highest office in the land.
> And so begins the Process,

With winnowing and sorting, winter to spring
With travel and talk and too much chicken à la king,
Till by the summer's end but two remain
To take the road again,

Traducing each other's patriotism, race,
And putative paternity, with one hand out
For the money the other throws away
On balloons and signs and party favors,

Till come November the survivor is allowed to say
That providence, and guidance divine,
Have brought him to the highest office in the land
And the greatest power ever known on earth,

Where he will be advised by expertise,
Instructed what to say and how to smile
While saying it; where he will be cartooned
And told to do this and that until
He either does it or he doesn't.

For this he gets to live in a grand house
Infiltrated by a thousand tourists in a day
And overseen by servants, while the same
Vain music is played wherever he walks—

Such is the Process. . . .

"I dare you to say this isn't how it is," Nemerov implies, as he exposes the Emperor's new clothes. And yet there's no real moral indignation here; Nemerov implies that all over the world some such process goes on in producing those who will be leaders of the tribe. This particular chicken-à-la-king version is ours; but probably there's a Chinese and an Icelandic version too. The "nothing to be done" syndrome is powerful in Nemerov, as in Larkin, and there is both exhilaration and depression in their exposés of recalcitrant human reality. Nemerov's poem "On Getting out of Vietnam" goes the mythological route in its ironic gesture toward human self-repetition:

Theseus, if he did destroy the Minotaur
(it's hard to say, that may have been a myth),
Was careful not to close the Labyrinth.
So After kept on looking like Before:
Back home in Athens still the elders sent
Their quota of kids to Knossos, confident
They would find something to die of, and for.

The despairing alternative to such a dispassionate and even forgiving gaze on human aberration was always present to Nemerov in the person of his sister, the photographer Diane Arbus, who saw the same grotesqueries as Nemerov, but ended up a suicide. There is a touching elegy to her ("To D——, Dead by her own Hand"):

And now you've gone,
Who would no longer play the grown ups' game
Where, balanced on the ledge above the dark,
You go on running and you don't look down,
Nor ever jump because you fear to fall.

Nemerov kept his own balance on that ledge, in part because of his great attachment to the beautiful (whereas Arbus could not see the beautiful for the deformed).

Nemerov's hymns to the beautiful include poems in praise of art. A Japanese artist of a thousand years ago painted *Fish Swimming amid Falling Flowers,* and Nemerov, suspending his wonted irony before the silk scroll, agrees

That carp did always swim, and always will.
In just that way, with just that lightning sweep
Of eye, wrist, brush across the yielding silk
Stretched tight with surface tension as the pool
Of pale gold water, pale gold watered silk.

Nemerov was a poet renewed by light and by what light did to the things of the world. He admired how Vermeer could render that process— "being in love with light / And the marvelous things that light is able to do":

> At one for once with sunlight falling through
> A leaded window, the holy mathematic
> Plays out the cat's cradle of relation
> Endlessly; even the inexorable
> Domesticates itself and becomes charm.

Even though most of Nemerov's fine seasonal poems are elegiac, it is natural beauty as much as its vanishing that prevails in them. In his late "Landscape with Self-Portrait," he shows himself formulating the difficult beauty before his eyes while he sits in a rocking chair on a porch:

> And there to watch the tarnished silver cloud
> Advancing up the valley on a wind
> That shudders the leaves and turns them silverside
> While shadows sweep over stubble and grass,
> And sudden the heavy silver of the first
> Raindrops blown slanting in and summer cold
> And turning continuous in silver strings.

There is a great deal more to say about this poem of "the life-defeated self," but all I want to notice at the moment is the balance, in this one small passage, between the entropic and the beautiful, the beautiful and the entropic. If there is silver, it is tarnished; if there is summer, it is cold; if there are leaves, they shudder; if they turn, yet the turning shows their silver side; if there is grass, it is shadowed; if there are raindrops, yet they are heavy silver; if the rain turns continuous, yet it does so in silver strings; if a cloud advances, it goes not down the valley but up. The perplexity of perceiving life from the perspective of death has never been better rendered.

There is a hope in Nemerov generated from light, confirmed by the mind's play in light. He said that about himself in the last poem in this book, the title poem, "Trying Conclusions," with the pun intended. He was dying of incurable cancer, his face already gaunt from it on the jacket picture of the *Selected Poems*. He had refused life-prolonging treatment, preferring to live out his days without the horrors of chemotherapy. In his last months, he remembered his tour of duty as a pilot in World War II, taking off down the runway and up into the sky, and wrote his own elegy:

What rational being, after seventy years,
When Scripture says he's running out of rope,
Would want more of the only world he knows?

No rational being, he while he endures
Holds on to the inveterate infantile hope
That the road ends but as the runway does.

That peculiar combination of gnomic stoicism and buoyant curiosity says "Nemerov" to us as we meet it on the page. If Nemerov was stubborn about not believing, he was also elated in his nonbelief.

What all this had to do with being Jewish was a question he himself raised from time to time—in a poem called "Graven Images," in another called "The Image and the Law," in a tender nature poem called "Acorn, Yom Kippur," and, more humorously, in an early Yeatsian self-defining poem called "Debate with the Rabbi":

You've lost your religion, the Rabbi said.
      It wasn't much to keep, said I.
You should affirm the spirit, said he,
And the communal solidarity.
      I don't feel so solid, I said.

We are the people of the Book, the Rabbi said.
      Not of the phone book, said I.
Ours is a great tradition, said he,
And a wonderful history.
      But history's over, I said.

We Jews are creative people, the Rabbi said.
      Make something, then, said I.
In science and in art, said he,
Violinists and physicists have we.
      Fiddle and physic indeed, I said.

Stubborn and stiff-necked man! the Rabbi cried.
      The pain you give me, said I.
Instead of bowing down, said he,

> You go on in your obstinacy.
> We Jews are that way, I replied.

The things Nemerov mentions here, even if satirically, as "Jewish," are qualities we find in him: the spirit, human solidarity, books, art, creativity, and history (of the Minotaur-mythological sort). They may not come in shapes the Rabbi is prepared to recognize—any more than the Bishop recognized St. Jerome in Crazy Jane's "Love has pitched his mansion in / The place of excrement"—but the influence of the rabbis (and Freud as their successor) in Nemerov is not hard to find, and will be explored as his intellectual identity is further examined. Still, for all his allegiance to the Law, his first veneration goes to language,

> Whose Gödelian and Delphic word has ever been
> *Don't look under the hood while driving the car.*

Now there's a Law for you, but not one that will be found in the religious Fathers. It is the sly poet's own, and one proper to those ambiguous authorities Gödel, who showed there could be no self-coherent system, and Apollo of Delphi, whose oracles were notoriously indeterminate. The fickle combination of inspiration and tinkering that is poetry escapes the more communal laws of social cohesion, and lives in "a dumbshow of predicaments untold / Moving familiarly among the worlds" ("A Blind Man at the Museum").

Where does Nemerov stand among his contemporaries? That will be clearer a generation hence. Like Bishop and Ginsberg, he found a style and kept to it; but he kept evolving, as they did, in emotional terms, though broadly within the same style. He was not so volatile or imaginative as Ammons, Lowell, or Berryman; and he was more controlled by irony than any of them, though all three had (in the case of Ammons, has) a plentiful supply of it. Though less imaginative than Plath or Ginsberg, and less technically inventive than either Merrill or Ashbery, he was better at satire than any of them, and funnier than any, gloomier than any. What he brought to American verse was a firm look at the worst, a Hardyesque atheism, a biting view of the political process, a Thoreauvian acuteness of perception, and a keen sense of the absurd. His is a poetry for grown-ups, free of illusion and unashamed of its intellectuality. He had no time for a sentimental populism or a falsely ingenuous "democratic" minimalism. Mind was precious to him, and he would not denigrate its tragic reverie. He knew, of course, that he would never be a popular poet:

> Now listen, Howie, if anyone ever read
> Those little verses that you sometimes do,
> It wouldn't have been because they wanted to hear
> About age, old age, and illness, and the grave
> Or all that there they know enough about
> Without your help, without your dubious help.

(from "Drowning the Book")

Well, some of us, Howie, like hearing about all those dark things; and the help you give is not dubious at all, not by a long shot.

HELEN VENDLER

Viper Rum

(for Deb Larson)

All day we had run-ins with jungle snakes.
Above my canoe, a tiny vine serpent
like a single strand of luminous-green linguini

moved in a quick, muscular S from black orchid
to unripe mango to strangler fig.
Back at the lodge, a coral snake on the stucco floor

sent an old Girl Scout rhyme slantwise through my head:
"Red by yellow, kill a fellow.
Red by black, friend of Jack."

The waiter caught it in a Hellman's mustard jar,
and we all stood around the bar
while it swayed hesitant behind the glass.

Once it curled back in on itself
the small knot of fear in my chest
unloosed. Over stew, the archaeologist

told how his friend surprised
in a ceremonial Mayan pot
the fer de lance or Tommygoff,

which never doesn't bite. "She made
a double tourniquet right off
and only lost the limb," he said.

Far off, a howler monkey pack started
the whiskey-throated roars
that maybe kept a jaguar back.

That's when the proprietress brought out the viper rum,
a gallon jug wide-mouthed enough
to fit inside the wrist-thick python

that circled there, flat-faced.
Shot glasses went round. The lid unscrewed
let out some whiff of Caribbean herb

that promised untold mystery unfolding in your head.
The python's lidless eyes were white, mouth
O-shaped, perfect for a cocktail straw, I thought.

Then naturally, I cast back to those last years
I drank, alone nights at the kitchen sink,
bathrobed, my head hatching snakes,

while my baby slept in his upstairs cage
and my marriage choked to death.
I should have wound up in a fetal coil

eyes scalded of sight, staring out
at the warped and vacant world.
What plucked me from that fate

can't yet be named, but I do reverence to it
every day. So with my untouched shot glass still
flipped upside down, I said goodnight. Outside,

the moon was a smoky disk, the path to my hut
loaded with white magnolia petals,
so every step sent up a fragrant mist

that wound up filling my circular
thatched hut—the flowers' flesh
got mashed in my boot soles.

My hammock cradled me in its knotted web.
All around a thousand radiant wings
were shimmering. The jungle hummed.

County Fair

On the mudroad of plodding American bodies,
    my son wove like an antelope from stall
to stall and want to want. I no'ed it all: the wind-up
    killer robot and winged alien; knives
hierarchical in a glass case; the blow-up vinyl wolf
    bobbing from a pilgrim's staff.
Lured as I was by the bar-b-que's black smoke,
    I got in line. A hog carcass,
blistered pink on a spit, made its agonized slow roll,
    a metaphor, I thought, for anyone
ahead of me—the pasty-faced and broad. I half-longed
    for the titanium blade I'd just seen
curved like a falcon's claw. Some truth wanted cutting
    in my neighbors' impermanent flesh.
Or so my poisoned soul announced, as if scorn
    for the body politic
weren't some outward form of inner scorn,
    as if I were fit judge.
Lucky my son found the bumper cars. Once I'd hoped
    only to stand tall enough
to drive my own. Now when the master switch got thrown
    and sparks skittered overhead
in a lightning web, I felt powered like some
    wheeling, furied Frankenstein.
Plus the floor was glossy as ice. Even rammed head-on,
    the rubber bumper bounced you off unhurt
and into other folks who didn't mind the jolt, whose faces
    all broke smiles, in fact,
till the perfect figure-eight I'd started out to execute
    became itself an interruption. One face
after another whirled shining at me from the dark,
    each bearing the weight of a whole self.

What pure vessels we are, I thought, once our skulls
      shut up their nasty talk.
We drove home past corn at full tassel, colossal silos,
      a windmill sentinel. Summer was ending.
My son's body slumped like a grain sack against mine.
      My chest was all thunder.
On the purple sky in rear view, fireworks unpacked—silver
      chrysanthemum, another in fuschia,
then plum. Each staccato boom shook the night. My son
      jerked in his sleep. I prayed hard to keep
the frail peace we hurtled through, to want no more
      than what we had. The road
rushed under us. Our lush planet heaved toward day.
      Inside my hand's flesh,
anybody's skeleton gripped the wheel.

The Wife of Jesus Speaks

Ours was the first inch of time.
The word *passion* hadn't yet been coined,
and I'd not yet watched my beloved

laid out to butchery and worshipped a virgin, son
of a virgin even. This was before the Roman
bastards hammered his arms wide

as for some permanent embrace,
before the apostles paid me to lie
he never shuddered to death in my arms, I never

feasted on his flesh that now feeds
any open mouth, and inside me he never released
with a shudder the starry firmaments

and enough unborn creatures to fill an ark
all in a salty milk I nursed on.
His god gave us no child,

and even the books of salvation have not seen fit
to save me. Not the first woman
a powerful man denied knowing,

I said no back, for eternity.
With a rope slung over a tree branch,
I put my face inside a zero,

and with a single step clicked off
his beloved world's racket. Now my ghost head bends
sharp to one side, as if in permanent awe.

When he came down to hell and held out
that pale hand, I showed him my back,
the snapped vertebrae like a smashed pearl.

So my soul went unharrowed.
In these rosy caverns, you worship
what you want. I have chosen that time

in time's initial measure, history's
virgin parchment, when with his hard
stalk of flesh rocking inside me, I was unwrit.

Before me, I hold no other god.

Four of the Horsemen (Hypertense and Stroke, Coronary Occlusion and Cerebral Insult)

Mother's on the sofa with her channel-changer raised,
aimed like a wrist-rocket at the last reality
she can alter. Her bearing's still imperial,

but each day she fades a little. Last winter a surgeon
reamed her heart out. He cut her leg from instep
to crotch for a vein, which left an inch-deep trench

I swabbed each day, then packed
with strips of medical gauze that looked like worms.
Lord God, it's sorry work.

She'd whimper *stop,* too frail
to pull away. Sometimes I sensed a presence
slinking the room's unlit perimeter. Its scaly tail

dragged shadows. More accurate, though,
Death lodged in her own ribcage,
which they'd pried open. Actual staples

held halves of my mother's chest
fast to the scarlet scalpel line.
Such meat hunks we are, such heavy corpses

borne up by frail breath, as Epictitus said
according to Heraclitus, for some dim wisdom
does filter down. Tell that to Mother, though,

on the sofa chain-smoking *More* s. She scorns
delivered wisdom: Ashtrays stud the room,
so unsquashed cigarettes she forgot she lit

send up curls of smoke like altar offerings,
steam from the entrails of sacred butchered birds,
Please don't die, I say. She rolls her eyes.

Once when she was sleeping I pressed my ear
to her bony chest as if to power up
that sluggish beat a bit. Instead I heard

the horsemen she prays to—not riding out at a lope
with silk capes blown back, but at a slow plod,
bent over their saddlehorns like tired commas,

animals unspurred, only coming at her behest.

MARY KARR

The Imaginary Friendships of Tom McGrath

Thomas McGrath. *Letter to an Imaginary Friend, Parts I & II.* Swallow Press 1970. 214 pp. Out of print.

Thomas McGrath. *Letter to an Imaginary Friend. Parts Three & Four.* Copper Canyon Press 1985. 128 pp. $16.00 $9.00 (paper)

Thomas McGrath. *Selected Poems, 1938–1988.* Edited and with an introduction by Sam Hamill. Copper Canyon Press 1988. 185 pp. $15.00 $10.00 (paper)

Thomas McGrath. *Death Song.* Copper Canyon Press 1990. 117 pp. $19.00 $10.00 (paper)

Thomas McGrath. *The Gates of Ivory, The Gates of Horn.* 1957. Another Chicago Press 1987. 128 pp. $7.95 (paper)

The Revolutionary Poet in the United States: The Poetry of Thomas McGrath. Edited by Frederick C. Stern. University of Missouri Press 1988. 199 pages. $26.00

Thomas McGrath: Life and the Poem. Edited by Reginald Gibbons and Terrence Des Pres. University of Illinois Press 1992. 238 pp. $29.95 $12.95 (paper)

"You only live twice: once in the mind and once
In the world."

Letter to an Imaginary Friend, Part II

The annals of friendship poetry go back to the earliest days of the art, with Babylonian and biblical verses exploring the relationship of man, friend, and God. Certainly one of the great themes of Greek poetry is that of friendship, among warriors, philosophers, poets, and pastoral types alike. The friendly spirit humanizes the poetry of Wordsworth and Coleridge; not merely Coleridge's "This Lime-Tree Bower My Prison" (addressed to Charles Lamb, and considered perhaps the friendliest poem in English), but the enormous enterprise of *The Prelude,* which is unimaginable without the friend—ideal reader and fellow poet—in mind. Friendship is one of Tennyson's great themes; the death of Arthur Hallam on which *In Memoriam* expatiates becomes the occasion for a more general meditation on faith, loss, and human frailty.

In America, Whitman is suffused with the spirit of camaraderie (sometimes erotic, sometimes just convivial), and if we were not a tribe that valued friendship, the poetry of Frank O'Hara, Ted Berrigan, and especially James Merrill would be well-nigh incomprehensible.

Thomas McGrath's *Letter to an Imaginary Friend,* the long poem that occupied him for over twenty years, fits well into this tradition. Wistfulness entwines with grandeur in the project because, like so many of us, McGrath is lonesome for people who don't exist. He wants an intimate, one who will listen (as Coleridge listened to Wordsworth, as the New York poets listened to each other) to his screeds and respond knowingly to his string of allusions—a revolutionary activist with a *Norton Anthology* in her jeans. In a poetic world extending across decades and 6,000 long lines (of six beats or better, leading Alan Swallow and later Sam Hamill to use an oversize format for the two volumes of *Letter to an Imaginary Friend*), an amiable tone of voice is one of the constants that keep the reader in tow.

Five years after McGrath's death in 1990, the bulk of his poetry remains in print, along with a novel and two collections of commentary on his work, *Thomas McGrath: Life and the Poem* (based on a 1987 special issue of *TriQuarterly*) and *Thomas McGrath: The Revolutionary Poet in the United States.* The complaints of his devotees notwithstanding, these tributary essays suggest that McGrath has never lacked an audience. Not that it has been easy: Barriers to McGrath's fame have included the isolation of his native North Dakota as well as the long-windedness of *Letter to an Imaginary Friend.* And McGrath has set up another hurdle: his politics. A dedicated leftist, a member of the American Communist party, he was no fan of consumer society. The liberal reader who sometimes feels sympathetic to McGrath's tone and perceptions is nonetheless regularly challenged by his social agenda.

In the best of his shorter work, McGrath's politics add ironic tension to his lyric structure. Take "Perpetual Motion":

> One, one
> Lives all alone,
> Shape of the body's
> Tree of bone.
>
> Two, two
> Can make the world do;
> In youth, in youth,
> But not in truth.
> · · · · · · ·
>
> Three, three
> Society,
> Will do, will do,
> But not for two
>
> Since two, two
> In love, withdraw;
> Wish to be one,
> To live alone,
>
> But all must come
> To the skeleton,
> And one and one
> Live all alone.

Strung on a two-beat rhythm, the short lines seem even thinner because of the long vowels and booming assonance. "Perpetual Motion" nods to folk tradition as well as to cavalier song. Within its little shape, it raises very big questions: What kind of a creature is man, and how does man or woman figure in the bigger picture? However we read "society"—as a society of two acting in consort, or as a society of many acting with common mores—the plangency of "will do, will do" is meant to be as apocalyptic as Frost's ice, which "will suffice." The lovers become crowded by society; they return, at last, to bone. However much the poet (or lover) may want to rebuild society, he contrasts it here with the human condition, expanding and contracting in perpetual flux.

The same notions are addressed in a later erotic poem, "There Is Also a Fourth Body" (first published in book form in the posthumous *Death Song*). It begins promisingly enough with the drowsy languor of a postcoital bedroom scene depicted by McGrath's long, almost weary lines:

> In the predawn light they are aware of another being:
> Who is themselves and not their own selves: an emanation
> Or ghostsmoke that arises from the sweat of their work and
> their sex—

Here, teased by the emanation, you begin to expect a Blakean vision, a generative act of Edenic proportions. Instead, the room begins to get crowded. The ghostsmoke "Rises on their breath and the breath of their children"—a healthy if unexpectedly quick step from sex to fertility. But open the doors wider: Out of the ghostsmoke also rises "their hopes and dreams and those of friends and comrades," whose approach might be more welcome did they not themselves deteriorate into a string of further abstractions:

> A longing
>   a desire
>   a pledge:
>   the third body: of Solidarity.

In the bedroom, yet! And the ghostly overpopulation does not stop there:

> And they have come to know that there is also a fourth body:
> Decaying but strong: decaying in the husk of the corn
>   making

The coffee bitter
        poisoning their children—
                            an evil being
With a distant accent coca cola and cowboy boots—
The spirit of capitalism and exploitation. . . .
The fourth body spreads its plague on all continents.

The third presence, "Solidarity," places the meaning of eroticism in a
larger context—society, in the terms of "Perpetual Motion." But the
fourth body reduces the young lovers' heat to nothing more than an
occasion for McGrath's complaint. The promise of sexual healing, the
redemptive power of the hypothesized children (the society of the
future), dissolve in the bitter lees of cliché. Is that a manifesto in your
pocket, or are you glad to see me?

Throughout the work are scattered promising poems whose impact
is lessened by an appeal to dogma, by allusions to popular styles or
common measures that dip into bathos. Many of the sentiments of *Letter
to an Imaginary Friend* are on display in an early poem, "The Heroes of
Childhood":

        The heroes of childhood were simple and austere

        . . . .

        We saluted the outlaw whose heart was pure
        When he stuck up the stage or the mail car—
        Big Bill Haywood or Two Gun Marx,
        Who stood against the bankers and all their works—
        They robbed the rich and gave to the poor.

        But we in our time are not so sure:
        When the posse catches us our guns hang fire,
        And strung up from the wagon-tongues of long reflection
        Our hearts are left hanging by the contradiction
        Which history imposes on our actions here.

A modest amount of verbal invention (the wagon-tongue of long
reflection), a set of allusions (cowboy movies, Haywood, Marx) that are

personal but not too obscure, a prevailing sense of irony—all come to less than we might hope, because McGrath resorts to dreary abstraction at the poem's end. What history? What action? We are indeed left hanging.

There are exceptions, of course, as in McGrath's series of occasional poems called "Praises," Neruda-like odes to bread, vegetables, women, and, perhaps most successful of them all, to beer:

> Guitars are distilled from wine: from the politics of moonlight,
> From the disasters of tequila and the edible worm in the deep well
> Of mescal.
>   But from beer comes banjos and jazz bands ecstatic
> Trumpets midnight Chicago early thirties Bix.
>
> It was Beer that invented Sunday from the long and salty days
> Of the workday week:
>   that from the fast beer on horseback or the warm
> Beer of the burning fields of the harvest, when the barley comes in,
> Fermented the sabbatarian leisure;
>   that, in the eye of the workstorm,
> For the assemblyline robotniki and the miner who all week long
> Must cool his thirst at the root of the dark flower of the coal
> Offered reprieve;
>   and for slow men on tractors (overalled
> And perpetually horny) turned off their motors for the Sabbath calm.
>
>   (from "Trinc: Praises III")

"Trinc" talks us through the days of the week ("It is farther from Sunday to Monday than to any other day of the week"), informs us about the brewing process, and hints at the real feelings of working people. In short, it is a friendly poem, albeit a mock-heroic one that celebrates the family values of the Sunday picnic, and the role of alcohol in the divinely ordained day of rest:

>   . . . the golden spirit of Beer
> Comes to lead us out of the net, if only for a moment,
> To where Possibility rolls out its secret roads

To picnic places where Potato Salad and the Olive and the Onion
And Ham-and-Cheese sandwiches position the kids on the grass. . . .

With the kids on the grass, it may be timely here to say something about McGrath's personal history. Born to an Irish Catholic farm family in North Dakota in 1916, McGrath grew up with an allegiance to old-time virtues and farmwork. He was converted to radical politics by a Wobbly organizer (much of this history is revisited in *Letter*), and he identified with the cause of the worker versus the bosses from his youth. An intellectual with a working man's hide, he went from the University of North Dakota to Louisiana State, where he earned his master's degree in English in 1940. During World War II most of his time was spent undramatically in the Aleutian Islands. His brothers Warren and Jimmy were killed in the war; elegies to them, and tributes to his other siblings, are to be found among the collected poems.

From the start, a sense of inner exile ruled McGrath;[1] he cast himself as an intellectual among farmers; as a Wobbly among more complacent workers; a poet among soldiers; a northerner among southerners at LSU; a workingman's friend among college students and intellectuals; an American iconoclast among English intellectuals at Oxford, where he studied on a Rhodes scholarship after the war; and (increasingly important in *Letter to an Imaginary Friend*) a Native American-sympathizer among Anglos. He had become active in the American Communist party in New York before moving to California to teach, and he maintained this affiliation throughout his life. His refusal to cooperate with HUAC led to his losing his teaching job, and for several years he supported his family with documentary film writing (usually anonymously), welding, wood carving, and union organizing. He returned to teaching at C. W. Post College on Long Island in 1960, before closing the circle with twenty years at North Dakota State (1962–67) and Moorhead State (1969–82), in the twin cities of Fargo, North Dakota, and Moorhead, Minnesota, not far from his birthplace. He died in Minneapolis in September 1990.

Besides the odes to his siblings, McGrath addressed poems to two of his three wives, Marian (married in 1942), and Eugenia (1960 till his death). (His short-lived second marriage, in 1952, is not commemorated.) By the evidence of the poems, the first marriage seems to have been a love match that ran its course ("I return to the hunt for something long buried / In Time . . . but [I] cannot reclaim my youth / Nor those lost violent years whose casual ignorant lovers / We were for a season"—from "The Repeated Journey"); the marriage to Eugenia was buttressed by mutual sympathies in politics and writing; they coedited the journal which McGrath had founded, *Crazy Horse,* for a number of years. His deepest feelings, though, seem to have been released by the birth of his son, Thomas ("Tomasito"), to whom he addressed dozens of poems, many of which are reprinted in the *Selected Poems.*

> All those years, alone,
> Married to the intense uninteresting life . . . [sic]
> And, until you came, Tomasito,
> I didn't even know my name!

("You Taught Me")

The reader gleans from McGrath's fitful biographical notes the sense of a life without spectacular events, of revolutions that did not occur. One epochal moment of *Letter to an Imaginary Friend* is in fact a fictionalized version of McGrath's and his brother's attempt, as children, to assassinate a banker who they believed was unfair to the local farmers—in the literal sense, a non event.

Although Sam Hamill, in his introduction to the *Selected,* praises McGrath's formal virtuosity, you could more accurately describe his movement from formal to free verse and from career to career (and back) as a symptom of doubt stemming from his late start as a poet.

The theme of tardiness crops up in "You Can Start the Poetry Now, Or: News from Crazy Horse," which debuted in book form in the 1964 *New and Selected Poems,* twenty-plus years after his first publication. Here McGrath adopts a dadaist or Brechtian technique of self-interruption. (It's a technique often used by Kenneth Patchen, with whom McGrath felt some kinship.) The mise-en-scène is a poetry reading where the refrain "You can start the poetry now" interrupts a harangue. Is the poet coaching himself, or is he being heckled by the crowd?

START THE POETRY! START THE POETRY NOW!!

> *—it's the quarters and halves or maybe the whole antelope Buck that*
> *gets me it's the cutting up of the Buffalo Bread it's* all *them*
> *goddam swimming pools full of shot horses it's Christ Indians*
> *and revolutionaries charging full-tilt at the psychiatrists'*
> *couches and being blasted with the murderous electrical hot*
> *missionary money of hell-by-instruments it's all of us pining*
> *and starving surrounded by the absolutely heavenly pemmican-*
> *charisma that Geronimo invented it's the—*
> *START THE POETRY!! GOD*DAMN IT!!
> *START THE POETRY*!! START THE POETRY NOW!!

The hyperactive punctuation and aggressive use of the upper case and italics let *us* know that *McGrath* knows his *speaker* is trying too hard. The political diatribe of the Geronimophilic narrator drowns out the objections of the more reticent, ironic poet of inner debate whom we have met in such lyrics as "Perpetual Motion" or "The Heroes of Childhood."

Reading through McGrath in chronological order, you get the sense that you are reading the same poem over and over. It's not just the constancy of his themes; often it's literally true: *Selected Poems* begins with excerpts from *Movie at the End of the World* (1972), which itself culls work from *First Manifesto* (1940) and "The Dialectics of Love" (from Swallow's *Three Young Poets,* 1942). The effect of this recycling is paradoxical, like so much of McGrath: conservative, thrifty, Scots-Irish, and old-fashioned—timeless yet stodgy.

Terrence Des Pres[2] and E. P. Thompson,[3] in their respective essays on McGrath, make much of the role of industrial work in his poetry. Given what usually passes for "work" poetry (semiconfessional subliterary musings), they are probably right. McGrath is an exception—a highbrow poet who takes the side of, if not the voice of, the industrial worker, including the farmworker in today's postpastoral environment. In our poetry, only Philip Levine (who recounts his own debts to McGrath in *Life and the Poem*) has made a career voicing similar sentiments.

Sam Hamill says that in editing the *Selected,* he tried to avoid a "greatest hits" list, but in fact McGrath does not anthologize well. He is featured prominently in *The Rag and Bone Shop of the Heart: Poems for Men* (edited by Robert Bly et al.), which is not likely to increase his reputation. McGrath's work is jury-rigged into a number of anthologies of antiwar poetry, but it's a bad fit, because McGrath is not so much against War as in favor of a Revolution that has yet to occur. His is a nostalgia for a world that never was.

Let us turn now to *Letter to an Imaginary Friend,* on which McGrath's reputation must depend. I remember when I picked up Parts I and II in the Gotham Book Mart, shortly after it first came out. I was spending much of my time those days reading Blake, Whitman, and Pound, with their contrasting versions of epic and their own calculated appeals to the reader. McGrath's lyrical epic, addressed to the imaginary, the ideal reader—to *me,* in other words, as I imagined myself then—excited me.

When I plunged in, I found a barrage of midwestern references, American heartland images, as well as a matter-of-fact literary quality that were comforting. This was not a Publishers' Row or Harvard Square book, not the voice of a St. Louis altar boy who had fled to England; nor was it that of a West Coast hipster or bodhisattva, but a voice proud to remain rooted in the farmland. There was something ordinary—friendly—to all of it:

> My father took me as far as he could that summer,
> Those midnights, mostly, back from his long haul.
> But mostly Cal, one of the bundle teamsters,
> My sun-blackened Virgil of the spitting circle,
> Led me from depth to depth.
> Toward the light
> I was too young to enter.
> He must have been about thirty. As thin as a post,
> As tough as whang-leather, with a brick-topped mulish face,
> A quiet talker. He read *The Industrial Worker,*
> Though I didn't know what the paper was at the time.
> The last of the real Wobs—that, too, I didn't know,
> Couldn't.

Played a harmonica; sat after supper
In the lantern smell and late bat-whickering dusk,
Playing mumbly-peg and talked of wages and hours
At the bunkhouse door. . . .

What he tried to teach me was how to take my time,
Not to be impatient, not to shy at the fences,
Not to push on the reins, not to baulk nor pull leather.
Tried to teach me when to laugh and when to be serious,
When to laugh at the serious, be serious in my laughter,
To laugh at myself and be serious with myself.

You can be an ordinary boy and a poet, this passage muses, learn conventional virtues and hang out with the grown men, and all the while stay true to your inner life. If you grow up to be a radical, you may be ostracized—saved only by language and humor. McGrath's best metaphors yoke common speech and literary turns: Virgil is sun-blackened; the fancy "bat-whickering dusk" is brought down by the colloquial mumbly-peg. McGrath teaches us to take literally every symbolic gesture in his political catechism, so that you will feel the hard ground under your hip when you fall off your high horse.

Who is the imaginary friend? As I suggested earlier, a congruence of ideal reader and ideal comrade. In this dream sequence late in the poem, the speaker summons a collection of people, "poets all":

The men are swapping Ralph Wristfed stories: *Rolf Ristvedt*
To give him his proper name—the archetypal Norwegian.
Bob Edwards is there—who, on the high steel,
Walked through the wintery skies of cities; and Dale Jacobson,
The tormented one; and Robert Bly of the Misty Isles.
And Martinson, David, and Mark Vinz and Sam Hamill,
Bert Meyers, Charlie Humboldt and David Cumberland-
    Johnson,
And Fred Whitehead and Richard Nichson with his gambler's
    smile.
Also Don Gordon, who'd left his mountainy perch
To join us in the mysteries of the joyous season; and Hart Crane

Who would later study the undersea life in deeps far
Far deeper, more fearsome, than those of the Mexican Gulf.
And there was our neighbor, Brecht, who sang both high and low
And mostly in German; and a small man who looked like a
    turtle and came from Chile.
Poets all of them. And my father, that quiet man, chief among
    chiefs—
Seemed to me in those green years: and now as I say it.

These men, living and dead, remembered and imagined, are among those for whom McGrath's dialect has been invented, Americans and internationals, one steelworker and many poets. Friends who will respond to tall tales (Rolf Ristvedt), puns (Brecht's singing high and low), and insider knowledge of poetry (Crane's deeper studies; Neruda's turtle-like looks), all the while practicing male bonding. Although radical women writers like Meridel Le Sueuer and Naomi Replansky are cited elsewhere in McGrath's writing, the imaginary friends in this dream are exclusively male. The tribe is led by the poet's father, here singled out perhaps more for his archetypal than his biographical significance.

McGrath stitches into *Letter* catalogues of game birds, rivers, minerals, and trees. Catholic, Buddhist, and alchemical imagery coincide; cowboy memories and Hopi rituals ride alongside one another. Political rants and parodies merge in macaronic lines with allusions to Yeats, Blake, and Longfellow. A personal creation myth is revealed, in mock-biblical rhetoric: "It was then that THE McGRATH / took Creation in hand. . . . It was the Time-clock and the check-in of the First Hour." (Reflecting McGrath's vacillation between lyricism and revolution, this line is amended a few stanzas later to read "And it was the Morning Glory and the Evening Primrose of the First Hour.")

Variegated as its surface may be, the essence of the *Letter* is simple. Parts I and II, from which the passage above about Cal, the Wobbly organizer, is taken, present a fairly straightforward fictionalized autobiography, a bildungsroman in verse. The more adventurous Parts Three and Four, in the manner of a dream vision, depict a few remembered incidents from youth, reconsidered by the writer at desks in Portugal and Minnesota fifty or sixty years later. In a prefatory note to this section,

McGrath equates the Hopi's belief in a series of worlds, each a cleansed and reborn version of the last, with his own political agenda. We now live, according to Hopi mythology (my source here, like McGrath's, is Frank Waters' *The Book of the Hopi*), in the fourth world. The Blue Star Kachina will inaugurate the fifth world, much better than our own:

> The Blue Star Kachina will help these spirits to bring the new world into being. I see this as a revolutionary act to create a revolutionary society. All of us should help to make this Kachina. I think of the making of my poem as such a social-revolutionary action. In a small way, the poem *is* the Kachina.

In the course of the dream vision, the poet/hero is led by a guide who is at times his son, at times his father, passing through nine imperfect heavens into a world in which the real work—the struggle to make the world better—is just beginning.

> And now, in my upstairs room at six-fifteen South Eleventh,
> In Moorhead, Minnesota, the snow in my paperweight
> (and in all this weight of paper) is sifting cold and slow
> Over the miniature farmhouse under its dome of glass
> And paper . . .
>   where the boy sleeps . . .
>   . . . .
>
>   *Bear him his gift*
>   *To bless his work,*
> *Who, farming the dark on the love-worn stony plot,*
>   *The heaven-turning stormy rock of this share-*
>   *crop world*
> *His only brother warms and harms;*
>   *Who, without feathers or fur,*
> *Faces the gunfire cold of the old warring*
>   *new*
>   *year—*
>   *Bless! Grant him gift and gear,*
> *Against the night and riding of his need,*
>   *To seed the turning furrow of his light.*

In this assonance-rich closing prayer, built around internal rhyme, alliteration, and a synesthesic use of parts of speech ("share-crop" and "gunfire" become adjectives; "heaven" an adverb; "riding" a noun), McGrath chooses images that are abstract and concrete at once. Although the revolutionary work may have unintended or paradoxical results ("warms and harms"), the work must be started, to bring on the light of the new world. McGrath's lyrical urge has outweighed his need to propagandize in these closing lines.

Would the common man whom McGrath professes to speak for appreciate the linguistic twists and turns of the *Letter*? Hardly. Would the fellow travelers who used to wait in bars and union halls to hear and cheer the latest of McGrath's popular rhymes in the late 1940s (according to a legend McGrath himself helped propagate) understand the allusions to Hopi ritual and belief? No, the imaginary friend is one of the literati, purer of heart and broader of mind even than those who crowd his honor roll, willing to put up with the insults of McGrath's prose and yet sympathetic to McGrath's politics and purpose. Imaginary indeed!

The American poet's flirtation with the left too often does not carry with it responsibility. Take Richard Jones's anthology *Poetry and Politics* (1985), in which decent poets like Stanley Kunitz try unconvincingly to equate poetic grace with humanism: "I think of the poet as the representative free man of our time." When Blake the visionary, Pound the fascist, and Williams the humanist offer the same message, all are demeaned.

E. P. Thompson and Terrence Des Pres argue that McGrath has somehow lost his reputation because of his Communism, not because his art was middling. It is a fact that McGrath's politics caused him to be called before HUAC and to be blacklisted, and to lose his academic job in the 1950s, with severe repercussions.

> I would say that the episode *destroyed* a life. But we all have several possible lifelines—maybe it was all to the good. But I would say that it was largely responsible for destroying a marriage [his second]

and a family because of lack of money to live on, lack of security, the resultant anxieties.[4]

I would argue that blacklisting has burnished McGrath's reputation. Although there were lost years—more accurately, a lost path through life—there was in its place what McGrath called in his elegy for his brother Warren "new planes of struggle, lords of organization / And the nodal point of qualitative change." Some of the statements in the Stern anthology are downright fawning, and I suspect that McGrath's reputation among poets is *higher* now than it would have been had his politics been simply "leftish." Blacklisting added a cachet and glamour to a career otherwise solid, but (if we were to base our judgment on the short poems alone—and who reads 6,000-line poems?) not extraordinary.

We are particularly susceptible to received opinion when we fail to recall its origin. The fact is, McGrath's blacklisting and his politics allowed him to slip permanently into a fruitful irony, knowing that he was and would remain an outsider. (And wise enough to know, for all his dreaming, that the New American Revolution would not come in his lifetime.) By the end of his career he seemed to recognize this freedom, as these excerpts from a 1987 interview with Des Pres indicate:

> **TDP:** Some of your early poems have a truculent aspect, as if you wouldn't mind insulting the reader—if it was the wrong, or the right, reader.
> **McGrath:** [Laughs.] Yes, right, that's true. Because sometimes—I went through *years* when I was writing poems that nobody wanted to publish, so *that* gave me a great freedom that most American poets have never experienced. . . . I published on the left, and I published in some of the lunatic magazines of the West Coast. But in effect I had gone on a blacklist. . . .
>
> But in any case, since I was sort of out of it, that gave me a lot of freedom, in a way; in a certain sense it was one of the things that helped in writing *Letter*. Because when I finally started it I had no idea that any part of it would ever be published anywhere, anytime. So, I said, well, fuck it, I just launched out.

In the years after the blacklist, McGrath's truculence mostly disappeared, replaced, perhaps, by the sardonic laugh noted in the interview.

By a curious twist, his master work, *Letter to an Imaginary Friend,* has been made possible by the blacklist.[5]

Trying too hard to shore up McGrath's reputation, Hamill equates him with Pound, linking the two through the person of Tu Fu, the eighth-century Chinese poet. Tu Fu was an exile, an innocent, a political victim of corrupt times, a poet of friendship, and—most important—far removed from us historically. If Pound and McGrath are each like Tu Fu, Hamill's syllogism goes, they must be like each other. Fascist equals Communist! Does moving the political fence back twelve hundred years truly remove one from responsibility for the contemporary consequences of one's politics? I don't think so.

> What is named
> Is known.
> By its disguises.

("The Need for Dictionaries II")

Let us see McGrath for what he truly was: an American poet with a fascination for the millennial, with the wit and good humor to produce one of the best paeans to beer since the early Irish bards, with a laugh that infects his art as well as his interviews. He must have been better company than Pound, Yeats, Eliot, or Stevens, and less inclined to mope than Crane or Lowell. He is part of the American tradition of bluster, like Whitman and Ives. His Communist beliefs and Hopi references are certainly less weird than Merrill's transcriptions from the beyond, and do not require a Scots glossary like MacDiarmid's equally Communist stew of world language and utopia. But, my friend, despite the real pleasures of reading *Letter to an Imaginary Friend,* McGrath is not the artist that any of these were, and no amount of fellow feeling should lead us to overstate the case. Remember McGrath as part of the tribe. Despite his honorable wounds, do not mistake him for the chief.

MARTY COHEN

Notes

1. This is not the literal exile of which Sam Hamill makes so much in his introduction to the *Selected Poems,* treating North Dakota as if it were a place of coventry. By inner exile, I mean to suggest a distance between McGrath's life and his ideals, a sense of detachment and self-masking that is glossed over by his humor.
2. In Gibbons and Des Pres, *Thomas McGrath: Life and the Poem,* pp. 158–192.
3. In Gibbons and Des Pres, pp. 106–157, and also in Stern, *The Revolutionary Poet in the United States,* pp. 158–192. An earlier version of this essay had appeared in Thompson's own *The Heavy Dancers* (1985).
4. From a questionnaire response quoted in Ellen W. Schrecker's *No Ivory Tower: McCarthyism and the Universities* (Oxford University Press, 1986), p. 302.
5. This may be the place to say a word about McGrath's novel, *The Gates of Ivory, The Gates of Horn,* which deals satirically with his appearance before HUAC and his blacklisting. Compared favorably to Orwell by E. P. Thompson, the novel in fact covers territory that has been handled better by dozens of science fiction writers and satirists. A reprint of some of McGrath's anonymous and pseudonymous screenplays might do his reputation more service than this trifle.

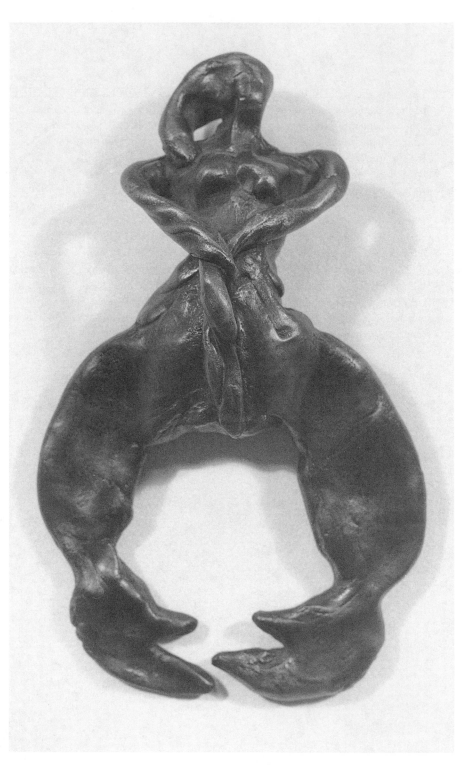

CLAUDIA DE MONTE
Bronze #6

Catullus: Playing with Prosody

> Idle yesterday, two of us saw fit to
> Share my notebooks and vie in writing poems,
> Treat amour in a wittily risqué way,
> Giving good as we got, with wine and laughter.
> All the while, improvising verse on verse, we
> Played with prosody—meters, this and that one. . . .

That would be one way to transpose into English the beginning of Catullus' poem (L) on the gleeful day he and a friend spent (*multum lusimus*) playing with various meters. It cannot have been the only time the greatest of the Roman lyric poets enjoyed such metrical recreation. In these increasingly toneless days, do young writers find any pleasure in playing with the meters?

What James Wright called "the difficult, the dazzling hendecasyllabic" (as illustrated in the lines above) is one of the favorite meters of Catullus; he used it in some 40 of his 110-odd poems. The only meter he used more often (some 50 times) is that of the elegiac couplet, familiar to us from Auden's many Goethean epigrams.

All of his poems are elegantly metered. Besides the two meters referred to, he used about a dozen others in the poems of his we have, and who knows how many he experimented with in his "notebooks"—which of course were not our spiral-bound pads but a few slim thong-attached boxwood panels coated with wax, in which words could be scratched and then thumbed out when not wanted. In those days, writing was a richly tactile experience.

One kind of fun we can have today is to see if the metric diversity of other times and cultures can be adapted to our language. What happens if we take the long and short syllables of Latin prosody and transpose them into our accented and unaccented ones? Can that introduce usable rhythms into our poetry? Ezra Pound thought it could. Whether the attempt succeeds or not, the pleasure remains, and presumably there is some gain for the writer in any exercise that makes language sit up and take notice.

The translation below is in one of the rarer meters of Catullus; he used it only once. Called "rollicking" by one classical scholar, it goes by the sexy name of Priapean, because of its use in hymns to the phallic god. It is made up of a glyconic (as in "Who's the | girl in the min | iskirt?") and a pherecratic ("Get her | telephone num | ber"). These rhythmical figures with the jawbreaking names are easily naturalized Nothing un-American in their cadences.

Most translations of Catullus give us no idea of the metrical verve he thought inseparable from poetry. Nor do they let us share in the way he revels in the expressive pleasures of sound itself, as in the beginning of the rowdily derisive poem XXV, in a rhythm called Septenarius, whose seven and a half iambic feet we can hear in a sentence like "I wish I knew a place to get a better cup of coffee."

> Cinaide Thalle, mollior cuniculi capillo
> uel anseris medullula uel imula oricilla . . .

Catullus
XVII

O Colonia, mad to dance
        all the length of your bridge, and
More than ready to do so now,
        only fearful the trembly
Piers supporting the poor old thing's
        salvaged rickety timbers
Might turn turtle and, wrong side up,
        founder deep in the marshes—
Heaven grant you a better bridge,
        true to specifications,
Where your Lords of the Dance, unharmed
        can cavort in their orgies,
On condition you do one thing:
        leave me doubled up, laughing,
When you collar this village fool,
        plunge him—*plunk*!—in the thickest
Scummy muck underneath your bridge,
        burbling, head over heels there.
But it's got to be where the bog's
        grimmest guckiest gumbo
Stinks to heaven as nowhere else,
        livid, color of corpses.
Him! He's dumbest of all dumb men.
        See that tot in the cradle?
Two years old, but when half asleep
        twice as bright as old stupor.
"Dumb? How so?" Well, his wife's a flower,
        fresh in bloom, in her springtime,
No young creature as rare as she,
        winning, warm—what a charmer!
Gardeners guarding their glossy grapes
        needn't keep such an eye out

As that husband of hers—but no!
               she's left free as a breeze to
Stray at will, and he doesn't blink,
               doesn't budge, like a tree trunk
In a ditch where the logger's ax
               crippled, cropped, and forgot it.
There, unconscious of all, it lies,
               focused nowhere, on nothing.
This clod, stupor itself, is such:
               hears not, certainly sees not,
In a fog as to who he is,
               if he is, if he isn't.
He's the booby I'd like to dunk
               upside down in your mudhole's
Dimmest depth, on the chance it might
               jolt him out of his coma,
Cling like glue to his sodden soul,
               leave it lodged in the wallow,
As the clutch of the sullen mud
               sucks the shoe from a jackass.

JOHN FREDERICK NIMS

To Turn Again

Stanley Kunitz. *Passing Through: The Later Poems, New and Selected.* W. W. Norton 1995. 175 pp. $18.95

Stanley Moss, Editor. *Interviews and Encounters with Stanley Kunitz.* The Sheep Meadow Press 1993. 241 pp. $22.50

When asked by Christopher Busa in *The Paris Review* interview if he felt differently about translating the poems of Baudelaire, whom he could never know personally, than about translating the work of various contemporary poets, Stanley Kunitz replied "I know Baudelaire too." Taken literally, Kunitz's contention might set a more speculative imagination to flights of wild conjecture. ("All poets are contemporaries," he has said.) Think of the possible combinations of acquaintance that such time travel would allow. What species of exquisite naughtiness could Hart Crane and John Wilmot hatch, left to their own devices in the Ramble in Central Park? Allen Ginsberg would not think it strange to see Garcia Lorca pricing summer fruit or Whitman pawing the ground chuck in the fluorescence of a Berkeley grocery. Mightn't Ovid have benefited from Archibald MacLeish's diplomatic acumen in helping to grease his return to Rome from Tomis on the Black Sea? Literary gatherings would take on added luster: "Wystan, I'd like you to meet Quintus Horatius Flaccus—Oh, I see you're already acquainted." Such reveries aside, Kunitz has something more serious in mind. To say that one may know poets long dead implies a transubstantiation between the flesh-and-blood poet and his incarnation on the page; this mystery manifests itself in the dual meanings of *corpus* —the physical body, a body of work (the Greek *soma* splits the same way). For his part, Kunitz has long been aware of the numerous intersections between the life and the work: "The life of a poet is crystallized in his work, that's how you know him"; or, as he put it on another occasion, "A poet's collected work is his book of changes"; and, finally, this Jungian distillate,

"[Poetry] has its source, deep under the layers of a life, in the primordial self."

At ninety, Stanley Kunitz has more layers to his life than most. Accumulated in those layers are the poems of nearly three quarters of a century, alongside which stand interviews and essays, the products of a mind occupied not only with poetry but the teaching of it. Traced accurately, Kunitz's pedagogical reach might encompass more contemporary American poets and poetry than any other living individual's; and, as his students and acolytes—Lucie Brock-Broido, Susan Mitchell, Louise Glück, and Michael Ryan among them—take on their own students (Brock-Broido now teaches in the Columbia writing program, where she once studied with Kunitz), his influence continues to grow exponentially. Marie Howe has said of his mentoring powers, "How can I tell you what he's taught us? I can't stand here and tell you that he fussed with my commas and line breaks. He changed my life. He changed the lives of so many of us." As many artists will attest, to work on technique is to work on the bugbears and shortcomings in the self; poetry is "interwoven with the tissue of the life." In Kunitz's Socratic phrasing from the preface to his most recent book, *Passing Through: The Later Poems, New and Selected,* the poet puts it this way: "Through the years I have found this gift of poetry to be life-sustaining, life-enhancing, and absolutely unpredictable. Does one live, therefore, for the sake of poetry? No, the reverse is true: poetry is for the sake of the life." If poetry and the life are inextricable, then there can be no summary division between Kunitz's work as teacher and his work as a poet. The heuristic impulse applies to the making of poems as to the teaching of them: both endeavors function as aides to discovery. While, of necessity, Kunitz's discussions of verse take on a character distinct from his poems, both are mined from the same vein. Where the poems are highly refined, their metal hammered to a near transparency, his broader, more sententious reflections on the writing life display both the raw materials and by-products of the verse. His numerous interviews trade phrases with the poems; poems crystallize journal entries and bits of conversation. Here we get a further sense of *soma*—the life/work as a whole organism as opposed to its discrete parts.

2. "I stand on the terrible threshold"

In the title poem of "The Layers," a section of new poems from *The Poems of Stanley Kunitz: 1928–1978,* published when he was in his seventies, the poet wrings the liquor from several of his apothegms quoted above:

> Yet I turn, I turn,
> exulting somewhat,
> with my will intact to go
> wherever I need to go,
> and every stone on the road
> precious to me.
> In my darkest night,
> when the moon was covered
> and I roamed through wreckage,
> a nimbus-clouded voice
> directed me:
> "Live in the layers,
> not on the litter."
> Though I lack the art
> to decipher it,
> no doubt the next chapter
> in my book of transformations
> is already written.
> I am not done with my changes.

Here, Kunitz animates the life/work connection through metaphor. Each phase of the life marks a chapter recorded in a "book of transformations." (All poets live contemporaneously; their quickening takes place on the page.) The final line of the poem, a credo of sorts, sounds as a refrain in Kunitz's interviews; with it he refers at once to himself and his art. This is powerful juju from a septuagenarian poet, who fifteen or so years down the line may now look back and see that he was right: His changes are not finished, and the ethos behind this continuous transformation shows no sign of flagging.

A telling facet of the poet's outlook glitters from "The Layers." Not only is change continual for Kunitz, but often his changes are "already written." Compare this generosity of spirit with T. S. Eliot, who in middle age could already envision a state where one "do[es] not hope to turn again." (Kunitz states his turning not once but twice in the poem.) As A. David Moody suggests, Eliot, in "Ash-Wednesday" resigns the "hope of a renewal of youth's joy and strength." For Kunitz, however, youth harbors the source of those primordial networks of images that give a poet the strength to live and write. Less a model than a foil, Eliot functions for Kunitz as a kind of influence manqué, someone to put his feet up against. Whereas the forty-year-old Eliot indulges his hopelessness, the seventysomething Kunitz exults from deep within the layers of the life.

This striking affirmation notwithstanding, Kunitz's sterling optimism, more of the hard-won variety than the cock-eyed kind, remains burnished. Here is the first half of "The Layers" leading up to the poem's pivotal line with its insistent "turn"s:

> I have walked through many lives,
> some of them my own,
> and I am not who I was,
> though some principle of being
> abides, from which I struggle
> not to stray.
> When I look behind,
> as I am compelled to look
> before I can gather strength
> to proceed on my journey,
> I see the milestones dwindling
> toward the horizon
> and the slow fires trailing
> from the abandoned camp-sites,
> over which scavenger angels
> wheel on heavy wings.
> Oh, I have made myself a tribe
> out of my true affections,
> and my tribe is scattered!
> How shall the heart be reconciled
> to its feast of losses?
> In a rising wind

the manic dust of my friends,
those who fell along the way,
bitterly stings my face.

For the writer of a personal book of changes, the scope of "The Layers" could not be much broader. Far from milquetoast lyric composed to commemorate a fleeting observation, the poem assays life in its entirety, viewed back to front. At the center of the poem gapes a doorway dividing the past from the future, a vantage point from which the poet may survey his surround; from this cusp Kunitz takes stock of his beginning and his end. Richard Jackson, in an interview with Kunitz, has pointed out the abundance of "thresholds" in the poems, as in "Open the Gates": "I stand on the terrible threshold, and I see / The end and the beginning in each other's arms." Again an echo of Eliot clamors from the wings, but even more nearly we hear the lines of the anonymous Scots poem "Ballad of Sir Patrick Spence," which Coleridge (another poet that Kunitz could claim to know) takes as an epigraph to his "Dejection: An Ode": "Late, late yestreen I saw the new Moon, / With the old Moon in her arms / And I fear, I fear, my master dear! / We shall have a deadly storm." Signs and portents.

A storm rises in "The Layers" as well, blowing the dust of "those who fell along the way" into the poet's eyes. The speaker stands between the jambs of "I turn, I turn," compelled to crane his neck in order to proceed forward. Behind, milestones dwindle into an expansive distance, slow fires trail; camps are abandoned, tribes scattered; the heart feasts on loss. The G-force on that tiny *yet* as it streaks into the atmosphere of the poem is nearly enough to squelch it. The turn is so tenuous starting out that it must be affirmed, gaining force in the repetition. Here the poet pivots in the doorway to peer forward again, but carrying the memory of what lies behind. Chilled in the penumbra of a recalled darkness, the speaker can exult only "somewhat," but the will to proceed remains intact. In the transformative light of the speaker's resolve, fate, that aloof prankster, appears robed like grace; at the close of the poem, the next chapter of the life "is already written," and in fact is being written as the poet peers past the lintel to utter at once a prophecy and a plea: "I am not done. . . ." A typographical representation of the poem would resemble one of Herbert's "Easter Wings." The panorama of the past narrows as the speaker approaches his peripety at the poem's center (looking back, angels—of history?—are scavengers on heavy wings); from there the view expands again, opening, however tentatively, to an assured future. Herbert, a poet to whom Kunitz has long acknowledged indebtedness, concludes his poem with this angelic feather: "Affliction shall advance the flight in me." Kunitz, in his, is similarly "compelled" to take stock of his afflictions before proceeding onward.

The next poem in *Passing Through,* from the 1985 collection, *Next-to-Last-Things,* provides another point of intersection with Kunitz's more general poetic concerns. Noticing two garden snakes sliding among the conifers in his Provincetown plot, Kunitz murmurs:

> I should have thought them gone,
> in a torpor of blood
> slipped to the nether world
> before the sickle frost.
> Not so. In the deceptive balm
> of noon, as if defiant of the curse
> that spoiled another garden,
> these two appear on show
> through a narrow slit
> in the dense green brocade
> of a north-country spruce,
> dangling head-down, entwined
> in a brazen love-knot.
> I put out my hand and stroke
> the fine, dry grit of their skins.
> After all,
> we are partners in this land,
> co-signers of a covenant.
> At my touch the wild
> braid of creation
> trembles.
>
> (from "The Snakes of September")

Compare the end of this passage with its prose corollary, which Stanley Moss cites in his introduction to *Interviews and Encounters:* "All myths are the same, all metaphors are the same metaphor; when you touch the web of creation at any point, the whole web shudders." Poetry for Kunitz aspires to the status of myth, and by placing us squarely in the center of received myth "Snakes" serpentines toward the creation of a new, personal one ("the effort is to convert one's life into legend"). The scene proceeds through dualities, a constant division of ones into twos. Structurally, the poem divides in half on the *volta*-like sixteenth line; here we read that it's noon, the hour dividing ante- from postmeridian. "September" situates the speaker in an equinoctial month, and one supposes it to be the 23rd, the first day of the fall (read *the Fall*); for in a garden where netherworldly serpents are "defiant of the curse / that spoiled another garden," how could it be otherwise? The poem turns on "not so," after which twos repair into ones: The two snakes twine together; the poet partners with the serpents; they become "co-signers of a covenant." At Kunitz's deft handling of *covenant,* the whole web of Biblical myth shudders, from Adam to Moses to Jesus.

In the structural complexity of "The Serpents," with its dense helix of images spiraling down through the poem, we may behold Kunitz's own braid/web of creation. If you prod one image in Kunitz, other poems register a reaction. "If we go deep enough," the poet explains, in his interview with Jackson, "we may discover the secret place where our key images have been stored since childhood. There are chains of other images attached to them, the accretions of the years. A single touch activates the whole cluster." This last bit is immediately recognizable as a second paraphrase of "The Layers." While many of Kunitz's poems rework the same "key images," poem calls to poem most explicitly in "Touch Me":

> *Summer is late, my heart.*
> Words plucked out of the air
> some forty years ago
> when I was wild with love

and torn almost in two
scatter like leaves this night
of whistling wind and rain.

The italicized first line echoes the poet's "As Flowers Are," from *Selected Poems 1928–1958,* the contents of which are sadly omitted from the current *Selected:*

Summer is late, my heart: the dusty fiddler
Hunches under the stone; these pummelings
Of scent are more than masquerade; I have heard
A song repeat, repeat, till my breath had failed.
As flowers have flowers, at the season's height,
A single color oversweeps the field.

Kunitz's images, his personal archetypes, surface and resurface throughout his lyrics; the effect can be understood, not by reading one poem as separate from another, but by considering the work—poetry and prose—as a whole. In midcareer the poet traded the masterly pentameters of "As Flowers Are" for the *sui generis* "functional stressing" present in the later poetry quoted thus far—a loose trimeter or tetrameter line with ample variation where the ear dictates the intervals. Early Kunitz, which comprises three volumes—*Intellectual Things* (1930), *Passport to the War* (1944), and the 1958 *Selected*—employs a syntax and vocabulary that to today's ear may seem wantonly mandarin. These, however, are among the poems that Yvor Winters recommended to his students at Stanford. For many of that generation, *Intellectual Things,* by the precocious twenty-five-year-old, with its fluent formalism and lush syntax, was a manual on how to write verse. In the mid-Thirties Theodore Roethke, who at that time had yet to publish a volume of his own, appeared on Kunitz's doorstep wearing a raccoon coat and sporting a copy of that arresting first book. Inside, after a few drinks, Roethke proceeded to pay homage by reciting several of the poems from memory.

Part of Kunitz's evolution has been to thin out the linguistic densities of his early work, finding instead a pellucidity of surface and diction; the complexities of the later poems are formed in the layers hidden from ready view, which Kunitz locates "below the floor of consciousness."

Psychological richness replaces the early emphasis on prosodic richness. One may regret (as this reader does) the loss in Kunitz of the linguistic challenges of *Intellectual Things*. Formal brinkmanship, daring to go too far, while not always successful, can on occasion result in lines that lodge unassailably in the mind. If *Passing Through* were Kunitz's first book, would a young unknown show up with it committed to memory? Lines, yes; whole poems, no. Willfully weeding the poems of their surface mystery, Kunitz has labored to cultivate a mysterious interconnectedness in the inner tissue of a given poem and even between poems.

As the redeployment of the line from "As Flowers Are" suggests, while the early style may have developed into its virtual opposite—hermetic lines in received meters replaced by a "transparent" free verse—strings of recurring images endure, clinging in the web of the work *in toto:* "If you understand a poet's key images, you have a clue to the understanding of his whole work." "Key images" is a felicitous phrase considering the extent to which locks and keys and doors operate in Kunitz's poems as just these kind of clues:

> "Dante!" I cried
> to the apparition
> entering from the hall,
> laureled and gaunt,
> in a cone of light.
> "Out of mercy you came
> to be my Master
> and my guide!"
> To which he replied:
> "I know neither the time
> nor the way
> nor the number on the door . . .
> but this must be my room,
> I was here before."
> And he held up in his hand
> the key,
> which blinded me.
>
> (from "The Illumination")

Set in a Paris hotel, the poem depicts a private heart of darkness, one in which the poet finds himself disconsolate, alone in a foreign city, his funds sapped. In this self-imposed exile from his native soil, the poet's most formidable demons conspire to haunt him: the parent he has denied, the friends he's failed, the hearts he's spoiled ("including my own left ventricle"). Out of this slough, poet calls to poet. An edition of Dante's *Inferno*, with engravings by Gustave Doré, which Kunitz knew in his childhood, figures in several of the poems, both early and late. As much as the Florentine's chthonic epic, the accompanying images by the nineteenth-century French engraver found purchase with the poet at that formative age. Doré's first plate in the *Inferno*, a depiction of Dante cowering in that dark wood, renders the pilgrim much as Kunitz does in "The Illumination": "in a cone of light." In the first Canto of the *Comedy*, the sun begins to rise, illuminating somewhat the savage wilderness and briefly bolstering Dante's spirits. Soon, Virgil, whom Dante calls *maestro*, appears. In "The Illumination" Kunitz paraphrases Dante's greeting in an address to *his* master; Alighieri's Paris incarnation, however, falters in his role as hoped-for Virgilian guide—he too is lost—and the key he proffers is blinding.

3. "The key which blinded me"

Each image within a given body of work operates as a valise containing not only denotative meaning but the connotations accrued from the poet's deployment of that image elsewhere; hence, the "green thought" in "The Garden" can be grasped only in terms of Marvell's use of "green" throughout the body of his poems. What, then, is this "key" that Kunitz refers to, and what is it that is locked? The image reappears in "The Testing-Tree":

> Once I owned the key
>   to an umbrageous trail
>   thickened with mosses
> where flickering presences
>   gave me right of passage.

As in "The Layers," the "flickering presences" of the past, in this case the spirits of Wampanoag Indians, provide Kunitz with right of passage, but, as he discovers in "The Illumination," the specters of the past, seen in that poem as private failings, can withhold imprimatur; in any case, they must be dealt with. In the early poem "Open the Gates," in which Doré's images loom large, the poet again confronts his past as a requirement for stumbling forward:

> Within the city of the burning cloud,
> Dragging my life behind me in a sack,
> Naked I prowl, scourged by the black
> Temptation of the blood grown proud.
>
> Here at the monumental door
> Carved with the curious legend of my youth . . .

Before being admitted, the poet must decipher the conundrum posed by his youth; the information he needs to untangle this curious legend— his life—he has carried with him on his back.

Depending from this chain of images rattles a passage from "The Portrait," which Kunitz has called, along with "The Layers," a poem of origins:

> My mother never forgave my father
> for killing himself,
> especially at such an awkward time
> and in a public park,
> that spring
> when I was waiting to be born.
> She locked his name
> in her deepest cabinet
> and would not let him out,
> though I could hear him thumping.

Locked as it is in the deepest cabinet, the specter of the lost father lurks as the oldest and most powerful in Kunitz's poetry of personal legend. Perhaps it is the mother's willful internment of the memory of her husband (later in the poem, she tears up her son's pastel rendering of his father) that has caused this ghost to pace the floorboards of Kunitz's poetry. The father, however, as in the last line of "Father and Son," often makes no reply; in answer to his son's entreaties for his return, the father offers only "the white ignorant hollow of his face." The image recalls Dante via Doré. In the *Vita Nuova,* a title Kunitz borrows for one of the poems written in his twenties, Dante employs his own "key" image: "Here me and then consider: am not I / The keep and key / Of all the torments sorrow can combine." Certainly this heartsick questioning lies in the same register as the description of the mother's locked cabinet with its grisly contents; it bespeaks the same desolate horror of that Paris hotel room; it feeds at the feast of losses glimpsed from the center of "The Layers."

4. "All myths are the same"

If there is a peculiarity, not quite a flaw, in Kunitz's later style of freighted imagery, it is the way a poem sometimes changes gears too quickly, leaving the reader behind, as the poem speeds on toward revelation. At the end of "The Snakes of September," the poet moves from the particular to the universal, as the "wild braid of creation trembles" at his touch. The poem earns its conclusion on the level of meaning, but there is something overripe about that "wild." This rapid tonal shift to an ecstatic register jars, and for an instant our attention is diverted to the machinery of the poem working slightly too hard.

In his best work Kunitz achieves these grace notes while sacrificing nothing in the build up. "The Wellfleet Whale," a jeweled tiara of a poem, crowns the poet's achievement, and restores some of the linguistic pomp of the early poetry. The poem carries a prose epigraph, a journal entry describing the poet's encounter with a whale stranded on the beach. The whale, now in its death throes, opens one prehistoric eye to gaze on the poet. While Kunitz's long poem should be read in full, this passage from the fifth and final section, carries the signature of the whole:

> Voyager, chief of the pelagic world,
>   you brought with you the myth

of another country, dimly remembered,
where flying reptiles
        lumbered over the steaming marshes
            and trumpeting thunder lizards
wallowed in the reeds.
        While empires rose and fell on land,
            your nation breasted the open main,
rocked in the consoling rhythm
        of the tides. Which ancestor first plunged
            head-down through zones of colored twilight
to scour the bottom of the dark?

· · · · · · · · · · · ·

            Master of the whale-roads,
let the white wings of the gulls
        spread out their cover.
            You have become like us,
disgraced and mortal.

The poignancy of the apostrophe, another of the poet's characteristic moves, derives from its personification of the doomed Leviathan. As with the September snakes or the titular salmon in "King of the River," this creature from the natural world provides the poet with an appropriate catalyst for verse. Through these beasts Kunitz may refer to the human animal: "You have become like us."

This suitability of the subject weds the suitability of the form; the concatenating tercets of "The Wellfleet Whale," with their restless forward motion, provide Kunitz the sweep he needs to work this scene into the necessary tonalities, from the epic to the personal. By discarding inherited prosodic forms in his later poetry, Kunitz may be likened to a virtuoso who has left off playing from score and begun to improvise. Rather than grappling with standard measures, the poet relies on his own sense of a line's musicality to set the needed length and number of stresses. Echoing Blake, an abiding poetic forebear, and fellow seer, Kunitz notes, in an interview, "I must create a system myself or be enslaved by another man's." Freed from rigid metrical contracts, this poet may better find the unique vessel appropriate to each poem. Oddly, Kunitz works out his two finest poems, "The Wellfleet Whale" and "The

Testing-Tree," in the same pattern of tercets wrought in numbered sections. This expansive form heightens the music of Kunitz's line:

> You have your language too,
>   an eerie medley of clicks
>   and hoots and trills,
> location-notes and love calls,
>   whistles and grunts. Occasionally,
>   it's like furniture being smashed,
> or the creaking of a mossy door,
>   sounds that all melt into a liquid
>   song with endless variations,
> as if to compensate
>   for the vast loneliness of the sea.
>   Sometimes a disembodied voice
> breaks in as if from distant reefs,
>   and it's as much as one can bear
>   to listen to its long mournful cry,
> a sorrow without name, both more
>   and less than human. It drags
>   across the ear like a record
> running down.

                    (from "The Wellfleet Whale")

Kunitz here submerges an *ars poetica:* "liquid song" sung "to compensate for the vast loneliness of the sea" could serve as the jacket blurb to this *Selected.* In the above passage we hear the whole symphony of Kunitz's musicianship: the pizzicatto strings of "clicks and hoots and trills"; the legato horn of "location-notes and love calls"; the tympanic percussion of "a record running down." All of this elegiac music, ostensibly for the dying mammal on that Cape Cod beach, borrows certain measures from the poet's life: as with Margaret in Hopkins's "Spring and Fall," it is *Kunitz* that he mourns for, making "The Wellfleet Whale," in its sweep and intimacy, the most far-reaching and potent of his many personal myths.

Part of the power of myths derives from our inability to pinpoint their exact meaning and message; they cannot be distilled to one-line thematic essences. Myth may be paraphrased, alluded to, stolen from, reworked, but its meanings resist the sound-bite; they are not fables with appended morals. In this sense, Kunitz's attempt to create a personal mythology, his legends of origin, has been wholly successful. More than isolated lyrics, the poems resonate, cross-pollinate, call to one another, and will not be reduced to incidental music. The dangers in writing a highly personal poetry of origins—dangers succumbed to by a number of Kunitz's epigones—include sentimentality and solipsism (the "who cares?" factor), which Kunitz's poems, happily, avoid. What registers instead emanates from the molten center of life-long experience, images transformed to poetry by their mystery and complexity, conveying human warmth, wisdom, and the poet's dearly held resolve to turn again, which is living itself.

DAVID YEZZI

Lee Friedlander
Cherokee, Louisville 1993

Exquisite Environments

Mary Oliver. *New and Selected Poems.* Beacon Press 1992. 255 pp. $20.00

Mary Oliver. *White Pine: Poems and Prose Poems.* Harcourt Brace & Company 1994. 55 pp. $11.95 (paper)

Mary Oliver. *Blue Pastures.* Harcourt Brace & Company 1995. 128 pp. $22.00 $13.00 (paper)

Gary Snyder. No Nature: New and Selected Poems. Pantheon Books 1992. 390 pp. $25.00

Gary Snyder. *A Place in Space: Ethics, Aesthetics and Watersheds.* Counterpoint 1995. 263 pp. $25.00

> The exquisite environment of fact. The final poem will be the poem of fact in the language of fact. But it will be the poem of fact not realized before.
> —WALLACE STEVENS, *Adagia*

Considering that she is one of the foremost laureates of American Nature poetry of the last decade, Mary Oliver exhibits a peculiar lack of genuine engagement with the natural world. Outwardly, her credentials are sterling. The thirty-odd years' worth of poems collected in *New and Selected Poems* and the volume that follows, *White Pine,* as well as the prose pieces in *Blue Pastures,* certainly reveal a profound admiration for the phenomenal world—for surface and scintilla, animal and plant. Oliver follows in the footsteps of other famous walkers in and musers upon Nature. Bashō journeyed on foot throughout Northern Japan, the Romantics wandered England's Lake District, even the urbane Wallace Stevens ambled through Hartford's Elizabeth Park, notebook and pen in hand. So Oliver tramps the shores, marshes, and woodlands of Cape Cod or Virginia, keeping her eyes peeled for the miraculous.

Like that of Blake and Whitman, both of whom this poet claims as influences, Oliver's art is driven by urgency and conviction. Yet the passion to sound an alarm, to rip veils from the eyes of the less perceptive is, if anything, among her less endearing qualities: The persona of the poems is always leveling a reproachful gaze and firing bumptious questions at the reader, such as "have you too / gone crazy / for power, / for things?"; or—more Thoreau-like—"Tell me, what is it you plan to do / with your one wild and precious life?"

Of course, curmudgeonliness is a time-honored trait of the nature writer. It's tolerable when, in other respects, Oliver's work seeks to record and respond to the minutiae of the immediate, and largely neglected, universe, and when she adheres to her own dictum that "our duty . . . as writers begins not with our own feelings but with the powers of observing." Among her plentiful gifts to the reader are an apostrophe to an owl that goes, "Dear, dark dapple of plush!"; the characterization of a black snake that "jellies forward"; the whimsy of "snails on the pink sleds of their bodies."

Nevertheless, these poems are not, to use Wallace Stevens' phrase, "poem[s] of fact in the language of fact," which that earlier nature poet had the prescience to identify as our century's compelling need in its dealings with Nature. "[T]he path to heaven," writes Oliver in "The Swan," is

> . . . in the imagination
> with which you perceive
> this world,
>
> and the gestures
> with which you honor it.

Despite the nod toward Romantic doctrine in paying homage to the imagination ("Wherever man is not, Nature is barren," wrote Blake), Oliver herself often depicts human experience as hopelessly paltry compared to that of almost any other creature and human presence as an unforgivable trespass.

Yet neither is she content to perceive and honor *this* world in all its ordinariness. No Aeolian harp quivering to every passing sensory breeze, she strains to maintain—and when necessary manufacture—an unwavering pitch of intensity, awe, and visionary ecstasy. The moments of revelation that crack the world open in, say, Wordsworth or Emily Dickinson, seem the windfalls of experience. Their poems rely on a firm foundation of the daily against which the visionary rises in shining relief. The unvarying tenor of Oliver's poems, by contrast, brings to mind Joyce Carol Oates's snide (but accurate) observation that Nature "inspires a painfully limited set of personal responses in 'nature writers'— reverence, awe, piety, mystical oneness."

Revelation in Oliver's poems breaks forth from a pattern of mannerisms: the tic of disbelief, the empty intensifier, the beatific generalization. Take, for example, "The Ponds," a poem that begins with characteristic incredulity:

> Every year
> the lilies
> are so perfect
> I can hardly believe
>
> their lapped light crowding
> the black,
> mid-summer ponds.

It could be argued that the vernacular "so perfect" is necessary to move the poem forward to the poem's central question that comes a few stanzas later—"But what in this world / is perfect?"—were it not for the regularity with which both the specious adverb "so" and the adjective "perfect" turn up in her poems. Elsewhere, a speaker is "so full of energy"; moths burn "so brightly"; scallops are "perfect fans"; a bear possesses "perfect love," and an owl is a "perfect, billowing instrument."

The answer to the posed question, which comes a few stanzas later, is first a catalogue of the blooms' flaws—

I bend closer and see
how this one is clearly lopsided—
and that one wears an orange blight—
and this one is a glossy cheek

half nibbled away—
and that one is a slumped purse
full of its own
unstoppable decay.

—and next the poet's wistful bid (how else to understand this?) for more
and better fireworks:

Still, what I want in my life
is to be willing
to be dazzled—
to cast aside the weight of facts

and maybe even
to float a little
above this difficult world.
I want to believe I am looking

into the white fire of a great mystery.
I want to believe that the imperfections are nothing—
that the light is everything—that it is more than the sum
of each flawed blossom rising and fading. And I do.

While it is marvelous to see eternity in a grain of sand and heaven in a
wildflower when fate and the weather conspire to afford glimpses of
them, to clamor and tug at Lady Nature's skirts for extra favors is
unseemly. Humans do not live by epiphany alone. "The Ponds" begins
in callowness but ends in complaint. The childlike bemusement that
marks the telling of the flowers ("and this one . . . and that one")
underlines the simple charm of the images: "a glossy cheek," "a slumped
purse." But the watery syntax and artless vocabulary of the following
stanzas smack of an odd stridency in the willful intrusions of ego ("I
want . . . ") and the piled-on infinitives. Longer and longer sentences

suggest a badgering aggravated by the repetition of "I want to believe." That culminating "And I do" seems self-congratulatory. (Is this a sham faith? The lady protests too much!). Mounting emotion might register as passion were it not diluted with a cliché ("the white fire of a great mystery") and a sweeping platitude ("the light is everything").

Many Oliver poems, clearly the products of a sensibility devoted as well as devout, exude a near-religious fervor couched in the language of light and conflagration. Natural elements shimmer and glimmer and blaze and shine: "the flowers burn"; a speaker in a poem longs to "become again a flaming body / of blind feeling"; the sea is a "roaring flamboyance"; first snow falls with "such / an oracular fever!" In an undoubtedly lovely vision, "the trees / are turning / their own bodies / into pillars / / of light. . . ."

The paradoxical effects of this approach—in *our* century's climate of general recklessness toward Nature and in a poet who is usually regarded as an exponent of the new nature poetry striving to respect Nature's integrity as "Other"—are difficult to untangle. On the simplest level, the passion for transcendence impairs the poet's powers of observation. Maybe it's true that Oliver's hummingbird "whenever there is a fuss / just rises and floats away." But the hummingbirds I've witnessed in my backyard are murderous little hellions who, for all their jewel-like demeanor, are rapacious for territory and become miniature MIGs when raiding each other's feeders.

Oliver's posture of awe, admiration, and envy distances her from the rest of Nature. A poem called "October," for example (one of the new in *New and Selected*), describes another woodland walk, this one resulting in the sighting of a black bear. The meditation ends this way:

> Sometimes in late summer I won't touch anything, not
> the flowers, not the blackberries
> brimming in the thickets; I won't drink
> from the pond; I won't name the birds or the trees;
> I won't whisper my own name.
>
>   One morning
> the fox came down the hill, glittering and confident,
> and didn't see me—and I thought:

so this is the world.
I'm not in it.
It is beautiful.

The impulse to somehow undo the profound damage humans, in their cruel swarm, have inflicted on this planet ("I won't touch . . . I won't . . . name") is understandable, worthy, and above all poignant. But extracting and isolating the human from Nature is just the other side of the same anthropocentric coin that values people as the crown of creation to the detriment of the rest of Nature; they are both grandiose, narcissistic delusions. Doesn't ecological wholeness depend on interaction and interdependence? Even if one has no argument with the literal sense of the passage, the poem's own gestures undermine its intentions. In her fervor to obliterate self, the speaker stumbles over the pronoun "I" no less than six times!

Along the same lines, an encounter with a deer which "in some kind of rapturous mistake, / . . . did not run away / / but walked toward me" further demonstrates Oliver's addiction to spiritual thrill-seeking. No animal would barter its own life and body within a world of change, as Oliver readily would, in exchange for a stasis in which ripe fruit never falls:

I have been, ever since,
        separated from my old, comfortable life

of experience and deduction—
    I have been, ever since,
        exalted—
            and even now,

though I miss the world
    I would not go back—
        I would not be anywhere else
            but stalled in the happiness

of the miracle—

The hushed reverence is "authentic" (to use the term most frequently applied to Oliver's work), but the focus on being "stalled in happiness" is troubling, as though we moderns were in the uniquely awkward position of simply having nothing to do with ourselves when out in Nature except walk around, gawk, and exult (that is, when we're not tearing it up with machinery).

In "1945–1985: Poem for the Anniversary," Oliver betrays a similar laxity of purpose, all the more disturbing since this poem, in a rare instance of historical specificity, commemorates the Holocaust:

> The way I'd like to go on living in this world
> wouldn't hurt anything, I'd just go on
> walking uphill and downhill, looking around . . .

The weak repetition of "I'd go on . . . "and the insouciance of the third line suggest a naiveté that, given the subject, seems inappropriate. It's difficult not to take complacency of rhythm and syntax, in this case, for complacency of thought.

One wonders what version of fellow-feeling for other creatures induces a poet to proclaim

> If I had another life
> I would want to spend it all on some
> unstinting happiness.
>
> I would be a fox, or a tree
> full of waving branches.

This imputation of "happiness" to foxes and trees recurs throughout Oliver's poems. A deer is "busy with her own happiness"; that spaced-out hummingbird we met above "comes / like a small green angel, to soak / his dark tongue / in happiness—"; wrens are "happy they are to be / diligent at last." What this "happiness" appears to celebrate is the creatures' ability to be wholly present to the fullness of their earthly (and only) existence. If this interpretation is on the mark, it doesn't make up for limp language that fails to embody complexity of thought.

In the end, the work represented by the *New and Selected Poems* and *White Pine* is, to resort to a valuation not usually within the purview of literary criticism, ecologically unsound. The last thing we need to do in the current urgency of reconsidering our relationship to the natural world is to "cast aside the weight of facts" and "float . . . / above this difficult world." This, finally, is what Oliver urges: not to see the world itself for what it is, but to see *through* it. Though her antennae are acutely attuned to the physical world, it is not so much the signal received that the poems transcribe as the rather manic motion of the antennae themselves.

Curiously, judging from her prose writings, Oliver knows better than to let her own reactions to Nature mesmerize her. *Blue Pastures,* a haphazard collection of essays, occasional pieces, aphorisms, and jottings from notebooks, gives fresh insight into Oliver's poetics, her philosophy of Nature, and the contradictions therein. The essay entitled "A Few Words" discourses wisely on the dangers of prettifying Nature:

> Nothing in the forest is charming. . . . And nothing in the forest is cute . . . Such words—'cute,' 'charming,' 'adorable'—miss the mark, for what is perceived of in this way is stripped of dignity, and authority.

One wonders, though, if the rhapsodic is not as lethal as the sentimental. This essay, like so many of Oliver's poems, ends in a transcendent vision of wholeness:

> Life is Niagara or nothing. I would not be the overlord of a single blade of grass, that I might be its sister. I put my face close to the lily, where it stands just above the grass, and give it a good greeting from the stem of my heart. We live, I am sure of this, in the same country, in the same household, and our burning comes from the same lamp.

This passage is lovely, but it is not of our time. We recognize Thoreau in its exhortations and analogies, in its assertions and metaphors, in its vocabulary (especially the word "overlord"), and, above all, in its cadences. But it does not answer to the needs of our own historical moment, or to the particulars of the late twentieth century's conflicts with Nature.

Finally, what is vexing about Mary Oliver's poetry is precisely that it does not suffice as poetry. A generic quality pervades language and landscape. Robert Frost's mended wall makes better neighbors in New Hampshire or Vermont; Robinson Jeffers delivers his rumbling pronouncements from the bluffs of Big Sur; James Wright (one of Oliver's mentors) breaks into blossom in a Minnesota twilight; but Oliver's hummingbirds and marshes and woodlands and deer and bear could be anywhere east of the Mississippi. Nor does her language hold up under the contradictions of her need for transcendence and her need to speak plainly. What is one to make of the banality of this assessment of human and individual aspiration:

> . . . a few people just trying
> one way or another
> to survive.
>
> Mostly I wanted to be kind.

If flatness of expression is meant to render some shy, "unmediated" experience of the natural world, if short lines and jarring line breaks reflect a wish to perceive every mote in sunlight and to speak of the details slowly, then how explain the particular form of "Mockingbirds"* in the newest collection, *White Pine?*

> This morning
> two mockingbirds
> in the green field
> were spinning and tossing

---

*Substitute a nightingale or a lark for the mockingbirds and we have the Romantic commonplace of the poet listening for revelations.

> the white ribbons
> of their songs
> into the air.
> I had nothing
>
> better to do
> than listen.
> I mean this
> seriously.

Because each line comprises a prepositional phrase or some other coherent syntactical unit, reading the poem is like scanning a series of freeze frames; this is to say that the form could yield a specific meaning. But the washboard syntax defies the fluidity of birdsong, as do the schoolmarmish last lines above: Should we mistake the occasion for a lighthearted moment, they reprimand us.

The opening stanzas of "Porcupine," in *their* line breaks, however, defy explanation:

> Where
> the porcupine is
> I don't
> know but I hope
>
> it's high
> up on some pine
> bough . . .

What this hiccuping aesthetic teaches is that if you put a lot of stark white space around a few very small words, those words had better be worth the dazzle.

White Pine includes what for Oliver is a new genre, prose poetry (the volume is subtitled "Poems and Prose Poems"). In feeling, sensibility, and diction these poems continue in the vein of Oliver's non-prose poems, some of them successfully enough, but they also point up the arbitrary form displayed by the earlier non-prose poems. "Fletcher Oak" begins

> There is a tree here so beautiful it even has a name. Every morning,
> when it is still dark, I stand under its branches. They flow from the
> thick and silent trunk. One can't begin to imagine their weight. . . .

In their monotonous syntax and uniformity, these lines replicate the
tactics of an Oliver poem. The weak passages of her prose-poems
encourage the droning intonation and pseudo-profundity of many
1960s adolescents' favorite poet, Kahlil Gibran:

> A dog comes to you and lives with you in your own house, but you
> do not therefore own her, as you do not own the rain, or the trees,
> or the laws which pertain to them.

With their self-doubt, backtracking, and endless qualifiers, Oliver's
poems betray an overall sloppiness. When John Ashbery interjects the
phrases "I don't know" or "and anyway," he is mapping the circuitous
progress of thought processes or deliberately mimicking fragments of
conversation. But Oliver's poems do neither of these. Regularly interrupted by expressions such as "I guess," "and anyway" and "so what,"
their stilted formality feels awkward. And when the poems pose
chummy, conspiratorial questions to the reader—

> Also I wanted
> to be able to love. And we all know
> how that one goes,
> don't we?—

we want to answer, "No, as a matter of fact, we don't know. Tell us, in
a language that suffices."

2.

> language as wild system, mind as wild habitat, world
> as a "making" (poem), poem as a creature of the wild
> mind.
>
> —GARY SNYDER, "Unnatural Writing"

Gary Snyder's *No Nature: New and Selected Poems* and *A Place in Space: Ethics, Aesthetics and Watersheds,* a collection of essays, talks, reviews, and occasional pieces, offer quirky, incisive critiques of mainstream American culture—and an alternative vision notable for its good-natured humor and off-beat erudition. They yield a fascinating contrast to Mary Oliver's poetry. Where Oliver yearns to merge with the natural world, Snyder, it appears, has never *not* been merged; he takes as a given our full citizenship in Nature's nations. His poetry embraces language and consciousness as adaptive, biological traits of our species and of our bodies as well as minds—not, as Oliver and the Western Romantic tradition behind her would have it, obstacles to some idealized, unmediated connection.

In Snyder's view, Nature shields no one from the corruptions of civilization, since by definition it includes them. "Nature also means," he writes in this volume's preface, "the physical universe, including the urban, industrial and toxic." The construct "Nature" as opposed to "Culture"—or mind as opposed to body, or any of the long metronomic list of Cartesian dichotomies—collapses in the big picture. The title, *No Nature,* gives the lie to artificial separations: *No Nature* because no *not* Nature.

If the title issues disclaimer and caveat, it puns on a command, as well: "Know Nature!" This collection charts one way to come by this knowledge, though Snyder warns at the outset that "we do not easily *know* nature, or even know ourselves." The caution implies a core belief: Knowing nature and knowing the self are closely aligned activities, so long as the latter is understood not in a narrow psychological sense, but as skeins in a web of relationships—to place, people, animals and plants, history and idea.

The barest facts of Snyder's life and influences explain his wild eclecticism. A lifelong environmentalist, he worked in his youth both on trail crews in Yosemite and as a shipmate on oil tankers. In his career as poet, Snyder has been buddy to bikers, rednecks, cowboys, and "whoring sailors," all of whom appear in the poems. He spent ten years in Japan pursuing Zen practice, studying in monasteries and translating Buddhist texts. A New World/Zen poet who figured large in the West

Coast Beat scene in the fifties, and who in one recent poem muses on "Europe forgotten now, almost a dream—," he nevertheless once lamented the frustrations of teaching poetry to students who have never read Spenser or Shakespeare.

The poems in *No Nature* comprise an autobiographical record, but always with an overlay of commentary and a nimbus of context. Their "I-do-this-I-do-that" narrative recalls Frank O'Hara; their learned, often obscure, fragmentary allusiveness recalls Pound. Amplitude of experience in the life is matched, in the poems, by a variegated, not to say motley, aesthetic. As in any well-functioning ecosystem, everything gets used; nothing is wasted; nothing is left out.

Of course, as anybody with a compost pile knows, the process of recycling can be messy. Materials break down at different rates en route to their new life as rich loam. Some things, like orange peel, just won't decompose, so they poke out of the soil. In its generosity and inclusiveness, in its tolerance for the undigested bits, in its attention to the whole rather than to parts, Snyder's work undergoes a similar process.

His constant is dedication to language. Nature, writes Snyder, is "An open space to move in, with the whole body, the whole mind. My gesture has been with language." For Snyder, no fan of current fashionable theories of language, words *link* us to what's usually thought to be "outside" the mind, including natural forces (which are, however, themselves often analogous to mental processes). Language is both natural and functional—"a wild system born with us," he says in an essay called "A Single Breath." Snyder vouchsafes no gap between the world of human imagination and the world of solid, physical fact: "Whatever made people think Mind isn't rocks, fences, clouds or houses? Dogen's* ingenuous question."

"Riprap," the title poem of Snyder's first published collection, remains an apt emblem for his poetics. Loose stones used to stabilize, say, a logging road, stand in for words laid down as a makeshift highway for the mind, as well as for the assemblage of the things of this world which, like Whitman, Snyder's poems affectionately inventory:

---

*Dogen is the priest who introduced Soto Buddhism to Japan in 1227.

> In the thin loam, each rock a word
>   a creek-washed stone
> Granite: ingrained
>   with torment of fire and weight
> Crystal and sediment linked hot
>   all change, in thoughts,
> As well as things.

While these lines admit no rift between "thought" and "things," in no way do they suggest that "things" are less real than "thought." "Our poems are full of real *presences*," Snyder asserts—doctrine anathema to any self-respecting deconstructionist. Language is a kind of granite foundation for human experience in the physical world; its molten explosive origins seethed within the Big Bang as much as those of any crystal or sediment. Elsewhere Snyder calls language "riprap on the slickrock of metaphysics." So it's a foothold and a pathway *through;* it doesn't *create* Nature.

"Riprap," a relatively arcane term to all but forest service employees, echoes the word "riffraff" as well, implying that in these poems there's plenty of room for what might be thought, in a more purist aesthetic, worthless, trashy, or ephemeral. One of Snyder's guidelines for what he calls a "New Nature Poetics" is that "it study . . . language as wild system, mind as wild habitat. . . . poem as a creature of the wild mind." "Wild," in this context, means self-regulating, not, as is commonly thought, dissolute or chaotic. Language, like wild ecosystems, is "richly interconnected, interdependent, and incredibly complex. Diverse, ancient, and full of information." This view of language as wild system leads to Snyder's hands-off poetic that casts its lot with verbal momentum rather than with integrity of line, stylistic adroitness, or deft turn of phrase. "Good writing is 'wild' language," writes Snyder; in other words, it takes care of itself.

"Bubbs Creek Haircut," a long (five page) poem from the early *Mountains and Rivers Without End,* points up Snyder's inclusive methods. It recounts the poet's preparations for trekking into the Sierra backcountry. The opening account of barbershop and barber—"High ceilingd and the double mirrors, the / calendar a splendid alpine scene— scab barber—in staind white barber gown"—gives way to a meditation on shopping for clothes at Goodwill, reminisces of other haircuts and shopping trips, detours into a description of hiking Bubbs Creek with a rowdy trail crew up to the glacial Forester Pass, breaks briefly into a song to Hindu deities, segues to a hitchhiking jaunt with Allen Ginsberg, switchbacks to the Bubbs Creek trek, and comes to rest finally back in the barbershop.

Embedded in the poem's jittery mobility is a sober consideration of what Snyder, in "Piute Creek," calls "All the junk that goes with being human," which he juxtaposes against the stark, inhuman beauty of the actual mountain looming over the whole poem. The detritus of civilization makes for both a reassuring continuity and a lot of rubbish as well. Thus, the barber, we find out, is familiar with Snyder's destination up Bubbs Creek: "Well I been up there. I built a cabin / up at Cedar Grove. In ninteen five." The Goodwill, though, boasts a roomful of "unfixed junk":

> All emblems of the past—too close—
> heaped up in chilly dust and bare bulb glare
> Of tables, wheelchairs, battered trunks & lamps
> & pots that boiled up coffee nineteen ten, *things*
> Swimming on their own & finally freed from human need. Or?
> waiting a final flicker of desire
> To tote them once more. Some freakish use.
> The Master of the limbo drag-legged watches making prices
> to the people seldom buy.
> The sag-asst rocker has to make it now. Alone.

The haphazard omission of articles ("heaped up in chilly dust and bare bulb glare"), abbreviated spellings ("High ceilingd," "staind"), jaunty vocabulary, and casual use of the ampersand all heighten, verbally and graphically, the poem's agitated, talky energy. But Snyder choreographs momentum with syntactical savvy. The long sentence tallying the room's contents glissades to pause at that anticipatory "Or?," accelerates with a series of shorter phrases, picks up speed with two full sentences, and pulls up short again on the single word "Alone."

In contrast to the Goodwill's human clutter, presided over by the gimpy "Master," stands the remote austerity of Forester Pass. At twelve thousand feet, the seemingly sterile "half iced-over lake" is "filled with leaping trout":

> the crazy web of wavelets makes sense
> seen from high above.
> a deva world of sorts—it's high
>   it is a view that few men see, a point
>   bare sunlight
>   on the spaces
> empty sky
>   moulding to fit the shape of what ice left
> of fire thrust, or of tilted, twisted, faulted
>   cast-out from this lava belly globe.
> The boulder in my mind's eye is a chair.
>   . . . why was the man drag legg'd?

Forged in the fires of geology, bare, empty, forbidding, and inhuman, the landscape briefly evokes the human in resembling a chair, maybe for a god. Sinuous, impromptu as dribbles in action painting, the schema of perception jags across the page in bursts of long and short lines. Unlike Mary Oliver's line breaks, which flatten affect and serve up thought in prissy tidbits, Snyder's lines cascade along in rushes of free association, the view forking between Hinduism ("deva world") and earth science. Hovering briefly over a contemplation of vastness and bareness, the passage's short lines hang appropriately suspended in empty white space—but not for long. Rather than remain "stalled in the happiness" of the panorama, Snyder moves the poem forward (*and* back to its beginnings) with the non-sequitur about the man in the Goodwill. The lines that follow could apply to the glacier and its master as well:

> King of Hell
>   or is it a paradise of sorts, thus freed
> From acting out the function some
>   creator/carpenter
> Thrust on a thing to think he made, himself,
>   an object always "chair"?

> Sinister ritual histories.
> is the Mountain God a gimp?
> The halting metrics   and the ritual limp.
> Good   Will?

Besides saluting the primal "otherness" of objects unfettered by human need or desire, "Bubbs Creek Haircut" tracks the byways and back-country of creativity itself. The poem proves how human creations (chairs, poems) assume a life of their own beyond the "creator / carpenter['s]" plans for them. The "halting metrics" and the "ritual limp" describe, and therefore unite, the gimpy Goodwill proprietor, the Mountain God, and the poet. Words, being wild, command multiple personae: So the Goodwill store invoked throughout the poem in a kind of ritual refrain mutates to a question: "Good Will?" Is the Mountain God benign? Is any creator? And what about created things?

Snyder's allegiances to an ecological world view run deep: The language of natural systems saturates his thinking about social relationships, history, the environmental crisis, and literature. But an equally useful framework for appreciating Snyder's poetry is to recognize that it takes its cues from oral and narrative forms and traditions: from folklore, myth, performance, conversation, anthropology. While his poems sometimes look like lyrics, they shun the lyric's conventions: the self-contained moment, often ending in epiphany, linguistically and semantically rounded off in closure. Snyder makes no attempt to dress up prosaic images, his Whitmanian catalogues brook no hierarchy. He aspires to what he terms "an elegant plainness, which we name the Zen aesthetic. . . . The idea of a poetry with minimal surface texture, with the complexities hidden at the bottom of the pool under the bank, a dark old lurking, no fancy flavor . . . "

A late poem entitled "Right in the Trail" shows how Snyder's talent for storytelling, despite "minimal surface texture," imbues a stroll in the yard with pleasure and significance:

> Here it is, near the house,
> A *big* pile, fat scats,

> Studded with those deep red
> Smooth-skinned manzanita berries,
> Such a pile! Such droppings,
> Awesome.

The exclamation and the adjective "awesome" (this last Snyder probably picked up from his sons) do not sound as contrived here as slangy constructions in Oliver do, because they occur in a context already chatty. But after this informal beginning, Snyder ups the ante by switching into the Haida bear myth of a young girl's kidnapping when she messes with bear scat:

> And I saw how
> The young girl in the story,
> Had good cause to comment
> On the bearscats she found while
> Picking blueberries with her friends.
> She laughed at them
> Or maybe *with* them, jumped over them
> (Bad luck!), and is reported
> To have said "wide anus!"
> To amuse or annoy the Big Brown Ones
> Who are listening, of course.

This tale of the girl who eventually "had some pretty children by a / Young and handsome Bear" is significant not only in Pacific Northwest ethnography, but in Snyder's personal history. As a young graduate student, he wrote a thesis on this myth that came to be a respected piece of scholarship in the field. The personal note chimes again in Snyder's emotional effusiveness, but rather than remain mired in it, he moves on to "read" the "text" the animal has left:

> Now I'm on the dirt
> Looking at these scats
> And I want to cry not knowing why
> At the honor and the humor

Of coming on this sign
That is not found in books
Or transmitted in letter,
And is for women just as much as men,
A shining message for all species,
A glimpse at the Trace
Of the Great One's passing,
with a peek into her whole wild system—
And what was going on last week,
(Mostly still manzanita)—

A clue in a detective story, the scat reveals a chapter of the bear's life story—her movements, her habits, her diet, her "whole wild system"— as well as a bit of natural history (she's eaten what was ripe and available that week, the manzanita berries). The "Great One's passing" alludes not only to the bear's sojourn in Snyder's woods, but also to her kind passing from our consciousness, and to the possibility of her species passing into extinction. The animal traces remind Snyder of the bear legends of the Northwest, a mythology whose origins arose from real people's encounters with real bears. In the spirit of those meetings, Snyder turns the occasion of the poem itself into a tryst with a bear by apostrophizing the creature in an irreverent praise poem, both teasing and entreating the Great Ones to stick around (we need them):

Dear Bear: do stay around. Be good.
And though I know
It won't help to say this,

Chew your food.

Affection leavens awe. Like a parent counseling an unruly yet cherished child, Snyder humorously speaks for the bonds that link Nature's extended family.

Bear "sign" (another word for scat) is itself a kind of scatological semiotics, a sign not transcendent but embedded in the very ordure of animal experience. Like the scat, Snyder's poems are studded with bright berries of evidence of all he has consumed and digested and recycled in his poetry of Indian folklore, natural history, personal experience, and the records of human-animal relations.

GYORGYI VOROS

The Pass

Long-haired in Walker County, driving
Home the week of Kent State, I worried
My green lid of homegrown marijuana.

This was deep in Klan country. There
Had been riots, bombs. George Wallace,
In three days, had called out the guard,

Then voided the semester. I drove slowly,
For the wind, the curves, and the coal trucks
Erupting unpredictably off side roads

Made the way perilous. For a few miles,
O. B. Emerson, that supremely delicate man
And epic bibliographer of Faulkner,

Rode behind me in his baby-blue Firebird.
Then there was nothing but curve and hill,
With, once in a while, a semi looming

And descending to meet me in a blunt gust
That took and flung me to the side.
When a young man drives alone,

It is as if a faithful animal holds the wheel
While he draws from the bounty of his ego
The wishful story of his life to come,

A saga of martyrdom and nudity, recited
By Ian Fleming in the alternating
Prose styles of Henry Miller and Henry James.

I thought my life would pass in erotic gentleness
And secret acts of philanthropy and heroism.
Then the old Plymouth swerved into my lane.

It wobbled, righted itself, and, dead
On my bumper, veered, bucked sideways,
Then flipped once before rolling

Behind me and vanishing in the pines.
I slowed, looked both ways, made a U-turn,
And pulled over in the grass. The wreck

Lay on the driver's door. The man inside
Groaned out to me. "Honey," he said,
"Get me some help," and I went running

Through needling briars. The ambulance
In Cullman was not twenty minutes away.
At the road, already the accident vultures

Were piling out. Then I saw him bending
From his car. "Dr. Emerson," I cried,
And a two-hundred-pound matron had his arm.

In those days, my friends and I worshipped
The accident, the joke. Each time we tripped,
Something would happen—a dwarf might

Stagger by, dragging a snarling Chihuahua
On a jeweled leash, or a line of mirrors
Would topple from a truck—so we'd feel

We'd tapped the mother lode of the absurd.
So the doctor explained himself, and roared off.
Back toward the wreck, I followed the crowd.

Three farmers had the hurt man like a rope.
"Wait," I said. "Don't move him. What
If his neck is broke?" And one said, "Damn

Hippie, we can't just let him lay there
Sufferin'." Very gently, they drew him out.
Then he found me. "Honey," he said,

"You come back. Come over here awhile."
I leaned down. "Closer now. There,
There," he smiled, and now he got my hand.

Not *that,* I thought, but this was getting odd,
The way he winked and swallowed long,
Nothing I could swear to, but the manner

Of it all, so I felt somehow I'd blundered
Into the gravity of a myth that wasn't mine.
Around us, the leaning faces made a wall.

Until the ambulance arrived, I'd sit there
Frozen in that thorny palm like a woman
Struck down in a field and ravished by a god.

A Slide of the Ladies Home Missionary Society Meeting

When I get down to the bottom of things,
It was a dark green, stiff-billed soldier's cap
Stamped with the white numerals of one
Of the enigmatic insignia of the Alabama
National Guard. Why keep it now?
The boy who wore it, Billy Don Boulden,
Has been a man out of prison for a long time.

We used to play a fast hide-and-seek
In the woods just south of the house
Where the Ladies Home Missionary Society
Sipped iced tea as they watched slides
Of African children spraddling to scoop
Handfuls of ants into their mouths.
Just once I brought him, thirsty, inside

The house, and the good ladies, taking in
The darkness of his nappy head, looked
So aghast you would have thought one
Of the heathens had stepped down naked
From the white bedsheet they were
Using as a screen and now was debating
Whether to eat their earrings or their ears.

You know what it is to be *it,* don't you?
Since I drove up toward a cemetery
With a girl and we lay down half-naked
And rose up naked, with the horns blaring
And the long row of headlights shining
In our eyes, I've studied to memorize
The ground rules in the South: (1) God's

Watching all the time; (2) Every cemetery
Hides a church. It's always the same
With the two naked bodies, one moment
Alone in the darkness, and the next,
Two families in convention at the ten
Upturned toes. Mothers, fathers,
Grandparents, aunts, uncles, infamous

And demented cousins, like patriots
Appraising every possible outcome
Of every possible war, or certain
Familiar verses of the national anthem
That the singer cannot quite bring
To the tongue. The time machine
That changes the ludicrously tragic

To the mildly preposterous will arrive
In twenty minutes. If luck holds,
No one mentions marriage or pulls
A gun. But if you're fifteen and
Black, and a white game warden
Comes on you with a white girl
In the woods, in Alabama, in 1964,

One of the things that might happen
Is murder. If the white man's dead,
And you're caught in his car with a gun,
The jury takes less than an hour,
And you're building years, lollygagging
And jawing over the café au lait
In one of the bistros of Kilby Prison

Before the time machine turns into a bus
And lets you off with the night shift
Outside a laundry in Montgomery.
Old friend, I think of you running
A brush across some senator's pajamas,

Then of the slide, kicking into the light:
Somewhere in the Congo, circa 1959.

The ladies click their dentures into smiles.
King hasn't marched yet. We've just
Stumbled in out of the sunshine.
It's that instant when we're blind
And passing through the beam.
The feast of ants is painted on your back.
It's like all the past now. It's black and white.

RODNEY JONES

Jiving Toward the Heart of Speech

William Matthews. *Selected Poems and Translations, 1969–1991*. Houghton Mifflin 1992. 222 pp. $19.95

From the unpromising dirt lots of an American workaday idiom, William Matthews has been conjuring a companionable, colloquial poetry that kicks sand in the face of the sweetly lyrical. By turns witty, wistful, jaunty, cynical, erudite, arrogant, meditative, and always with the biting emotional clarity of the blues, his work points to "the bad marriage of mind and body" and the violence that each perpetrates upon the other. Even language, the poet's hedge, becomes for Matthews a poor indemnity; this difficult truth lends a fine pathos to much of his work. To read through Matthews' *Selected Poems and Translations, 1969–1991* is to trace the refinement of a style that cleaves to "the truculent heart of speech." His commitment to the cutting, unembellished phrase seems almost a moral choice, as though only this can justify the fierce ways of the world to man. With almost no frontal artifice, Matthews has laid down hard, fluent lines on everything from potatoes, lust, and Freud to baseball, Auden, Nabokov, and jazz. His lines register what you say, if you are articulate and educated, when you speak offhandedly with a double shot of bile and adrenaline held in check by some practical wisdom and a feel for the corrosive.

While Matthews favors a cool and easy vernacular, he makes room for a comparatively elevated diction. He holds, in effect, a sort of dual citizenship. If he hangs out in dives listening to Bud Powell ("Two bucks for a Scotch in this dump, / I thought, and I bought me / another"), it doesn't stop this smartest of poets from ruminating eloquently in his book-lined study ("How much of the great poetry / of solitude in the woods is one / long cadenza on the sadness / / of civilization . . .). Matthews is wary of forfeiting either of his passports, and it's his pleasure to talk his way across frontiers and keep us guessing. He disarms the critic by referring to his own work at one point as "genial chatter." "Genial" does convey his warm talkativeness, but if the poems partake of "chatter," it is only in their quick, quirky treatment of what they "talk about." Consider "Lust," an early poem from *Ruining the New Road* (1970), his first collection:

> It is a squad car idling
> through my eyes, bored,
> looking for a crime to crush.
> Two tough cops drive it,
> three years on the same beat,
> sick of each other.
> To it I am no better
> than a radish.
> I hear its indolent engine
> grump along in second gear,
> feel both cops watch me
> walk with stiff ankles,
> a nun among drunks.

The tone here comes off as casual, even jokey ("Two tough cops drive it, / three years on the same beat, / sick of each other"). It's something you might conceivably hear in a bar, though of course "indolent" is our tip-off that this is no mere Bud guy. The conceit itself, comically ingenious, reveals a talent for metaphor and a sophisticated degree of antic self-perception, the speaker playing victim to his own steamrolling libido. It's a highbrow figuration ("To it I am . . .") dressed down for a night in the Village.

As a brief, psychological snapshot, "Lust" is characteristic of Matthews' early phase. His later poems consistently admit a more supple syntax and a breadth of rhetorical form better suited to his talkative style. In "Familial," the speaker imagines heaven as a never-ending forum for evening talk:

> I want my place in line, the way
> each word in this genial chatter

has its place. That's why we call it
grammar school, where we learn to behave.
I understand why everyone wants

to go up to heaven, to rise,
like a ship through a curriculum
of locks, into the eternal light

of talk after dinner. What I don't
understand is why one would balk to die
if death were entry to such heaven.

(from *A Happy Childhood,* 1985)

At key junctures, as in the final two lines above, Matthews assumes a more mannered diction in order to drive home his point. Also typical is the flash of a striking simile, that ship rising through its "curriculum of locks," amid the mostly mundane. Some readers may be put off by his idiosyncratic jumps, as in the second stanza above, which awkwardly telescopes grammar school and "behaving." Of course, it's a condensed witticism: In grammar school we learn to behave, just as we learn to make our grammar behave, and he wants his own words to stand obediently in line. But the aside, jammed into the stanza, creates a sort of kink in the smooth continuity of thought and risks seeming gratuitous.

If Matthews can do the avuncular, he can also modulate effortlessly to the hard-edged and dark, as in this draconian passage:

You have the right to be silent, blank
as an unminted coin, sullen or joyfully

fierce, how would we know? What's truly yours
you'll learn irremediably from prison.

You have the right to clamp your eyes shut,
not to assent nor to eat nor to use our only

> toilet in your turn, but to hold your breath
> and frail body like secrets, and to turn blue
>
> and to be beautiful briefly to yourself.
> And we have our rights, too, which you can guess.

(from "Right," *A Happy Childhood,* 1985)

Under the pressures of subdued rage, "irremediably" gavels down with Latinate authority, while a sublimated growl ripples among the r's in "truly yours," "irremediably," "learn," and "prison." The excerpt expresses what, in Matthews' universe, the wary body might say to the prodigal imagination, seen as disreputable because of its parasitic and subversive liberty.

This mind-body schism underlies much of Matthews' work. But the dual national, again, plays both sides. If he sometimes gives himself to imaginative flights, he also clocks a lot of time on the ground, talking about sports. Baseball, basketball, and skating all do extra duty as metaphors through which he articulates his thoughts on art and life. "In Memory of the Utah Stars" (from *Rising and Falling,* 1979) meditates on the now defunct professional basketball team famous for recruiting the *Wunderkind* Moses Malone, one of the few basketball players ever to go straight from high school to the pros. I quote it in its entirety to illustrate a closure characteristic of many Matthews poems, which begin with observation or commentary on particulars and then move toward a generalized reflection, in this case on burnout and loss:

> Each of them must have terrified
> his parents by being so big, obsessive
> and exact so young, already gone
> and leaving, like a big tipper,
> that huge changeling's body in his place.
> The prince of bone spurs and bad knees.
>
> The year I first saw them play
> Malone was a high school freshman,
> already too big for any bed,
> 14, a natural resource.

You have to learn not to
apologize, a form of vanity.
You flare up in the lane, exotic
anywhere else. You roll the ball
off fingers twice as long as your
girlfriend's. Great touch for a big man,
says some jerk. Now they're defunct
and Moses Malone, boy wonder at 19,
rises at 20 from the St. Louis bench,
his pet of a body grown sullen
as fast as it grew up.

Something in you remembers every
time the ball left your fingertips
wrong and nothing the ball
can do in the air will change that.
You watch it set, stupid moon,
the way you watch yourself
in a recurring dream.
You never lose your touch
or forget how taxed bodies
go at the same pace they owe,
how brutally well the universe
works to be beautiful,
how we metabolize loss
as fast as we have to.

Not Adam's curse but Malone's, who also labored to be beautiful, now a "prince" of injuries, "already gone / and leaving, like a big tipper." That tragicomic phrase is quintessential Matthews: fluid, demotic, deceptively simple, yet forceful. A master of tonal coloration, Matthews here enriches and complicates that phrase by what he plays around it. The way we hear it is subtly inflected by the stanza's rueful final line, which bodes ill for the exotic, starry-eyed misfit—and for all of us trapped inside "taxed bodies" for which we'll soon have to pay. This unrehearsed surge of feeling imparts a hint of solemn nobility to the grotesquely large, doomed, and departing big tipper. There's no artificial mediation in the language—it's all spontaneous verve.

By hewing close to the conversational, Matthews sacrifices the Rilkean raptures, but he spins out alternative advantages from the "used and casual beauty" of the plain style. Aware that its "stern exclusions" limit him to a narrower lyrical range, Matthews fondly quotes Dizzy Gillespie: "You only have so many notes, and what makes a style is how you get from one note to another." Here is Matthews doing plain-deal riffs on poet and pig:

> Behind its snout like a huge button,
> like an almost clean plate, the pig
> looks candid compared to the author,
>
> and why not? He has a way with words,
> but the unspeakable pig, squat
> and foursquare as a bathtub,
>
> squints frankly. Nobody knows
> the trouble it's seen, this rained-out
> pork roast, this ham escaped into
>
> its corpulent jokes, its body of work.
> The author is skinny and looks serious:
> what will he say next? The copious pig
>
> has every appearance of knowing,
> from his pert, coiled tail to the wispy tips
> of his edible ears, but the pig isn't telling.

("Photo of the Author with a Favorite Pig," from *Foreseeable Futures*, 1987)

It's hard to resist this comic affection for the "unspeakable pig"—a wordless keeper of the poet's secrets—or the charm of Matthews' empathy: "Nobody knows / the trouble it's seen, this rained-out / pork roast." What he gains with such archly homespun diction is an unassailable credibility. By the end of the *Selected*, the reader swears that Matthews can smell a clumsy lie from two miles away. His work betrays no false beats or affected flourishes. The genteel poverty of his loose, unrhymed tercets—as with his quatrains and couplets—points back again to a literate sensibility steeped in the prosy popular as well as the Tradition. Sometimes Matthews tests himself, yielding to a Romantic urge, but never for too long, and always, like a sly performer, with an eye to the well-timed effect. Here he contemplates the night sky from the back of a boat:

> . . . How com-
> modious the dark universe is,
> and companionable the stars.
> How drunk I am. I shake
> my shriveled nozzle and three
> drops lurk out like syllables
> from before there were languages.

(from "Pissing off the Back of the Boat into the Nivernais Canal,"
Flood, 1982)

In seven lines we witness a head-on collision between Wordsworth and Catullus. Hiccuping his way through "com- / modious," Matthews rights himself in time to manage "companionable." Overall, it's an idiom so attractively insouciant that unless we see it on the page, we forget we're hearing poems.

To say that jazz is the key to understanding Matthews' poetics—and it is—invites danger, since discussions of this sort bring to mind, among others, the Beats, whose bumptious application of jazz proved, with the exception of Ginsberg's *Howl,* far too patently self-conscious to be persuasive. In "The Metamorphoses: Jazz and Poetry,"[1] Michael Collins enumerates the "deadly sins" to which jazz poets are inclined. Prominent among them is that of structural misperception, a sin of naïveté, in which the poet, blinded by "the deceptive freedom of good jazz," trashes all structural principles, including the "embedded rhythms of sentence structure and syntax." Matthews is far too savvy, as poet and jazz aficionado, to indulge in such vandalism. Nor does he rely on the anaphora and the cheap-and-easy surrealism that some provincials still think of as groundbreaking. With Matthews, the poetry-jazz parallels are more fully thought through. In an interview published in *The Georgia Review*,[2] Matthews explains:

> It's a sense of procedure rather than subject matter that is the deep link between jazz and poetry. I happen to write frequently about jazz because I write about what I love, but it's the procedural link that interests me most.

That procedural link involves the patter and wanderings of the talking voice. No surprise, then, to find that the musical dimension animating Matthews' poems is of the improvisational order, not the melodic. It is as if Matthews distrusted the false consolations of the mellifluously lyrical—he rarely relies on phrasal ornamentation to fill out a fixed rhythmic pattern or rhyme scheme, nor does he toy ostentatiously with vowel textures. Instead, he inhabits loose rhetorical forms (narrative, anecdote, aphorism) and adjusts his phrasing, tone, and rhythm to re-create the natural habitat of the voice. Again, from the same interview, Matthews on Matthews:

> . . . jazz gave me permission to begin composing a poetic language based on the rhythms of the speaking voice: the voice rationalizing to itself, jiving other people, trying to seduce a comparative stranger, explaining why a paper is not ready on time, doing puns and jokes and imitations—in sum, doing the real emotional business of daily life, full of weird quirks and odd lilts.

Faithful to this working model, Matthews' crafty lines jive, seduce, and "do" the emotional stuff of daily life: Like the darkest blues, they console by virtue of their emotional accuracy.

Matthews takes care, however, to distinguish between musical events on the page and on the stage. In the interview, he explains the difference:

> . . . something happens in the course of a poem that doesn't happen in a piece of music. Words have conventional meaning, and so something's being proposed—to the reader at least, and in many poems to an implied listener, some second character of the poem beside the one we usually call "the speaker." Is it believable or not? Interesting or not? There are issues of persuasion and consent raised

by any given poem that I believe are important sources of improvisation in the writing of poetry.

Because Matthews' vernacular improvs are believable and engaging, he wins our consent. He certainly does so in one of his most important poems to date, "It Don't Mean a Thing If It Ain't Got That Swing," from his 1989 collection *Blues If You Want,* the last of his books represented in the *Selected.* A playful discourse on language, writing, form, and seduction, it fully articulates his esteem for "small-talk," a linguistic analogue of jazz:

> . . . love is woven
>
> from language
> itself, from jokes, pet names and puns,
> from anecdote, from double entendre
> (already invaded by *tendre*), until
>
> our lovers are a kind of literature
> and sole mad scholiasts of it.
> *Inventors at Work,* a sign on the bedroom
> door might say.

For Matthews, these intimate murmurings—"jokes, pet names and puns"—"aren't sweet nothings, / they're the very dial tone love's open line makes." Although the diction here is slightly more elevated (scholiasts studying double entendres) and the voice more literate, the colloquial pace and punch remain. The severe enjambment simulates the rough edge of speech, luring the reader with the promise of the genuine. Matthews then speculates on the proto-nature of language before the invention of writing:

> Language was young and sad. She could
> implore and charm, she could convince and scathe,
> pick laughter's lock,
> she could almost glow with her own powers,
> but she was the wind's,
> like jazz before recordings . . .

> *. . . Oh, I'd give anything,* she cried,
> *if I could be memorable.*
>
> *Anything?*
> intoned the opportunistic devil from
> behind a papier-mâché boulder. *Yes,*
> *anything,* she said, and thus the deal
>
> was struck, and writing was invented.
> But to be written down she gave up
> pout, toss, crinkle,
> stamp and shrug, shiver, flout and pucker,
>
> the long, cunning lexicon of the body,
> and thus what we lazily call "form"
> in poetry,
> let's say, is Language's desperate
>
> attempt to wrench from print
> the voluble body it gave away
> in order to be read. . . .

Matthews here describes the aspirations of his own poetics: to give back to written poetry the sensuous, voluble feel of *speech*—witty, gritty, intelligent speech that moves as unself-consciously as a smooth run of unrecorded jazz. (The sexual pun that haunts "cunning lexicon" is typical of Matthews' sense of innuendo.) His choice of the word "voluble" is perfect, since its Latin root, *volvere*, meaning "to roll," describes the movement of the voice through the enjambed lines.

That lovely, unstoppable roll can be heard in another key poem from *Blues If You Want,* this one about jazz musicians on an all-night bus ride between gigs. Note how the cadence and word choice achieve the pungency of actual speech, while the controlled phrasing and the delicately subdued metaphors and simile lift the poem above the sloppy ramble of what we "really" say:

> The way some of us played cards and some drank
> and some of us ran the tiny motors of talk long

into the night—so many needs and habits, don't
you know?—you'd think there'd have been at least
one of us awake at any hour of the night, but then
sometimes I'd wake at dawn and miss the idle
hum that we give off when we're awake and know
as steadily as the bus droned on and sleep
drained out of me, I and the driver were the only
ones awake. Even the boss, who used to sit
like a night-light directly back of the driver,
where we couldn't see him in the rearview mirror,
had withdrawn his interest in the world.

(from "Every Tub")

By this point Matthews has come a long way from the "curt" Polaroids of his early phase. The long, enjambed lines allow the voice to billow and relax into a much richer anecdotal style. Along with a latent blues-bitterness, these are signatures Matthews has clarified and refined in his later work, which continues to probe "the truculent heart of speech."

Why, though, would the heart of speech be "truculent?" An answer is suggested if we look at this telling phrase in context:

A phalanx of cabs surges uptown in tune
to the staggered lights and two young black
men spurt across the dark avenue (two A.M.)

ahead of them: *We're here, motherfuckers,*
don't mess up. Three of five cabs honk: *We're here*
too, older and clawing for a living, don't

fuck up. The cabs rush uptown and the lights
go green ahead like a good explanation.
Everyone knows this ballet. Nobody falls or brakes.

Tonight I talked for hours and never said
one thing so close to the truculent heart of speech
as those horn blats, that dash across Amsterdam,

not to persuade nor to be understood but
a kind of signature, a scrawl on the air:
We're here, room for all of us if we be alert.

("107th & Amsterdam," from *Blues If You Want,* 1989)

The heart of speech here turns out paradoxically to be a prelingual place, located in the unself-regarding urges of physical and psychological survival—maybe somewhere in the blues. It can just as easily give rise to shouted execrations as to a blast of car horns, an ecstatic dash across a late-night, big-city avenue, or a sultry jazz lick. Here it makes itself felt in the urgency of Matthews' language: The opening's heavy falling rhythm ("A phalanx of cabs surges") accelerates into long lines that crackle with the energy of consonantal repetition ("uptown in tune / to the staggered lights . . ."), while the choppy line breaks and rough monosyllabic verbs ("surge," "spurt," "honk," "fuck," "rush") force the reader forward through syntactic traffic. Matthews bridles the sound of necessity, and necessity, with its unrelenting demands, *is* truculent, the Latin root *trux* meaning "fierce."

"Ferocity," "fury," and "rage" loom large in Matthews' lexicon. Part of the poet's makeup, they fortify him to survive the withering pursuit of excellence. This is expressed memorably in a baseball poem, "Masterful" (from *A Happy Childhood,* 1985):

They say you can't think and hit at the same time,
but they're wrong: you think with your body, and the whole

wave of impact surges patiently through you
into your wrists, into your bat, and meets the ball

as if this exact and violent tryst had been a fevered
secret for a week. The wrists "break," as the batting

coaches like to say, but what they do is give away
their power, spend themselves, and the ball benefits.

When Ted Williams took—we should say "gave"—
batting practice, he'd stand in and chant to himself

> "My name is Ted Fucking Ballgame and I'm the best
> fucking hitter in baseball," and he was, jubilantly
>
> grim, lining them out pitch after pitch, crouching
> and uncoiling from the sweet ferocity of excellence.

Matthews' baseball metaphor enacts the grim, driven work of writing, to which one submits—an excruciating apprenticeship—until one's poems, "marinated in misery," as Matthews might say, crouch and uncoil, like Ted Williams' swing, with the pent-up "ferocity of excellence."

The fourteen lines of "Masterful" also show how Matthews subordinates formal features to the ad hoc rhetorical demand of securing an idiom to match his subject. Here he covets actual spoken rhythms rather than primly perfect iambs and disowns the artifice of rhyme. His enjambed lines help the cause, marking off phrases that fall believably within the sayable. The rangy cadences packed into couplets embody the easy, tensile stride of a confident athlete. Formally, the "sonnet" is such only by the skin of its cowhide. The fourteen lines cage the poem in a small space out of which it can illustratively explode, spitting its plosive b's and p's as Ted spits nails. Even in this most well-bred of forms, Matthews pledges allegiance to down-and-dirty diction, which best captures the violence and immediacy—the truculence—he seeks: "My name is Ted Fucking Ballgame and I'm the best / fucking hitter in baseball." This is vintage Matthews.

So, too, but for other reasons, is this moment from "Every Tub" (from *Blues If You Want,* 1989), quoted earlier:

> . . . See,
> the reason I'm a musician is, Language and I,
> we love each other but we never got it on,
> so as the saying goes, we're just good friends,
> though I surely love to talk.

These lines voice a congenital anxiety in Matthews' imagination: the poet's rocky marriage to his medium. Even in the very first poem of the

Selected, "The Search Party" (from *Ruining the New Road,* 1970), Matthews grumbles about figurative speech. After he sets the scene, a search through the woods for a child presumed dead, he belligerently turns:

> Reader, by now you must be sure
> you know just where we are,
> deep in symbolic woods.
> Irony, self-accusation,
> someone else's suffering.
> The search is that of art.
>
> You're wrong, though it's
> an intelligent mistake.
> There was a real lost child.
> I don't want to swaddle it
> in metaphor.
> I'm just a journalist
> who can't believe in objectivity.
> I'm in these poems
> because I'm in my life.

Despite his candor, a journalist who can't believe in objectivity is perhaps a bit tormented, like a poet who can't endorse the Romantic belief in the redemptive powers of language. As poet, Matthews lives by definition through figures of speech, but he is too clear-sighted to indulge overmuch in confections that would artificially sweeten the real world of thorns, colitis, divorce, and vasectomy. The standoff, then, between literal and figurative lends astringency to many of his poems.

Whatever his doubts, Matthews still amiably confesses that "I surely love to talk," and so he goes on, inventing conceits of great ingenuity, though they're pitched at times in melancholic, even bitter keys:

> . . . Remember "Reckless
> Blues"? Bessie Smith sings out "Daddy"
> and Louis Armstrong plays back "Daddy"
> as clear through his horn as if he'd
> spoken it. But it's her daddy and her

story. When you play it you become
your part in it, one of her beautiful
troubles, and then, however much music
can do this, part of her consolation,
the way pain and joy eat off each other's
plates, but mostly you play to drunks,
to the night, to the way you judge
and pardon yourself, to all that goes
not unsung, but unrecorded.

(from "The Accompanist," *Foreseeable Futures,* 1987)

Attentive to the accompanist's supporting role, he implicitly acknowledges the poet's less than ideal commerce with the Muse, who often
enough abandons the poet to his own shabby court of appeals.

Matthews expresses another of his fundamental anxieties in
"Nabokov's Blues" (from *Blues If You Want,* 1989). After spending an
hour amid the revered stylist's quasi-sacred butterfly collection, the
speaker ambles out into the winter streets: "I stood up to my ankles in
sludge pooled / / over a stopped sewer grate and thought— / wouldn't
you know it—about love and art. . . ." This is the typical Matthews
double vision: one eye on the sewer grate, the other on the Muse.

By the end of the *Selected,* we are in the presence of a "sure and casual
rapacity"—a major contemporary voice—that has mastered the games
of persuasion and consent. We follow that voice, knowing it will not
disappoint. Whatever dross there may have been is gone, and the
delivery has been perfected: "If time is money, teachers are shabbiest /
of all the summer rich. The rest of the year we rejoin / the poor we
refused to use our educations to escape." While Matthews has more than
fulfilled the promises of expressive power made in an early poem, which
raged that we are truly a nation "Because grief unites us, / like the locked
antlers of moose / who die on their knees in pairs," this connoisseur of
mood can also captivate us toward the end of the *Selected* with a
mellowed lament for a house as loved and lived-in as the language itself:

. . . The way cops "lift"
fingerprints, that's how I touched the house.

The way one of my sons would stand in front
of me and say, *I'm outta here,* and he would mean
it, his crisp, heart-creasing husk delivering

a kind of telegram from wherever the rest of him
had gone—that's how I laved and scoured
and patrolled the house, and how I made my small
withdrawals and made my wan way outta there.

(from "Housecooling," *Blues If You Want,* 1989)

And when Matthews tells us in a late, unguarded moment that his work is "a reverie on what I love, and whom, / and how I manage to hold on to them," we admire the Horatian equipoise, tinged with Coltrane, that has led us eloquently through furies and frustrations we know to be our own.

JOHN FOY

Notes

1. Michael Collins, "The Metamorphoses: Jazz and Poetry," *Parnassus: Poetry in Review 19,* No. 2 (1994): 49–80.
2. William Matthews, "Jazz and Poetry: A Conversation," *Georgia Review* 46 (Winter 1992): 645–61.

Rabbi Jose the Angel

A miracle is an embarrassment
Rabbi Jose the Angel said, shyly
furling his. His parents were human—we know that—

his father a vintner
of the tribe of Judah, his mother a Levite
who could drive a bargain.

The Talmud records only one discussion
of the wings that sprouted from his shoulders.
Rabbi Jose said they meant

that even to reach the Earth
he would need to ascend;
Rabbi Pinchas cited Daniel;

Rabbi Asher laughed;
Rabbi Tarfon taught, in the name of his teacher,
that a winged one is born in every generation

to see if the Flood has receded yet.
Flight was painful to him.
His wife, Tzipporah, a Moabite prophetess

with turmeric eyes, said
as much as she loved his wings
she preferred the rest of him.

His ambition was to reconcile
suffering and perfection,
or at least to deepen

the contradiction.
As he prayed his wings would open,
creaking sleepily, like sails.

He taught that humans were created
so that wherever there was a chasm
there would also be a bridge.

The implications weren't lost on the Romans,
who hunted him like a bird, with nets.
The rumor that he ascended,

like Elijah, in a blaze,
is reasonable, under the circumstances.
The Romans soaked him with oil

and touched a torch to him.
Trailing translucent, soaplike ash
he flew over occupied Jerusalem,

tracing a psalm of smoke
that's come down to us in Aramaic;
no one knows the end. Another source

has him fleeing to Egypt,
earning a modest reputation
as a carver of crystals, maker of mirrors

and baker of oddly shaped breads.
They say whatever he wore smelled burnt
like the back of a seraph's neck.

Shortly before his death,
the Emperor wrote to him.
Tzipporah warned him not to answer;

Romans dine on tongue, she said.
He dreamed the sea
was a trough of fire

and a wind walked the land mumbling *kaddish*
and the mountains shifted like uneasy sleepers
sharing a single bed.

Certain scholars still insist
that the Rabbi is based
on the roughly contemporaneous

Jose the Pious, who kept a dovecote near Nazareth
and was considered, for a Galilean,
to have a peculiarly beautiful head.

The fact of the matter is this:
in the first century of the Common Era
a man with wings wrote

"Power is a matter
of interpretation," in perfect Latin
on the skin of a sheep.

As Tzipporah foresaw, the Emperor was displeased.
The night before the soldiers came
the Rabbi gave a feast,

setting each place
with a cruse of oil
he had pressed with his feet.

His heart skittered like a spider
as he glided above his guests
and his eyes closed, and his hair blew back

in the oleander wind. Rabbi Tarfon says
he wasn't afraid of heights
but of the solace

of watching the world collapse
into patterns of light and dark
like the shadow of wings on parchment

or the gold and ebony strands
woven from human heads
into the carpet of conquered gods

that cushioned the Emperor's steps.
Rabbi Asher argued
that since Jose didn't know Latin

his death was miraculous;
Pinchas agreed with reservations;
Tzipporah the prophetess wept.

Rabbi Jose the Angel said
life is a seal on a letter.
The wax is broken.

We have reached the text.

JAY LADIN

The Wizard of Wichita

Albert Goldbarth. *Across the Layers: Poems Old and New.* The University of Georgia Press 1993. 217 pp. $16.95 (paper)

Albert Goldbarth. *Great Topics of the World.* David R. Godine 1994. 193 pp. $22.95

I could begin by comparing him to Heraclitus' river, thus: We can and cannot step in the same Goldbarth twice, for lo, he is always there yet just as constantly on the move and morph. Or I might liken him to the Roadrunner, all flirtation, resourcefulness, and infuriating speed; woe to the Wile E. Critic who would make a meal of this bird, for when you think to appraise him in his tracks, *beep beep,* the scamp is gone, another book published before you can opine on the last. It's hard to say which of these analogies would please Goldbarth more—he admires cartoon characters at least as much as pre-Socratics.

What's certain, however, is that Albert Goldbarth constitutes a one-man movement, an -ism unto himself. Almost a quarter-century into his career, he seems to be only now hitting his stride, which resembles a sturdy hiker's tramp crossed with some waddle copped from Monty Python's Ministry of Silly Walks. That he will persist at this megaerobic pace seems hardly less certain than gravity or television; he probably thinks writer's block is a Legolike toy for insouciant scriveners. We won't be able to take stock of Goldbarth entire until he's safely six feet under, and even then he'll doubtless manage to afterfax his poems to whatever avatar of Merrill is then receiving them.

At times I jealously suspect a subtractive side to Goldbarth's fecundity, for when my own poems flounder I know he's out there, deep in his Kansas lucubrations, hogging the finite fuel. I curse him at such moments, sure, but mostly I grow grateful that the world's occurrences have met their match in Goldbarth: No quark is small or trivial enough to duck his omnivorous appetite. Being prolific isn't just a fact about Goldbarth—it's an aesthetic and an astronomical imperative. Goldbarth expands because the universe does too. With a squillion juicy ephemera to collect, collate, and comment on, how could he be other than effusive? And if he is therefore our most cornucopian poet, he is also the least bored or boring. This list of superlatives could go on and on. In fact, I think it will: Goldbarth is the Sultan of Sanguinity, the Earl of Extroversion, the unchallenged Godfather of Goof; few bards are less flappable than he, or hornier; he's at least in the running for Tenderest, a savagely contested laurel.

As you can see, Goldbarth has a knack for tempting his observers astray into imitative fallacy. One cannot describe him without resorting to the same mock-exorbitant manner he has so friskily perfected. Because the surface of a Goldbarth poem is typically an outrageous neon purple, we may overlook the humbler slate beneath. Don't be hornswoggled: Minus the proverbial smoke and mirrors, our wizard is, you guessed it, an ordinary Joe. Indeed, this nakedness most endears him to me. If the pyrotechnics didn't dependably give way, time and time again, to a boggled wonder at the brute strangeness of our lives, their engineer would remain just that: a mere technician, a word wonk, or (to borrow Jarrell's affectionate jab at Dylan Thomas) an idiot savant of the English language. Far from keeping his sentiments in purdah, though, Goldbarth wants us, even needs us, to detect and relish them. He has dowsed the source of his own originality, which gushes not from what he feels—pretty much what we all do—but from how he gussies each emotion up; the antic correlatives chosen for the inner life, not the life itself, distinguish him. It is our pleasure to watch his zany trelliswork accumulate, and sometimes poignantly collapse, around the simplest of givens: the universe's unfathomability; the rich enigma of the past; the excellence of sex; midnight amazement at a sleeping wife; Kaddish for a dead father.

That last bereavement dominates *Across the Layers.* In a rather self-congratulatory preface, Goldbarth explains the book as a compendium of "filial gestures." He lifts its title from a poem called, in vintage Goldbarthese, "The Dynamics of Huh," where he laments about wanting "to call my father, across the layers of shale, / / worm-warren, and motherlode coal that separate us"— a peculiar notion, as if his father had resumed a chthonic state beneath the crust, but a crucial one to

Goldbarth's worldview. Possessed of an almost tribal taste for "the crackle of ancestor-plasm" (although not, apparently, for its snap and pop), he thinks of human history in terms of—what else?—ice cream: "now he's part of the parfait striations I'm singing of." Lineage constitutes for him the Vishnu Metamorphic Complex, as the basement stratum of the Grand Canyon is marvelously known—the bedrock, the stuff. There is a touch of Stephen Jay Gould about Goldbarth; a Gould liberated from scientific rigor might bust loose with freewheeling fugues like these:

> . . . The ever-ravenous protozoa
> in the rumen-goop of that bull I earlier mentioned, burbling
> away at their cellulose walls . . . by one hashbrowns-surrounded
> breakfast steak, they *are* connected to some soul-weary
> salesman in 1929 pulling in to a roadside diner . . .
> Let the sign of that connection be the thready, heady
> olfactory-waft of ant saliva the anteater rides like radar
> unto its repast. And so there *is* a mode, an almost diagrammable
> order, albeit on levels sub and supra . . .

I think it's safe to surmise that no other poet would crown bug spit as his epitome of cosmic symbiosis. Yet I would also maintain the underlying seriousness of such whimsy. For when Goldbarth gropes toward his father via filet, he puts into practice an eccentrically beautiful theory of relationships, which holds loved ones reachable, and perhaps savable, by way of spirited association. This belief finds its fullest and most affecting rehearsal in "Again," a poem whose very stanzaic pattern—stations of eight—seems fashioned to seduce eternity. At his father's sickbed, Goldbarth declares the poem

> . . . a relegation of breath to that preliterate
> place faith comes from—something meant to be a chain or list
> of small lights through his darkness. So I thought of Japan,
>
> the *Sheet of 1,000 Buddhas:* how a single woodblock stamp has meant
> so many duplications of the same small holy figure—each,
> its nimbus; each, its dole of glow to keep back its commensurate
> dole of benightedness . . .

> . . . And if I digress right now to the story
>
> of Chunosuke Matsuyama . . .
> it doesn't mean I've forgotten that hospital bed, my father
> dwindling in it, or the mission of this poem.

"A chain or list of small lights": exactly the remedy George Bush prescribed. But the slightly more articulate Goldbarth wants incantation in the ancient sense of warding off evil. His reticulum of lists and ancestry harks back, of course, to the Old Testament; much as his father's "heavy ledgers in the basement . . . were *this* / world's Torah," Goldbarth's poems, with their biblical fix on generation, teem forth like a mutant host of begats. The Byzantine asides build the poem, and the pullulating poem, in turn, becomes a talisman against rot. Here ontology enters the ring with oncology:

> . . . I'd stand there trying to think myself
> immeasurably into the cells, the sick ones, down the fundament
>   of what
> we are, to where it all begins, and by such empathetic thinking
> burnish the bastula of him clean . . .

The gallows irony of Goldbarth hoping to sparkle his father up by cogitating down the ass of what we are preserves, if not, sadly, the patient himself, at least the poetry from mawkishness. That concern is tackled head-on in "Sentimental":

> Is it sentimental? Oops . . .
>   . . . And will it make us run
> for the picklier taste of irony rolled around protectively on our
>   tongues
> like a grab of Greek olives? . . .
>   . . . If a balled-up fidget of snakes
> in the underbrush dies in a freeze is it sentimental? No,
> yes, maybe. What if a litter of cocker spaniels? What
> if we called them "puppydogs" in the same poem in that same
>   hard,
> hammering winter? When my father was buried,

the gray snow in the cemetery was sheet tin. If I said
that? Yes, no, what does "tone" or "history" do
to the Hollywood hack violinists who patiently wait to play
the taut nerves of the closest human body until from that
lush cue alone, the eyes swell moistly, and the griefs
we warehouse daily take advantage of this thinning
of our systems, then the first sloppy gushes begin . . .

This passage illustrates the tonal brinkmanship at which Goldbarth excels. Pretending to operate within the cool parameters of the hypothetical, the poem slyly licenses its own sappiness; "what if" is a *carte blanche* gambit, since it allows Goldbarth to go straight over the top . . . but not "actually." Needless to comment, the bluff's very transparency makes it work. The reader ends up being offered a kind of double contract: Goldbarth will play the lachrymose clown for us so long as we mark the realness of his makeup-smearing tears.

Circus metaphors inevitably somersault into view when dealing with such a high-wire freak, and highlight his remarkable childishness. Both valences of that last adjective are intended here, for Goldbarth's immaturity is at once conspicuous and fine. Nor, thankfully, has he ever seen fit to outgrow it. Only someone with one sneakered foot still in adolescence could seize it as wankishly as Goldbarth does in this passage from "The Future," the last essay in *Great Topics of the World:*

> But *I* wasn't going to die. No, I was thirteen and I was going to live forever! I was thirteen, I was fried each day in the alternating current of cocksure swagger and inadequacy. I dreamed. I stormed. I played with my dick, my impetuous other. I wondered: God, sure, okay, why not, but who made *God* then? I practiced a sullen stare. My brain wasn't big enough for my body, my body wasn't big enough for my ravenous heart, my heart would have *drooled* if I'd held it up to the light. It would bounce. Hell, *I* could bounce, like a man on the moon one-sixth the weight blah blah. I'd get a tattoo. I'd weep for the starving. I'd win the affection of Phyllis Kirschenbaum, third row, fourth seat, our tongues would squirm the squirm of mating snails.
>
> At night I gawked at the covers of pulp mags—*Startling Wonder Stories, Amazing, Superscience Monthly*—staring as if my eyes could

knock against that tacky artwork like two knuckles, and I'd be admitted. There were pitted, fire-coned planet landscapes, soared across by the regalmost armadas of patrolling rockets, and populated chiefly by women so perfect their bodies were pure Euclidean shapes befleshed, and then the flesh beglittered in the crisscrossed silver spaghetti-straps of "thermo-cling," which seemed to be the loose, louche fashion choice of space seductresses. I wasn't stupid and *still* I'd tilt those covers as if a different angle might let me ogle a bosom better.

Where most writers are content with (or limited to) vague nostalgias, their evocations, whether sprightly or wistful, made from an adult distance, Goldbarth gets right in there. His inner kid never was—the brat has always been out, at large, and in need of a good spanking. Unthinkable that Goldbarth would blush at earlier versions of himself, since the boy who leers at sci-fi Amazons and the man who follows Euclidian tangents are, at a key level of sensibility, one and the same; a single, running fascination links the two.

The above lech-a-sketch also bears a faint resemblance to a pud-pulling literary cousin: Alexander Portnoy. Although Goldbarth doesn't whimper over *shikses* and has never, to the best of my knowledge, fucked the family dinner, what with his logorrhea, his Willy Lomanesque, insurance-peddling dad ("some soul-weary/salesman in 1929"), his onanism, and the general scope of his lust, he seems from certain angles a dead ringer for Roth's antihero. Often he sports a charmingly sophomoric, yo-dude-smell-my-fingers bravado, as when in "Delft," another essay from *Great Topics,* he conjures up

> . . . that amberthatched snickerdoodle between her legs that enjoyed my own gargoyley thing . . . her lips a remora on me, mine improvising red-hot jazz on her chickfuzz ocarina.

¡Ay caramba! Cunnilingual prowess is a minor yet cherished theme in Goldbarth's quiver, as witness this second oral affidavit, wherein the self-proclaimed Coltrane of the Clitoris plays a bizarre riff on another famous American pervert, Faulkner's Vardaman:

> . . . I was a fish once. Even

now I like to lick women where they come
closest to gill.

Gold- may act the rank -fish at times, boastfully "dipping the dingus,"
but he can also impersonate a civilized -barth. In this passage from
"Delft," crass Yankee porn submits (although not totally) to the more
Continentally sophisticated aspect of his sexual persona:

> "Fleas are so much a German erotic specialty," Brendan Lehane
> writes, "that two learned Teutons, Herren Hugo Hayn and Alfred
> N. Gotendorf, applied themselves at the turn of the century to
> compiling a bibliography of the literature. *Floh-Litteratur,* they
> called it," from the sixteenth century up. But the Germans have no
> monopoly here; and by the sixteenth century, something like the

> > . . . flea
> > mankind one morning stared to see
> > on Catherine Desroches' bared breast
> > sucking imperturbably

> is a well-established folk *motif de prurience.* A poem ascribed to
> Ovid has its narrator imagining he can—*poof*—become a flea at
> will, and so spelunk flesh grottoes. Long after, a character in
> Marlowe's *Faust* says, "I am like to Ovid's flea. I can creep into
> every corner of a wench." Lehane: "There is in fact a whole class of
> erotic flea art." Night: a candle: an off-white cambric shift up-
> rumpled in search of some coven of spiky-snouted scoundrels, and
> there you have it: the two full moons and the fertile crescent, the
> nasties, the nougat, the grail.

And there we have as well Goldbarth in miniature, the donnish allusiveness gleefully sabotaged by upstart "nasties." To leaven his formidably
seasoned intellect, he jettisons adult jadedness, restraint, and etiquette;
the ensuing counterpoint of scholasticism and impish truancy sets the
tempo for much of his work. You see, Goldbarth doesn't just wear his
Widener's-worth of learning lightly—he likes to strip and go yipping
butt-naked through the musty stacks. Not for him high dudgeon or
philippics Rothian; where Portnoy's early promise withered from acidity

Goldbarth's thrives in sweeter soil. His is an output of precociousness fulfilled, the sublime homework of a higher geek.

In fact, even Goldbarth's vocabulary, for all its polish and leviathan scale (thesaurus nuthin'—he owns a *brontosaurus* of English synonyms), betrays the giddy, inkhorn excess of late high school and early college, when we proudly learn to say "commodious abode" for "big house," "mammalian protuberances" for "breasts," and "veritable" just because we can. Like a poetic Ponce de Leon, Goldbarth splashes noisily in the fountain of eternal folderol:

> Miss Needlepoint Maxims, Miss Funeral Shovel, Miss Semenburst,
> Miss Everything, Miss Spider-Of-Blood-In-Its-Bodywide-Web.
> We hate you. We're telling you now: we're ashamed,
> Miss Amalgamated Canning Concerns, Miss Taxidermy, Miss
> Soybean Dealers. Miss Generating Stations with the tiara
> of flashing lightbulbs in your platinum hair . . .
> We value you, with incredible passion. Miss Loosened Burnoose
> in the Deepening Desert Sunset, Miss Tonsils, Miss Lesbian Love,
> Miss Verdigris Glimmering Beautifully On A Hull Though No
>   One Sees It,
> Miss Guava Bushelboys Of The Tropics, Miss Beef, we want you,
> come nearer, be ours, Miss Manmade Fibers, Miss Avocado, Miss
> Charge-Built-Up-About-A-Lightning-Rod-Like-A-Vigorous-
> Sweetheart-Imagined-Around-The-Dildo . . .

As Umberto Eco has observed, there is nothing quite so wonderful as a list. This time around, the chain winds its way through nobody's darkness—Miss Generating Stations sees to that. It jubilates along instead for the pure, prankish hell of it, a bedizened testament to Goldbarth's rage for linguistic pageantry, and to his disdain for the inch when the buxom yard is within reach. I challenge those readers who are always locating "silence" in poems to find any here. "Miss Guava Bushelboys Of The Tropics, Miss Beef": Why stir just a few leftovers into the soup when you can snarf them all? That's the gustatory wisdom behind many Goldbarth recipes, which call for the entire candy store to be looted.

Once again, however, I would aver the grownup importance of the infantile where Goldbarth is concerned. Cradle-bursting curiosity has much to do with what makes Goldbarth Goldbarth; not until computing the breadth and vim of his interests did I realize the comparative sluggishness of most other poets', or my own. He chaperones a mind so promiscuous that every idea can enjoy a fling with it. The thousand and one subjects of this "*wunderdabbler*"—from Dürer to tarpans to "flying saucerania"—span a *mille-feuille,* day-glo spectrum with Mickey Mouse at one end and Rabbi Loew of c.1600 Prague at the other. In Goldbarth's magic kingdom, it's a small world after all, but a dauntingly enormous one as well:

> . . . Because
> we're little—people born into a giant's land
> of bureaucratic backrooms and, beyond it, the universe
>
> stacking matter and antimatter—we have these secret
> handshakes, satchels of family heirlooms, private songs , . .
> whatever it takes to personalize and console.

Having climbed the quantum beanstalk and found himself amidst the relative, anonymous turrets of space, wee Goldbarth lives by his wits. He emcees, with chutzpah, foxiness, and immigrant pluck, improbable Masonic colloquies between the disparate superheroes of his ardor—this to personalize and console. The mere act of bringing Amy Lowell, George (Krazy Kat) Herriman, and his own grandfather (!) together in Arizona (!!), as Goldbarth does in his essay "Worlds," is breathtakingly ballsy, since it hoists a defiant middle finger to the universe and its red-tape causalities; just because such and such didn't happen, Goldbarth reasons, doesn't mean it couldn't have. So shielded by his idiosyncrasies, he outsmarts the faceless, fee-fie-foe-fumming goon bent on the blood of an . . . American?

And they *are* quintessentially American, I think, these Goldbarthian sweeps of the paw, taking in as they do "snaggled cairns / of curios" no well-bred Englishman would countenance. Cruising the "Byways of Possible Combination / one pi-meson wide," Goldbarth follows in his father's mercantile tire-tracks, a hawker of gewgaws and "every Babel of junk," a purveyor of smoothly fraudulent patter straight out of Twain. He is perhaps our most persuasive advocate of kitsch, the leading archivist of our kookiness, of macaronic and cheese our greediest consumer. Materialistic in the best, bauble-loving sense and healthily contemptuous, in the classic native way, of distinctions between "high" and "low," he will try to pass off on you, with his auctioneering and flea market ekphrasis, a virtual yard sale (or "clutterscape," as he names it) of crap.

Goldbarth descends, in other words, from a venerable brood of American bullshit artists, whose most prodigal poetic sire can only be Whitman. I'd hoped, for once, to skirt the Camdenite's ensnaring beard, but there he is. Besides the obvious shared enthusiasms for long lines, the *kosmos,* concupiscent fluids, and most of all themselves, Goldbarth succumbs with Whitman to a weakness for hyperbolic enumeration. He too harbors multitudes:

> Here come the jokers, the jackoffs, the jerks,
> the festive wearers of lavishly tasseled fezzes,
> here they come, no *more* and no *less*
> than the owlishly bespectacled, the labsmocked
> and the bibliocentric sent by Fate to weigh this otherwise
> soapbubble planet in studiousness,
> and by their garb, and by their jargon, they know
> their own, by nametag and by intricate ritual handshake,
> here come Dykes on Bikes and here come Moms Against Bombs,
> the clans, the banded-together, and by their squirting
> pinky rings and by their prayershawls, similar spirits
> hearken and conjoin, and be they rabbis, hey or be they
> flingers of cowpies, each seeks mirroring in peerage, don't they
>   now o
> reader of poetry, o fellow reader of poetry?

Note the secret handshakes again: Something in Goldbarth longs to join a Moose Lodge. Likeminded schmoozing is an oft-touted felicity in his work—a previous essay collection was called *Sympathy of Souls*—and I wonder if, self-ostracized to Wichita, he doesn't turn for convivial persiflage to the exclusive treehouse of the page, where *he* can dictate the terms of membership (again, curious resonances with Merrill and his immortal *Monopoly* board.)

Who, then, are the swankest members of Goldbarth's club? In whose peerage does he most anxiously seek mirroring? The above passage drops some clues. Right away, the announcement "Here comes" summons in, along with Dykes on Bikes, Joyce on foot, accompanied by HCE, the *Finnegans Wake* protagonist whose cipher yields "Here Comes Everybody." Goldbarth is indebted to Joyce in several currencies. First and dearest, he has borrowed from Joyce a foppish, frequently salacious habit of coinage, studded with portmanteaux; Miss Semenburst surely spewed from Joyce's scrotumtightening sea. Like Joyce, Goldbarth views English as an inheritance to be ostentatiously spent, but also one to reinvest in the blue-chip stock of neologism. No tightwads of sound or syllable, both writers put back what they take, and then some. Theirs is an active, risk-taking stewardship of the language, not the timid management practiced by so many.

Next, Goldbarth seems to have learned at Joyce's knee his manner of jocular lyricism, and how to apply it to every topic under the sun—and galaxies. The following passage from "The History of the Universe Is Important to This Story," which features Rabbi Loew, Kepler, and Tycho Brahe getting sozzled together, owes much to the scene in the "Ithaca" chapter of *Ulysses* where Bloom and Stephen stargaze while pissing:

> The banker of stars. And his colleague their architect, building now his little pee arch while he yodels up at that band of sheer grandeur.
> And now a hound in the yard picks it up, and gives out with its own doggy yodel. And then another hound, and another, and three men singing an old folk ditty together "The Jolly Voyagers," three exotic feathers jauntily cocked from the hat Castle Benatek makes in silhouette on the moonflooded country.

This baying congress makes for yet another chain, further evidence of "the unbreakable code of social knottednesss and night sky / we inherit," as Goldbarth rhapsodizes elsewhere. What is the canon, after all, but several millennia of neighborhood mutts barking at or to each other, fighting, humping, sniffing hindquarters, spraying their scents for later dogs to smell and embellish on? For his part, Goldbarth runs with a boisterous pack led by the likes of Rabelais, Swift, and the archrake Lord Rochester, trailed by younger pups such as S. J. Perelman and William S. Gass. ("Delft" is, by the way, the best bit of entomological literature I've read since Gass's "Order of Insects.")

That the majority of those just named have lifted their legs to fiction emphasizes both the dearth of first-rate comic poetry, and the glut of Goldbarth's extra-poetic allegiances. Turning back to the Moms Against Bombs sonnet, let me harp on the throwaway "hey" near the bottom, because it calls attention to one of Goldbarth's strongest ties: to Jewish-American humor in general. "Hey, Las *Vegas*," Goldbarth could be hamming on a strobe-lit stage, or to a bunch of old biddies in the Catskills. As Dr. Johnson said of Burke, "Talk is the ebullition of his mind." Goldbarth's spiel is a kind of highbrow vaudeville, a telling of the daffy things that happened to him—or to his picaresque brain—on the way to the typewriter. So I would elect to his pantheon, in addition to the aforementioned Roth, Herriman, and Perelman, the whole range of Semitic funnyguys from Groucho Marx to Woody Allen.

Then there's the array of anti-Semitic characters known collectively as Ezra Pound. Although Goldbarth displays none of the tell-tale signs of an Ezuversity education, a rough comparison can be fruitfully made. Like Pound, Goldbarth is his own esoteric subject. Maximalist magpies both, they delight in stonking us from above with an endless rain of arcana. Yet Goldbarth's is a far more user-friendly, less bludgeoning and didactic style of erudition. Pound imperiously wields the scepter of a king; Goldbarth, that of a jester. His syncretism serves no political agenda beyond the mirthful desire to entertain, touch, and dazzle the populace. Planet Goldbarth is a democracy of tropes:

> In Nepal, a poacher reams a spoonful of musk
> from that orifice near the urethra, holding—with his other
> gloved hand—the deer's small death-kicks steady; and in
> mid-Manhattan at 3 A.M., at Chico's place, the Pimp Prince
> enters swimming in coke, with one frou-frou dewy-cunted
> acolyte on each eelskin sleeve, and he reeks of a vial
> of musk. I'm singing the rings-in-rings song of the planet,
> its milks, its furnaces, its chlorophyll links. . . .

Where Pound shanghaied Fenollosa to help him raid Cathay, Goldbarth embarks on *his* Asian excursion with one arm crooked around the Pimp Prince and the other grasping for a Gurkha.

The Pimp Prince hustles, like Goldbarth, in a poem called "How the World Works: An Essay," the brazen authority of whose title Heimlich-maneuvers the Restoration, an age besotted by essay poems. While it's hardly the first analogy to spring to mind, Goldbarth does profit from an Augustan confidence about what can be gotten into a poem, not to mention from Wit and Fancy; that spoonful of musk could just as easily have ended up perfuming Belinda's boudoir in "The Rape of the Lock." Pope himself hunches in for direct homage with "Radio Pope," an extensive series of sonnets (or sonnet-length poems) that includes the much-cited jerk-and-jackoff piece. In his research for the sequence, Goldbarth has dug up a recklessly rockhound side to the coupleteer:

> This is, I think, a fine, a *salient,* place at which to leave him.
> Pope is in receipt of a bucketful of *petrifacted ferns,*
> they look like molds for the making of faery ladders.
> Every spore-hung rung of them, miraculously detailed!
> They arrived as a happy gratuity with a linen-wrapped basket
> of Jersey shells, a gift from Aaron Hill, and this
> confluence of affinities is—as much as the sought-for
> specimens themselves—a good reason *the Rhapsode rises up*
> *in my Pip-squeak Carcase today and crows!* Lord Bathurst,
> Baron William Digby, Martha Blount . . . his weave
> of kindred spirits, ever tighter, ever more fantastickall. Yes, this
> is a fitting place to leave him, jigging with meticulous steps,
> around the bucket, composing a letter of thanks in his head
> . . . *which I have found most grottofying . . .*

"His weave / of kindred spirits, ever tighter, ever more fantastickall": Can poets dote on other poets without simultaneously preening themselves? Can they explain themselves otherwise? Tributes are to the poet what masks, in that stageworn theatrical truism, are to the actor: red herrings, switcheroos, handy disguises for narcissism. Not that Goldbarth takes pains to obscure his real subject, and not that he should. He's right, after all: His own poly-brocade fabric of ilks *has,* over the years, grown ever tighter, ever more fantastickall. Goldbarth's fondness

for the word "braid" illustrates the almost Celtic intricacy of his margi-
nalia; no one doodles more densely in the scriptures.

If Goldbarth's affinities have struck an agreeably piquant equilibrium,
his prosody persists at civil war. This seems as good a point as any to air
my one major, festering grievance against him: Goldbarth is an erratic
prosodist, and a positively dismal enjamber. Behold the evidence:

> . . . He's writing a poem
> in my mother, called "A Second Son," she's
> writing a poem around my father
> as if he were its subject. Hers, a
> revision of his, called "Daughter," a final version. The
> night means sparks in darkness, the day
> means shadows like black silk slips around models' ankles.
> The world says *bougainvillea,* the world says *cement,* the
> planet an epic. . . .

Now look at the clumsy miscreant again, caught *in flagrante delicto:*

> . . . She
> renews the inflatable lobster, pig and bee; he keeps the working
> 1940s windup jug band working. So these objects
> are the nuclei in a body of viable love. The rubber
> Paddy the Penguin figurine, the poodle lamps, the loosely
> oviform goldspecked aqua-trim formica end tables . . . "Albert,
> if you ever see a near-mint Paddy the Penguin set of coasters . . ." or
> posters or toasters or whateverthehell—they're
> collecting. They're bricking their love in safe. They're
> whipping themselves exquisitely toward completion. Mo,
>
> the Mickey King of St. Louis, once ushered me upstairs . . .

Before mauling Goldbarth's sense of the line, I should confess my own.
I cavil as one for whom the righthand perimeter of a poem must be a
Great Wall of Stress, a barrier against the invisible barbarians crouched
just beyond the last letter's pale, waiting in the page's white. Wimpy
little articles and pronouns, such as Goldbarth posts at his frontiers,

won't hold back the hordes. Besides, how ever would one read these passages aloud, the voice squeaking out a final "the" or "she" before dashing ignominiously to the next line's refuge? And why would one repeatedly terminate sentences within sight of the end, only to begin new ones with "The," "She," "They're," or "Mo," left dangling there like an embarrassing afterthought? It flummoxes the noggin, especially in a poet so lavishly attentive to his phrasing.

To be fair, few stretches in Goldbarth are as choppy as those I've singled out above. Still, he has a noxious penchant for rude, sudden, jerky enjambments, which taints his poetry with an inappropriate stutter. The revving diction calls for an agile, unimpeded read, but the line-breaks keep gumming things up, putting random hurdles along the vocal path. Goldbarthian syntax and prosody don't mesh the way they deliciously can in Hopkins, say; the words bottleneck, logjam— bottlejam, logneck—impatient to surge on. In Display #2 above, for example, we have lines concluding with "the working," "The rubber," and "the loosely," and virtually every line has a long caesura toward its close, the final three in an identical, awkward spot. I might buy this monotony (excepting "they're"/"They're," which I wouldn't bed down with if it were the last repetition on Earth) as a sort of metrical anaphora, but I doubt it's intended that way, if it's intended at all.

Alas, I question how many line-breaks in Goldbarth *have* been adequately fussed over. Probably no fewer than most poets', probably more than some. Yet with Goldbarth's idiom the object of such "consummate care," as he says, the relative neglect of its vessels stands out. Even when he does conspicuously mold the verse, it can look hideous:

> Now
> here he was, in the sackcloth walls, with Shakespeare
> on the signboard outside. And the books, of course.
> And Beach.—Would she accompany him
> to Stein's? and to his publishers?—He
> didn't speak French. But here we was,
> Sherwood Anderson, author of *Winesburg, Ohio,*
> think of it, and his wife for chrissake named Tennessee
> —*Tennessee!* In Paris.

All of them, so many
names, so many years . . .
Beach recalls their appearances,
Stephen Vincent Benét
("very serious-looking")
Archibald MacLeish
Janet Flanner
John Dos Passos
("always on the go")
Anaïs Nin
Allen Tate
Thornton Wilder
Henry Miller
Thomas Wolfe

Phooey. This is from *Different Fleshes,* which Goldbarth calls a "novel-poem" and which, as he announces in the introduction to *Across the Layers,* he is thrilled to see in print again. To my thinking, he should have left the damn thing deliquescing in its grave. Its inclusion constitutes the one serious misstep in *Across the Layers,* and, plopped down like a bouncer at the very front of the book, this eighty-page zombie could scare away readers before they make contact with the jauntily alive denizens of the interior. I won't attempt to recapitulate its "plot," involving a transsexual from some dipstick town in Texas hobnobbing with the Lost Generation in Paris, but the above passage alone signals Goldbarth's estrangement from his element. In fact, there's nothing characteristically Goldbarthian to this spree of shameless namedropping; it's just one more hackneyed daydream about a posse who may once have been lost, but who've now been found by every American writer nostalgic for a literary Camelot in exile. And as for shape, George Herbert it's not. The vaguely alar arrangement of names responds to no formal fiat I can deduce. It seems, rather, an indulgent caprice, entertained to further brighten the already luminous personages, as if a cuneiform roster were somehow more glamorous than an ordinary one.

I hope I'm venting more than my own grudge against mess when I say that Goldbarth writes best under a self-imposed discipline. "Steerage," for example, is neatly fractured into tercets, and while the poem still makes decisions I would quarrel with, it features a basic integrity of line, a wholeness, which its scattershot cousins lack. That poise of completion extends, moreover, to the poem's argument, whose logic leaps forward in quick yet prudent increments. Goldbarth appears most dapper when dressed Metaphysically, when he strays only to return. He nearly always cajoles, and occasionally whips, several creatures under a single yoke, which may or may not restrain them. To momentarily reanimate my circus metaphors of yore, here's another: The multiplex, man-and-beast extravaganza that passes for the average Goldbarth poem can take one of two courses. Ideally, it will present an ingenious spectacle of simultaneous diversion, the three hoops spinning out a well-oiled harmony of spheres. But on bad days, all Miltonic hell breaks loose: The lion decapitates its tamer, the elephant goes berserk in the stands, the man on the flying trapeze goes splat, the bear porks the Lippizaner, the ringmaster is gruesomely crushed by the human cannonball.

Never do such outbreaks of anarchy plague the essays, though. While I wouldn't go so far as to say that *Great Topics of the World* is a better book than *Across the Layers* . . . Then again, maybe I would: Unmarred by mangled appendages like *Different Fleshes* and without shaggy line-breaks to distract you from its glorious prose, *Great Topics* has a hard, lapidary sheen missing from *Across the Layers.* It comes alarmingly close to being a perfect book, each essay a little world made cunningly, each sentence a just-so sweep of the compass. This is not to suggest, God forbid, that Goldbarth should shift his attentions non-fictionward. His fundamental disposition is, was, and always will be that of a dyed-in-the-acrylic bard. And yet I like best to ponder him as the maker of *sui generis* "writings," not in the pretentious French sense applied to Artaud or Jabès, but rather as a disciple of "Mordecai of Delle, the court's alchemical poet," mentioned in "The History of the Universe." As his auriferous name suggests, Goldbarth might be *our* court's poetic Paracelsus, always testing and teasing the base genres toward some purer kryptonite, or our household Kabbalist, performing his slick *gematria* with letters.

So ductile is Goldbarth in *Great Topics* that the bland term "essay" hardly delimits his hothouse transmutations, a more general sense of which I'd be remiss in not offering you. Let's take "Delft" as a representative specimen. It concerns, over thirty-four "blood-stuffed, psyche-whomping" pages, Leeuwenhoek, the Dutch microscope pioneer; fleas in history; Vermeer; Goldbarth's collegiate swiving of a certain Cynthia (shades of Propertius); and an ancillary cast that includes (in order of appearance or citation) Columbus, Diane Arbus, Donne, Pliny the Elder, Thomas Moufet, John Aubrey, Mary Herbert, Countess of Pembroke, Herodotus, Marco Polo, Henry VIII, Jesus Christ, Buddha, Mohammed, Cleopatra, Madame Curie, Isadora Duncan, Defoe, Frederick Turner, Prof. Leroy Heckler of Hubert's Freak Museum, Prof. Len Tomlin, "struggling impresario of . . . Britain's one remaining flea circus," and Paddy the flea champion, giver of "52,850 consecutive performances." Got that? Astonishingly, not only does this mad congeries of material hang together, it rises into a clarion call to minute attentiveness, a sort of twisted hymn to all things dinky:

> For the spit or the snot below his exemplary lenses is a living turkish *[sic]* rug, is a paisley of armies and harem houris, brigands, flagellating pilgrims, hosts and hordes, upon their skimpy cellular business. Say it LAY-wen-hook: with his pseudopods and gastropods and all other podners in the enterprise of being alive at any glimmering instance on this planet. . . .
>
> Yea, I lift my pen as baton to all of the congregate proboscises of the globe, that join in one blatted honorific bombastic cockadoodle, for he is Leeuwenhoek, he has studied the spires and bristles, the mitred tips and galley-oared bellies, that pass beneath our notice. . . .
>
> Leeuwenhoek made the world larger by making it smaller.

Puniness is one of Goldbarth's pet great topics. Like a designer of high-tech parkas or astronautwear, he tinkers with novel methods for "[t]he nubbling of extra texture into the breath-thin lining of life," and those experiments can yield ravishing advances such as this one in "Worlds": "Life is never the past, the present, or the future. Life is moments the size of the Thailand bumblebee bat that weighs less than a penny." Isn't that *lovely?* I'm especially smitten by the absence of a comma after "bat"—Goldbarth could have written ". . . bat, which weighs . . ." But *sans* punctuation, the sentence is doubly evanescent; it flits by with the haunting alacrity of life itself.

While acknowledging with one hand that "we're a piffle of elements strung in empty air," Goldbarth has never been cowed by the colossal,

which he scrappily assaults, à la David, with the brass-knuckled other—
"as if infinity could be grabbed by its vasty lapels and dragged closer."
He exhibits a Texan gusto for scale, and sudden, telescopic swoops from
the micro to the macro (or vice versa) are one of his signature spasms;
"by that final cursive gaiety, we understand him." Coleridge discerned
in Sir Thomas Browne "the Humorist constantly mingling with &
flashing across the Philosopher"; with Goldbarth, I'd change the last
word to "Astronomer." In him, the two vocations mingle and flash into
a single aurora: comic astronomy, whose keynote preposition is "across"
(space, time, the layers).

Reading Goldbarth can be like watching the classically campy, high-
school science film *Powers of Ten,* in which the camera pulls away from
a picnicking couple on Lake Michigan to take in Chicago, the eastern
U.S., Earth, the solar system, the known universe; then plummets back
to the white-bread pair nibbling their deviled ham; and for the climax
goes deep inside them where, at ten to the minus yatta yatta, their
all-American protons buzz contentedly. A born connoisseur of distance
and its paradoxes, Goldbarth measures

> the width of the border between a man and a woman
> —slickness atoms-thick? or something so
> large as prehistory and we'll never cross it
> in this life?

and concludes that intimacy, the holiest of tellurian grails, can seem
remotest when apparently most close. I bet it satisfies him that his wife's
name is Skyler, for he has often spoken of women and the heavens in
the same reverent breath; both enthrall by evading definitive capture.

But that doesn't discourage Goldbarth from pursuing them, and
countless lesser quarries, with every fiber (whether natural or man-made)
of his warm-blooded being. The hunt for affectionate proximity—to
the living, to the dead, to the fragrant oddities all around—remains the
robustest activity of his writing, and leads, I would venture, to its
centralmost sanctum. *Connection* is his subject of subjects, the last
Russian doll you reach, waiting there at the heart of his artichoke, not
a final fiction but the ameliorating Truth, which in Goldbarth retains
the majuscular certainty Keats graced it with. Tenaciously optimistic,

he has an unbudgeable faith in the virtue of joining, and in imagination as its deftest instrument. To the debatable extent that Goldbarth can be read as a religious poet, the doctrine of his sect implores us to obey a simple creed: "Thou shalt forge links." And so, to set a good example, he undertakes a kind of ecumenical diplomacy with whoever (and whatever) will receive his gregarious embassies; no less potent for being provisional, Goldbarth reckons, are such transgalactic alliances.

If ever the Martians do pay us a courtesy call, I will nominate Albert Goldbarth as an ideal ambassador. He is as well-versed in their customs as in our own (see "Worlds" for a summary of Edgar Rice Burroughs and other "Barsoomian" literature), and on ace terms with fellow starbuffs from Aristotle to Hawking; collects model spacecraft; has gone on record as finding a time warp no weirder than time; and is hiding, I'm convinced, waggly antennae under all that hair. Besides, what better Earthling to regale the little green visitors, during the long voyage back to Mars, with tall tales of our exploits, our splendid tomfoolery, our love?

BEN DOWNING

That Awkward Grace

Ted Berrigan. *Selected Poems.* Edited by Aram Saroyan, with an Introduction by Alice Notley. Penguin 1994. 145 pp. $12.50 (paper)

Alice Notley. *Selected Poems of Alice Notley.* Talisman House 1993. 138 pp. $11.95 (paper)

Alice Notley. *The Descent of Alette.* Penguin 1996. 166 pp. $12.95 (paper)

Ron Padgett. *Ted: A Personal Memoir of Ted Berrigan.* The Figures 1993. 101 pp. $10.00 (paper)

Halfway through Alice Notley's new *Selected Poems*—both in length and in emotional trajectory—lies a wry domestic sequence, "Waltzing Matilda." Its protagonist has her hands full. Her writing isn't going well, she complains engagingly, since "the words aren't jostling each other glitteringly in a certain way & they all have referents I think if that is a trouble." Her little boy, meanwhile, has a fever. Whenever her poem gets into a down and dirty Ovidian groove, he throws up, or begs to be tucked back into bed. ("Real-life juxtapositions are the most tasteless," she sighs.) As for her husband, also a poet—well, he's yelled at her, but nothing that makes sense, which leaves her more puzzled than hurt. "He has always in the past been excessively careful with words," she writes to The Adviser. "We both read L=A=N=G=U=A=G=E magazine." They make up, make love, go to poetry readings, wake up "hungover / & chagrined." "I see little difference between you & your husband," The Adviser shrugs in response. "You're both big and awkward sentimental truthtelling fuckups." As for all that referential writing? "Buy yourself a Fischer-Price Activity Center, some glue and scissors etc. & get on with it all."

"Waltzing Matilda" first caught my eye as a snapshot of the Berrigan-Notley household: a lucky, productive *ménage* that lasted from 1971 until Berrigan's death in 1983. I've come to suspect its cheerfully fractured self-portrait. (Both poets are more furtive than they appear.) But The Adviser's comments yield a helpful headnote to their work. On the one hand, Berrigan and Notley love to come across as "big and awkward sentimental truthtelling fuckups," affable, benign, endearing, blithe. So what if The Adviser goes on a word too long, bobbling his crisp, predictable "get on with it"? As in baseball, an error here and there keeps you awake. And yet, as they invite you to dote on their work not *despite* the occasional miscue, but *because* of it, they also insist you treat them as artists, "excessively careful with words." "Ted was ceaselessly interested in what you might call technique," Notley writes in her introduction to the new *Selected* Berrigan; he "probably talked about it more than any poet or academician in America." "Technically, she is impeccable, & / If She is clumsy in places, those are clumsy places," Berrigan returns the compliment. That stumble wasn't just a sign of life; it was a deliberate aesthetic gesture, a quick impasto swipe that calls your attention to the "jostle" of paint on the canvas—and, a moment later, to the hand that held the brush.

The risks of this approach are obvious. You don't have to read far into either Selected to find work that steps on your toes or nudges your elbow, calling you a killjoy if you don't grin back. Such poems can try your patience, whether for the jitter and clutter of their verbal surface or the baldness of their sentiment. (To get the pleasure of these poets you need a sweet tooth, and an appetite. "I like to use a lot of words," says Berrigan; and Notley calls her muse "that blabbermouth.") At their best, though, the twinborn personae invoked in "Waltzing Matilda" team up in a comic and appealing *pas de deux*. The sentimental truthteller saves the craftsman from pretension—the sort you'd find in (let's be wicked) *L=A=N=G=U=A=G=E* magazine. The artist bails the fuckup out of bathos. You can wear your heart on your sleeve, they reassure each other, as long as you wear your art there, too. Leaning together for balance, they make their way from line to line, in the dance that Berrigan once called "that awkward grace."

If Berrigan and Notley simply kept asking "Can I do *this* in a poem?" their work would be entertaining, even to a formalist like me. Not a goal to be sniffed at. ("Can entertainment have ceased to be a value in poetry?" Notley wonders in her Introduction to Berrigan—a question worth asking, expecially of "experimental" poets.) But as I acquired a taste for their work—Notley charmed and impressed me more quickly, I'll confess—I was struck by how that "Can I do *this?*" grows out of a more searching, savory root. "Can *I* do this in a poem?" Berrigan wonders: I, a "bumpkin with a master's degree," as he saw himself on his arrival in New York. "Can *I* do this," asks Notley: I, a woman determined to write in the "Mainstream American Tradition" of Williams and O'Hara while still "a slave, well mildly, to a baby." Although I will have less time than I'd like to speak of Notley's recent work—she's turned her back on playfulness, out for epic game—I want to trace the different ways each poet "gets on with it all." Cutting and pasting, Activity Centers writ large, they turn initial worry into awkwardly graceful art.

"To me," said Berrigan in 1970, "it's an incredible achievement that I could write a poem." Born into a working-class Irish Catholic family in Providence, Rhode Island, in the Depression, Berrigan grew up in a world he loved, but felt estranged from. "I never told anyone what I knew," he would recall in "Cranston Near the City Line," "Which was that it wasn't / for anyone else what it was for me." He kept those mixed feelings alive in the varied diction of his work, sometimes delicate, touched by hesitant detail—"one chipped glass Scottie; an eggshell teacup & saucer, tiny, / fragile, but with sturdy handle; a gazelle?"— sometimes brusque and selfconsciously masculine: "The piano was black. My eyes were brown. I had rosy / cheeks, every sonofabitch in the world said. I never saw them" ("Cranston Near the City Line"). In "Last Poem" he conjures two totemic objects from his earliest memory: "a glass slipper & a helpless blue rose." They peg him as, at heart, a Cinderella, forced to scrap and scrape to get along, waiting for escape and transformation. Hence, perhaps, the dream announced in "Personal Poem #9":

> I think I was thinking
> when I was ahead I'd be somewhere like Perry Street
> erudite dazzling slim and badly-loved
> contemplating my new book of poetry
> to be printed in simple type on old brown paper
> feminine marvelous and tough

The poet's O'Hara-like ideal self, "erudite dazzling slim," contrasts with the more sentimental description of his ideal poem, "simple type on old brown paper / feminine marvelous and tough." The latter hits closer to home.

Berrigan attended Providence College briefly, did poorly, dropped out. He joined the army, served in Korea, then went back to school in Tulsa, Oklahoma. In his genial short memoir of love and resistance, *Ted,* Ron Padgett recalls that Berrigan was "somewhat cowed" by the poets and artists he met in Tulsa. They were "scornful, elitist, atheistic, and angst-ridden": hardly the model or community for a man inclined to be exuberant, populist, enthusiastic, and religious in the gentle, sometimes mawkish way of another former altar-boy, Jack Kerouac. The "I" of Berrigan's later work gets "high on poems, or pills" primarily to regain his "simple awe that loveliness exists" ("Words for Love") and to affirm his status as a man "ordained to praise / In ordinary places" ("Heloise"). Poems by Frank O'Hara and the Beats gave him an alternative, more temperamentally appropriate model for what it meant to be an artist: not just "Strolling, sassy, dashing, brilliant!" ("Sandy's Sunday Best") but "completely interested" ("Frank O'Hara").

At the end of 1960 Berrigan left Tulsa for New York City "to become this wonderful poet, to become a poet," as he put it twenty years on. This mix of braggadocio ("to become this wonderful poet") and more reflective ambition ("to become a poet") suggests the hope and insecurity that spurs his work from those days—an emotional mix equally evident in the note he sent returning his Tulsa University M.A. diploma, "Dear Sirs: I am the master of no art." "How many times I heard Ted describe himself as a bumpkin, socially inept, unsophisticated," Padgett muses. If he was "cowed" by the coolness of Tulsa poets, he was still more "cowed" by the artists he met in New York, whose "dazzlingly witty conversation," writes Padgett, "made him feel cloddish. A combat boot among ballet slippers." To feel himself a poet, a *real* poet, he needed both to be confirmed by others and to achieve a relationship to art other than that vexed ideal of mastery. Consider "Hearts," an early sonnet sadly cut out of the Penguin *Selected:* "At last I'm a real poet," it begins, excitedly:

I've written a
ballade a sonnet a poem in spontaneous
prose and even a personal poem   I can use
punctuation or not and it doesn't even
matter   I'm obscure when I feel like it
especially in my dream poems which I never even
call   Dream Poem   but from sheer cussedness title
Match Game Etc. (for Dick Gallup) or something like that

For example, take this poem, I don't know how
to end it, It needs six lines to make it a sonnet, I
could just forget it and play hearts with Joe and
Pat and Dick, but lately I'm always lethargic,
and I don't even like hearts, or Pat, or Joe, or
Dick or / and especially myself, & this is no help.

Like the singer of the sixties' Motown hit "Do You Love Me (Now that I can Dance)?" Berrigan's "I" shouts "Watch me now!" He wants us to cheer him as he does the Ballade, the Personal Poem, the Mashed Potato, the Twist, a little scared that we'll say "no" when he asks, *Do you like it like this?*

I don't mean naively to equate this speaker with the poet. In the Author's Note to *So Going Around Cities*, a New and Selected collection that Berrigan edited in 1980, he says that his ambition has been to create "a character named *I*." I believe him. But the systole and diastole of "Hearts" capture the extremes that Berrigan's work always pulses between: the love of poetic forms and genres and "tricks" for their own sake, as things to *do*, and the fears of solitude, ineptitude, and lethargy that all this *doing* aims to assuage. Berrigan's "Things to Do" poems enact this movement from lassitude to action, or the reverse. "Things to Do in Providence" thus starts out flat, words scattered glumly on the page: "Sit / watch TV / draw blanks / swallow / pepsi / meatballs." It kicks into high gear as the "character named *I*" decides to "give [himself] the needle," and four packed pages of conversation, musings, amusements, and finally peacefulness follow. "Things to Do in Anne's Room," by contrast, starts by strutting a Williams three-step across the page— "Walk right in / sit right down / baby, let your hair hang down"—only to dwindle to a fetal curl: "get into the bed / be alone / suffocate / don't die / / & it's that easy." Writing poems usually breaks the "character named *I*" of his sullen mood, especially when he can turn to the reader, the "you," for reassurance. This turn, straight out of *Calamus,* makes for some of Berrigan's most winning moments. At the end of "Many Happy Returns" he finds himself "about to be / born again thinking of you"; and in "Ann Arbor Song," a bantering, burlesqued, and somewhat corny poem listing things that will never happen again, he promises his reader that "you'll find me right here, when you come through, again." Such confessions of a faith in being read certify what's come before as written by a "real poet." The poem's value, and more important, the *poet's,* are both guaranteed by the exchange.

The poems that earned Berrigan the reading he longed for, both from older New American Poets and from himself, were *The Sonnets.* Written in a flurry, sometimes several a day, these poems are a cut-and-paste collage of new material, earlier work, translations from Rilke, Michaux, and Rimbaud, and lines clipped from Ashbery, O'Hara, and Shakespeare. At times they exhibit Berrigan's earlier anxieties, as at the end of sonnet LXXV, where the "character named *I*" is a boy playing a losing game of pin-the-tail-on-the-modern: "looking for today with tail-pin. I / never place it right, never win." This time, however, he can say that "It / doesn't matter," since "The cooling wind keeps blow- / ing and my poems are coming." That the sonnets kept coming, despite interruptions, freed the poet of his worry over being the master of an art. "I wasn't trying to be the master of that form," Berrigan later recalled, "I was just trying to write my works and the form made itself available to me, in fact it forced itself upon me."

Berrigan credited his interest in collage not only to the usual avant-garde suspects (Cage, Burroughs), but also to T. S. Eliot, whose *Waste Land* he "fell in love" with when he returned to school. When the "he" of *The Sonnets* does the police in different voices, of course, the clash between grand allusion and garrulous demotic does not signal a cultural decline. It's meant, instead, to exorcise the ghosts of aesthetic pretension, as when Sonnet IV begins by quoting Rilke ("Lord, it is time. Summer was very great") only to turn simply silly: "All sweetly spoke to her of me / about your feet, so delicate, and yet double E!!" I'm no Tulsa intellectual snob, such lines proclaim—but I'm no Tulsa bumpkin, either. The most telling allusion comes in the final sonnet. Now that the "aery charm" of making *The Sonnets* is finished, he writes, "I'll break / My staff bury it certain fathoms in the earth / And deeper than did ever plummet sound / I'll drown my book. / It is 5:15 a.m. Dear Chris, hello." Unlike the end of "Hearts," where the private game of art proved an inadequate substitute for the communal game of hearts, the "Final Sonnet" mounts an allusive, masterful performance by disowning mastery and turning to the presumably smaller accomplishments of the social. Since even that final gesture is accomplished in words familiar from earlier sonnets, the last line seems as much a *da capo* as a coda. It foreshadows Berrigan's later interest in occasional poems, poems on postcards, "personal poems" in the Frank O'Hara style: poems as convivial as they are "constructivist." As soon as it was published in 1964, Berrigan mailed copies of *The Sonnets* to poets he admired: Dear Creeley, hello; Dear Aiken, hello. (Padgett quotes Aiken's urbane response: "Thanks for sending me your book, which is fun, I think, but not quite my cup of Mescal.")

Perhaps to end with that genial "Dear Chris, hello," the Penguin *Selected* saves its selection of *The Sonnets* for last. This is, I think, a mistake. The poet rightly saw these poems as a turning point in his career: his "first and last adolescent work," he agrees when Clark Coolidge suggests the phrase, but also a substantial achievement, after which he felt "a tremendous desire to be slight." Read in chronological order, many of the poems that follow seem an effort to keep in motion, to see what can be done now that one's "book," as if dictated by magic, has been written and drowned. Can I bring the torque and unpredictability native to the collage of *The Sonnets,* Berrigan asks, into a longer and lighter, not to say "slighter," work? Can I pack the speed and looseness of the longer "field" poems into a single bulky, even balky stanza? Can I build a poem worth rereading out of chewy mouth-music and layered non-sequiturs ("An Orange Clock"), or do I need to air it out with rhymes and a cheery address to a dedicatee ("So Going Around Cities")?

"If you're the kind of person who thinks that everything a poet writes should be perfect," Padgett warns, "then yes, Ted wrote too much. But that was his job, to write. And even the lesser works always have some purpose; he liked to experiment, try out new moves, new tones, and new shifts of tone." Is it our "job" to read such works? Should they be included in a *Selected?* Padgett's answer would probably be *yes.* To sift them out is to belie the poet's faith that writing was, in Padgett's words, "something you did when you read the sports page or ate a donut. It was something you did when you sat at your desk and thought about the gods. It was something you did with scissors and Elmer's glue." It is also to mask the formal achievement of the poems where the new moves and tones suddenly seem instinctive, effortless. By the time you've read fifty-some pages into the *Selected Poems,* for example, you've heard Berrigan experiment with the rhyming and clashing "hits between words" that build up a poem's "surface," watched him stretch out on the page in "Bean Spasms" and "Tambourine Life," and noted his increasing facility with poems that make themselves up as they go along, enacting the discoveries and shifting moods (often the growing relief) of their composition. Some of these poems, like "Things to Do in Anne's Room," are already accomplished work; others, like "February Air," seem successful labtests, their results yet to be tested on more demanding emotional terrain. Then you reach "Peace," a delicate poem elbowed out of anthologies by the flash and glitter of *The Sonnets.* It starts with the question behind so much of Berrigan's work: *What to do?*

> What to do
> > when the days' heavy heart
> > > having risen, late
> in the already darkening East
> > & prepared at any moment, to sink
> > > > into the West
> surprises suddenly,
> > & settles, for a time,
> > > > at a lovely place
> where mellow light spreads
> > > evenly
> > > > from face to face?

When Berrigan chats with Tom Clark about "that awkward grace," this is the poem they have before them. He has his eyes on vowels at first: open *ehs,* various *as,* "settling" eventually into a self-conscious, soothing rhyme. Next he plays with pace, rushing and slowing his lines, tossing in an awkwardly inverted simile, threading his beads first on one set of rhymes, then another, then a third:

> The days' usual aggressive
> > contrary beat
> > > now softly dropped
> into a regular pace
> > the head riding gently its personal place
> where pistons feel like legs
> > on feelings met like lace.
> > > Why,
> take a walk, then,
> > across this town. It's a pleasure
> to meet one certain person you've been counting on
> > to take your measure
> who will smile, & love you, sweetly, at your leisure.
> > And if
> she turns your head around
> > like any other man,
> > > go home
> and make yourself a sandwich
> > of toasted bread, & ham
> > > with butter,
> lots of it
> > & have a diet cola
> > > & sit down
> & write this,
> > because you can.

One of Berrigan's least strenuous and most accomplished poems, "Peace" makes a small, believable claim about the pleasures of making and proves it, expertly. The poem makes no bid for broader mastery; indeed, the little stumbles of "the head riding gently its personal place" (as opposed to its impersonal one?) and "she turns your head around / like any other man" (*she's* like any other man? your head is?) seem designed to lower expectations, keep it all casual. They set up, by contrast, the last lines' quiet faith.

My favorite poems by Berrigan share with "Peace" a counterpoint of sentiment and surface. Aram Saroyan seems to agree; or, at least, he finds such poems the best way into Berrigan's work. He opens the Penguin *Selected* with "Words for Love," the poem where Berrigan declares himself "in love with poetry." Love means you tally lists of words and names, and let the "minute detail" that "fills [you] up" fill up your poems, even if the clock is a little off. (Somehow it's 2 o'clock in Houston when it's 12:10 in New York.) Love commands that you scuff the surface of your work through twists of diction, cantilevered rhymes, and spotlit repetitions of sound. "I go my / myriad ways blundering," Berrigan declares, breaking the line so that you say, "my, my, indeed you do." Saroyan follows this with "Personal Poem #9," the "feminine marvelous and tough" poem I quoted a few pages ago, and then the gentle New York pastoral "For You," dedicated to James Schuyler—a poem that wages this tug of war between formal device and emotional appeal to good effect:

> New York's lovely weather hurts my forehead
> here where clean snow is sitting, wetly
> round my ears, as hand-in-glove and
> head-to-head with Joe, I go reeling
> up First Avenue to Klein's. Christmas
> is sexy there. We feel soft sweaters
> and plump ruffled skirts we'd like to try.
> It was gloomy being broke today, and baffled
> in love: Love, why do you always take my heart away?
> But then the soft snow came sweetly falling down
> and head in the clouds, feet soaked in mush
> I rushed hatless into the white and shining air
> glad to find release in heaven's care.

Some readers will find more "mush" here than they'd like, especially in the last five lines. I find the pun of "hand-in-glove," the play between "Klein's" and Christmas, the double-sense of "plump" as adjective and verb, and the mannered, nagging, burlesqued repetitions of sound throughout this almost-sonnet piquant enough to balance the sweetness. And, to be honest, I prefer Berrigan at his more "feminine," trying on the skirt of sentiment, to the giddier, self-interrupting poet who writes so much of *The Sonnets*, "Bean Spasms," and "Tambourine Life."

In Berrigan's later work, the question is no longer "what to do" but "how long do I have to do it?" Several of his strongest, most memorable poems were written in his last six years—in *So Going Around Cities,* the earlier New and Selected, you find them in the section entitled "Not Dying." It's odd to read these poems in the Penguin *Selected,* with nearly a third of the book still safely tucked under your right thumb, but it's exhilarating to see the poet's gift for brag, there from his earliest poems, suddenly take root and blossom. "I am 43," he writes in "Red Shift": "When will I die? I will never die. I will live / To be 110 & I will never go away, & you will never escape from me" since "I'm only pronouns, & I am all of them, & I didn't ask for this / You did." Such lines give a newly self-questioning spin to the poet's turns to "you" for reassurance; they make me wish that "Living with Chris" had been included, with its earlier tragicomic final question: "For god's sake, is there anyone out there listening?") The Monday morning editor in me wants to slip "Red Shift" into a closing cadence, and to close the book with Berrigan's "Last Poem."

Measured and assured, "Last Poem" glances back to memories of the "glass slipper & helpless blue rose," mulls over how the poet "verbalized [himself] a place / in Society. 101 St. Mark's Place, apt. 12A, NYC 10009." It also includes enough awkwardness to shake you out of any easy elegiac mood. (I can come up with four good reasons why the line "I once had the honor of meeting Beckett & I dug him" isn't a pratfall, starting with the reference, a line before it, to "several new vocabularies," but I'm not sure I believe them.) Unlike the "Final Sonnet," which calls on Shakespeare to stage its farewell, "Last Poem" seems an authentically Prosperian moment: a poem where "what strength I have's my own." That Berrigan envisions himself dying while writing, finding his words, sums up his faith in poetic *doing;* that he claims to have died while "next to you in bed" suggests how far he's come from the social and artistic anxieties of "Hearts." Of the poems that follow in the *Selected,* at least until you get to *The Sonnets,* one is tender, one is funny, and three are slight, stabs at new moves and new tones. None makes as fitting an ending as this:

> The pills kept me going, until now. Love, & work,
> Were my great happinesses, that other people die the source

Of my great, terrible, & inarticulate one grief. In my time
I grew tall & huge of frame, obviously possessed
Of a disconnected head, I had a perfect heart. The end
Came quickly & completely without pain, one quiet night as I
Was sitting, writing, next to you in bed, words chosen randomly
From a tired brain, it, like them, suitable, & fitting.
Let none regret my end who called me friend.

When Ted Berrigan died on July 4, 1983, Alice Notley had been publishing books of poetry for a decade. Like Berrigan, Notley schools herself to relish and attend, although her invocations of "the Goddess who created this passing world" and of the world itself are spikier, sprightlier. Her speakers, like his "character called *I*," aspire to be "Not saints but always pupils / pupils dilated fully black in full achievement of / gut feeling. Joy." ("Gut feeling"? Yes. She, too, deploys clichés. I find the assonance that links "achievement" and "feeling," and the jump from eyes to guts, sufficient excuse.) Most important, though, reading Notley reminds you what it's like to be, in Berrigan's words, "in love with poetry," particularly from the poet's side of the affair. Making poems is a pleasure in itself, especially when your stitching and restitching aims at a nobbly or appliquéd texture, all rhinestones and fringe, not at smoothness. How odd, how delightful, works of art can seem, especially when conjured from a bare cupboard. A baseball player's name, plunked notes, a jump-rope rhyme? Run through Notley's Activity Center, they come out as "Margaret & Dusty":

>   Margaret wrote a letter
>   sealed it with her finger
>   put it in her pocket
>   for the Dusty Baker
>
>   Dusty was his bat
>   Dusty was his moustache
>   Dusty was Margaret's pocket
>   They both got all dusty
>
>   If I had a flower
>   If I had a trinket of gold

> & silver & lapis
> If I had a medal & a trophy
> & a fullup sticker album
> I'd rather be all dusty
> Like those two friends of mine

"Can I do *this* in a poem?" Notley asks, then adds a "the" to the name of an early-80s L.A. Dodger, spinning it into an increasingly abstract, not to say awkward, second stanza. (The line "Dusty was Margaret's pocket" certainly comes out of deep left field. But then, those were "Baker's Acres.") How tickled she seems at the iamb-iamb-trochee Western legato of "They both got all dusty," or the adolescent rush of that "trinket of gold"! How touched by the way those shifting phrases and rhythms lend sincerity to the otherwise purely nominal friendship mentioned at the close.

In a talk entitled "Because Words Aren't Language," given around the time she wrote "Margaret & Dusty," Notley elaborates on the link between being "in love with poetry" and writing poems with an "awkward grace." She starts by insisting, correctly, that "a poet is a person who has a special relationship with words, not with life but with words." She turns this familiar insight into a winsome manifesto, a lecture by Gertrude Stein rewritten by *Bull Durham*'s Annie Savoy:

> Poets are in love with words. They are totally in love with words. They are these people who are in love with words. [. . .] A poet loves a word. She loves words singly, and then together, but singly because each is itself and unique like each thing or person in your world. Two lovers get in bed and lick each other all over for hours. Is that stranger than a poet making a poem out of words? I don't think so, I like to do both. What is language? Language flows, goes past, says, "I want to lick you all over right now!" Words hold still for it. In a poem you can admire and stroke each word the way you might try to attend to each being in all of creation, if only you could, or to each part of his body: knee, instep, mole, ring, twitch, dimple, sac, soft, rougher, smile, smell, indentation, sheen, blacker. Aren't those nice words? [. . .] What pleasure to draw each word out, like . . . like taking a baseball sticker out of its package, looking

at it, peeling it off the card it adheres to and placing it in your sticker album—and it's so shiny, and bright colors, and look at that face!

Notley helps herself to Stein's poetic of "caressing and addressing the noun," but she's ready to "admire and stroke" verbs and adjectives, too. Awkwardness makes words "hold still"; it catches your attention on details that would otherwise get lost in an amorous shuffle. As for that last exuberant analogy, the word as baseball sticker—well, it ties this talk to "Margaret & Dusty" and identifies the childhood sources of this languorous, tactile, lexical romance.

According to Notley's slim memoir of growing up in Needles, California, *Tell Me Again,* the slip between words and their referents was an early pleasure. "When my father picked up the phone at the store," she recalls, "he said 'Needles Auto' instead of 'Needles Auto Supply,' and I was always delighted at that phrase which made no normal sense." Many of her poems invite you to share that delight, which grounds the most unnerving, "experimental" uses of language in the giggly pleasures of childhood word-play. When Stein makes this hospitable gesture, she touches base with baby-talk:

> Here is a bun for my bunny.
> Every little bun is of honey.
> On the little bun is my oney.
> My little bun is so funny.
> Sweet little bun for my money.
> Dear little bun I'm her sunny.
> Sweet little bun dear little bun good little bun for my bunny.

> (from *Lifting Belly*)

In Notley's "January," by contrast, the poet starts by recording odd exchanges with, presumably, her own children. Their playfulness recalls the freedom with language that lies at the heart of her art, even as their demands for her time keep her from writing, except in jots and scraps, quick musings and diary entries of muddled, free-associative spills:

> Mommy what's this fork doing?
> What?

It's being Donald Duck.

What could I eat this?
                                        Eat what?
This cookie.
                            What do you mean?
What could I eat it?

          . . . .

I'll look up "love" in the dictionary. They're beautiful.
Bodily they're incomprehensible. I can't tell if they're
me or not. They think I'm their facility. We're all about
as comprehensible as the crocuses. In myself I'm like a color
except not in the sense of a particular one. That's
impossible. That's under what I keep trying out. With
which I can practically pass for an adult to myself. Some
of it is pretty and useful, like when I say to them
"Now I will take you for a walk in the snow to the store"
and prettily and usefully we go. Mommy, the lovely
creature. You should have seen how I looked last night,
Bob Dylan Bob Creeley Bob Rosenthal Bob on Sesame Street.
Oh I can't think of any other Bobs right now. garbage.
It perks. Thy tiger, thy night are magnificent. . . .

As its title suggests, "January" is a poem about both beginnings (the children's discovery of language) and cold spells (the mother's frustrated "garbage"): a month stranded between the past pleasures of Christmas and a hoped-for flowering. Surely her children's "incomprehensibility" and her effort to "pass for an adult to myself" will prompt new poetry. But for a poet committed to poetry as the enactment of the moment, devoted to dictionary searches and drawing words out like baseball cards, the poem that results keeps dwindling to the stuffing that her children "distribute / . . . to the wind." Not that the season looks entirely grim. Notley may use the "woozy" nonsequiturs of "January" defensively, against the expectation that women will be "pretty and useful." But she's also fond of them for their own sake, as mechanisms of delight. By the time "January" ends Notley seems to have determined that if winter comes, spring will not be far behind. "I am one with the wind," it ends, "and unwinding / am wonderfully useless to you."

In the course of the Notley *Selected*, worries over the relationship between poetry and motherhood serve the same artistic purpose as Berrigan's worries about being "a real poet." Of the first six poems in the book, four take up these fears directly, while a fifth, "30th Birthday" prays, simply, "May I never be afraid." Perhaps the word "fears" puts the matter too strongly. Notley rarely seems worried that being a woman and a mother will get in the way of her becoming "a real poet," at least in her own eyes. When the Holy Ghost demands, in "January," whether Notley likes her life, the answer is bemused: "how could / you dislike being a poet?" she wonders, "and having / children is only human." She doesn't even seem all that anxious about being one of "Dr. Williams's Heiresses," a woman in the masculine line that runs from Williams to O'Hara, and from there to a number of poets, including Berrigan. The scrappy speaker of "But He Says I Misunderstood" thus takes exception to her drinking companion's claims that "No women poets are any / good" and "Poe is greater than Dickinson," both echoes of Williams's *In the American Grain.* Her answer is certainly in Williams's beloved American idiom—"Well that latter is an outright and fucking untruth," she snorts—and she quickly turns her attention to what she's written so far ("6-line stanzas / Open though some?") as if to remind us that she, too, *makes* her poems, hammering them out of the speech that surrounds her. After two more six-line stanzas, all in insistent Americanisms, the poem grows wry, self-ironic, and ties itself off with a shrug and a boast: "All I can say is, / / This poem is in the Mainstream American Tradition."

Writing in that Mainstream American Tradition set Notley apart from the two most obvious models for feminist poetry in the early 1970s: the fierce, resistant mythologizing handed down from Plath; and the feminist exploration of women's "essential connection" to each other, to their mothers, and to their children, sponsored by Rich. The earliest poems included in her *Selected,* which proceeds in chronological order, glance at both models for guidance. What can I take from the first? she seems to ask. Maybe a metaphor like "I am the Dark Continent," with the adoption of Freud's mystified term for women, although that seems a bit melodramatic. From the second? Perhaps the chance to consider, then reject, the solitude of self proposed in Emerson's "Experience," such an uncomfortable model for a woman whose body feels the "quickening" of a baby inside it and the tug of identifying with both husband and child? Or, if that feels too overtly literary, why not a commonplace longing for more life "experience" before motherhood makes her feel herself taken over, a mere container—even, perhaps, a nightmarish living coffin? I speculate, of course. But Notley's poem "Dear Dark Continent" hangs these familiar thematic elements on the flustered, knotty inflections of a likable, singular voice. "Dear Dark Continent," she writes:

> The quickening of
> the palpable coffin
> fear so then the frantic
> doing of everything experience is thought of
>
> but I've ostensibly chosen
> my, a, *family*
> so early! so early! (as is done always
> as it would seem always) I'm a two
> now three irrevocably
> I'm wife I'm mother I'm
> myself and him and I'm myself and him and him
>
> But isn't it only I in the real
> whole long universe? Alone to be
> in the whole long universe?
>
> But I and this he (and he) makes ghosts of
> I and all the *hes* there would be, won't be
>
> because by now I am he, we are I, I am we.
>
> We're not the completion of myself.
>
> Not the completion of myself, but myself!
> through the whole long universe.

The pleasure here lies in particular phrases, the Western swing of "whole long universe," for example, and the slippery way the uppercase *I'm* tumbles into the lowercase *him,* and the wink that turns echoes of Rich's "Diving Into the Wreck" ("I am she: I am he") into the clutter and puzzle and sudden grand refusal of "I am he, we are I, I am we. / We're not the completion of myself." But I'm mostly drawn by Notley's lightness of touch. Where another poet would ask the drama of the *situation* to hold my attention, Notley trusts that I'll want to listen to this character, to watch her come into focus through her busy, breathless repetitions and jumpy typography. When I turn the page to the second poem, "Your Dailiness," and hear that voice again, though calmer, in the opening lines, I'm hooked:

> I guess I must address you
> begin and progress somewhat peculiarly, wanting
> not afraid to be anonymous, to love what's at hand
> I put out a hand, it's sewn & pasted hingewise &
> enclosed in cover. I'm 27 and booked, and my
> grandfather

The stanza breaks off. But already I know that the "peculiar" progress of this voice will involve quick unpredictable jumps of association ("at hand" to "put out a hand" to "put out," as in published), and that as it aspires to "Intimacy with / all, spreading," I as the reader will be part of that charmed circle. By the time I get halfway through the poem, say to the point where she notes "I just fed the / baby for the third time today, I must do these things / daily," I know that Notley has decided to try Frank O'Hara's blithe, self-interrupting style as a formal model, without sacrificing her interest in the relationship between art and motherhood. (She draws on more disjunctive techniques in her early long poem, *Songs for the Unborn Second Baby,* but the results are hard to come by. Like her study *Dr. Williams's Heiresses, Songs for the Unborn Second Baby* is not excerpted in the *Selected.*)

The poems I have treated so far center on a poetics of address. "Dark Continent" addresses the self, "Your Dailiness" its eponymous goddess, and "January" closes with an apostrophe to the "Matador" Notley meets in a children's book: a figure for the way her art will dodge motherhood's goring (galling plus boring?) demands on her time. Like Berrigan, Notley is primarily a poet of voice, not of description; unlike him, however, she has a playwright's love of voices and characters far from her own. Turn from his *Selected* to hers and the variety is particularly striking. At times she strips Williams's love of the American idiom of its dated nationalism and dresses it in her childhood love for slippery reference. A woman who made a mistake "really fucked old Shep," a character sighs in "Waltzing Matilda," then snaps, on second thought, a quirky curse: "Fuck her inner ear." (As a playwright, she's more Mamet than Molière.) Elsewhere the diction stays chaste, the tone, serene. Consider "Sonnet," with its Pop Art clarity of syntax. In the poem's sad sestet, George Burns plays straight man to Gracie Allen one last time:

> In her fifties Gracie Allen developed a heart condition.
> She would call George Burns when her heart felt funny and
>   fluttered
> He'd give her a pill and they'd hold each other till the palpitation
> Stopped—just a few minutes, many times and pills. As magic fills
> Then fulfilled must leave a space, one day Gracie Allen's heart
>   fluttered
> And hurt and stopped. George Burns said unbelievingly to the
>   doctor, "But I still have some of the pills."

This poem owes something to Kenneth Koch, just as the voice of Notley's "The Prophet" owes something to Koch's "The Art of Poetry" or "The Art of Love." But in both cases, Notley stamps the poem as her own. Koch could have written "If you're reading / Plato, the part / Where he seems to say women are a lesser order of beings than / men, don't / Stop reading. A character is speaking." But he would never have advised his reader that "It is precisely a tremulous new April day."

Notley's theatricality suggests a certain resistance to the notion that writing poetry, let alone "women's poetry," is a matter of finding or forging a distinctive "voice." Selfhood is a matter of performance, "playing me for you," as she puts it in "A True Account of Talking to Judy Holiday, October 13." In *Tell Me Again* she describes her decision to be baptized, despite her lack of faith, as a matter of "accepting the fact that I had to make a show for others, as they did for me, of who I was and what I called myself and what I worshipped." Rather than condemn this as an imposition of conformity, to which the poet must, like Dickinson, stand in refusal, Notley links it to her later vocation. "How could I have ever written a poem or published or read it for others," she writes, "if I hadn't been able to take part in this ordinary church-member's ceremony?" Many of her best poems include characters who "make a show for others," whether deliberately, as the loopy correspondents of "Waltzing Matilda" and the masquerading isolatoes of "September Song" are forced to do, or inadvertently, like the overheard speakers whose words she will shape into a collage. " 'Baby, maybe *you* can. *Maybe,*' " the poet hears on the street, and pricks up her ears at the cadence. "The words hang in the black air for a long time. Thinly etched white ice writing. My love" ("Because Words Aren't Language"). The model for such omnium-gatherum poems is Apollinaire's "Lundi Rue Christine," with its Parisian charm; wherever they are set, they live or die on their ability to match the uncanny, unconscious call-and-response of talk in a park or café. Such poems are hard to pull off, but Notley has the touch. Here's the start of "As You Like It," a poem from *Margaret & Dusty* that I miss in the *Selected:*

> I'm so with it I can't believe it.
> Well yeah some were but I have this folder I keep.
> Certainly.
> Hi. You going out today?
> You tell Mommy buy you ice cream.
> You tell Mommy go fuck self.
> Hi.
> Okay.
> Tell Bobby to call me up some time, there's a girl who's gonna
> kill herself if Allen doesn't come to her farm.
> Okay.
> Listen when she's hypnotizing you let your mind do whatever
> it wants & it'll all happen by itself.
> Okay honey, have fun. Bye bye.

The poet will stay "with it," the first lines promise, tucking sentences into her "folder." We, meanwhile, are invited to "go out" into a world laced with greetings and reassurances ("Certainly," "Hi," "Okay") where coherence seems to "happen by itself." A mention of ice cream echoes in a later reference to a farm. A vendor's annoyance gives voice to the sexual undercurrents between Allen and the farm-girl—and, perhaps, to the surrender of being hypnotized. Is Notley the "Mommy" here, and we her children, clutching her skirt but itching to head out on our own? Surely that last line is meant for us: "Okay honey, have fun."

Reading Notley's poems *is* fun. They're rangy, whimsical, warm, sexy in an offhand, unself-conscious way. The *Selected* also chants a suite of moving elegies, testing her poetic resources against the loss of her husband the way her earlier work tested them against the gain of becoming a mother. Perhaps a song would be best, stitched from the fragments of a broken voice, unable to finish its thought:

> I can't think of that
> Let me help and one
> Green is for always then
> Let me lay my head upon
> I will not fasten it
> Will not hold you to me
>
> You to it . . .
> ("Love,")

To "fasten it," granting the poem a syntactic shapeliness to match its music, would not only be to clutch at the dead; it would imply the power of art to triumph over, or at least compensate for, an inconsolable loss. Notley prefers to start and stop, invoke and retreat, launch her voice on the paper airplane of a phrase and see how far it will carry her before the drag of sorrow overcomes it. The broken music of "At Night the States" builds on this approach, even as its loose, improvisational melody calls Berrigan's own experiments in writing-against-mortality. I've heard Notley read this poem, on the CD included in the *Exact Change Yearbook, 1995*. It's a hypnotic performance. Phrases hang together, tumble apart, start to make sense and then fail, returning to the title phrase for the start of the next stanza. I have a harder time reading the poem myself, except aloud, when it can inflect my speech. The final

stanza is well worth quoting, however, and not just because it brings it
all back home:

> At night the states
> you who are alive, you who are dead
> when I love you alone all night and
>   that is what I do
> until I could never write from your
>   being enough
> I don't want that trick of making
>   it be coaxed from
> the words not tonight I want it
>   coaxed from
> myself but being not that. But I'd
>   feel more
> comfortable about it being words
>   if it
> were if that's what it were for these
>   are the
> States where what words are true
>   are words
> Not myself. Montana. Illinois.
>   Escondido.

Notley has wrestled loss before, notably the death of her father, which
stands behind "Alice ordered me to be made" and, I think, "Poem (You
hear that big land music)." By the end of "At Night the States," however,
she seems uneasy with her facility at "that trick of making / it be coaxed
from the words." If she has always been, as she says to Foster, "interested
in doing something with words and truth," here the scales of interest tip
towards truth, with words scrambling downhill to find where it lies,
buried in the emotional "state" of feeling "Escondido" (Spanish for
"hidden").

I read the end of "At Night the States" in the light cast by Notley's
most recent work, particularly the long poems published in *The Scarlet
Cabinet*, the "Compendium of Books" by Notley and British poet
Douglas Oliver that appeared in 1992. In the Introduction to *The Scarlet*

Cabinet Notley insists that "one is no longer entitled to write down every thought, rush it straight into print." "All achievement, writerly & poetic achievement included," should aim to be "invisible." ("*escondido*"?) "One feels that this personal 'I' is too well known by now," she testifies, but a poetry of words alone won't do for the alternative. ("The mannered tracing," she calls it, "of a mind which, by constantly denying its own existence as 'someone,' becomes of interest only to translators of difficult discourse, to critics.") Her conclusion: "*Someone,* at this point, must take in hand the task of being everyone, & no one, as the first poets did. . . . There must be a holy story."

Like her love of slippery reference, Notley's interest in "a holy story" goes back to her childhood. She grew up in a bible-reading Protestant community, a town where "you had a text, a literature to quote from, that was sonorous enough to pleasure you and to satisfy you as to its containing the truth," she reminisces in *Tell Me Again*. When she discovered poetry, reading Dickinson and Blake, she turned to them "looking for something with as much resonance as the Bible to 'know by heart'—some words that could seduce me into a place of truth-knowing, but a place that gave a lot more comfort than the Bible ever had." In *Tell Me Again* Notley's focus is still on the pleasures of words, not the truth-value of story—"first there were the words, which one by one were beautiful," she says—but in the last decade her poems and reflections on poetics have taken a decisive turn away from the love of jostling and glittery words and towards questions of how, as a woman, to write "continuous narrative": to write a "woman's epic" ("Epic and Women Poets"). Even her lyric works, poems like "Beginning with a Stain" (*The Scarlet Cabinet*) and "Red Zinnias" (in the *Selected*), lie miles away from the crazed, layered surface of a piece like "As You Like It."

To read Notley's introductions and explanations of her recent work is to hear an eerie echo of New Formalist and New Narrative manifestoes. "Part of what interests me in continuous narrative is the skill required to write it," she confesses in "Epic and Women Poets," "how difficult it feels to do it after a century gone counter to that, & therefore how worthwhile it feels. The old twentieth century forms are now becoming too easy; continuity at length is now hard." The narratives she has in mind are allegorical, an alternative that should appeal, she writes, to poets "tired of this century's lyric 'I,' or tired of fragmentation, disjunction, literary theory, & hipness." As for form, poetry "is a formalized distortion of the sound of speech," and as a narrative poet "you choose an artifice, you accentuate it as artifice, as music—as the Greeks did with dactylic hexameter." Another minute and she'll be sipping a dram of Old Pentameter with Frederick Turner—but when you see the poems that enact her new interests, their measure is distinctively untraditional, with roots in Notley's earlier work.

Here is the first stanza of "White Phosphorus," Notley's first attempt to answer the question "how could a woman write an epic?"

> "Whose heart" "might be lost?" "Whose mask is this" "Who has
>   a mask,
> & a heart?" "Has your money" "been published, been shown?"
>   "Who can &
> can't breathe?" "Who went" "to Vietnam?" ("We all know who
>   died *there*")
> "This was then" "Is now." "Whose heart?" "All our heart" "the
>   national
> heart" "Whose mask?" "has its own heart?" "A mother's" "mask"
> "Whose money" "do we mean?" "A woman's money"
>   "Woman's money"

The indistinguishable voices here, each speaking a phrase, sound like a tragic chorus whose script has been revised by Samuel Beckett. They might be the strollers of "As You Like It," forced by horror to tell one story only: that of a woman and her son, overcome by memories of the war. "White Phosphorus" thus answered one of Notley's demands. Like the poems of Homer, it managed to "tell a public story," and even the story of "a rather strange faraway but shattering war," as she explains in the quick manifesto, "Homer's *Art*." Yet although she felt she'd found the measure she needed, it was not until she chose different models, those of Dante and of the Sumerian myth of the Goddess Inanna, another traveller through the underworld, that she found the story she wanted to tell.

The Selected Poems of Alice Notley includes book three of Notley's four-book epic *The Descent of Alette*.* The story recounts Alette's journey through the underworld: an infernal subway on which rides "a world of souls." Alette's adventures, like Dante's, are thus largely a matter of listening to others' stories, told in full, or (to end a section) partial quatrains pulsing with quotation marks. From the point of view of technique, Notley *has* found a measure that supplies a "formalized distortion of speech." I don't prefer it to the throb of a pentameter, in part because I hear a distinct push at the start of each "speech unit," for lack of a better term, and stumble when an enjambed one spills over into the following line. As for her success as a storyteller, a weaver of myths? Some passages are haunting: the " 'mother' '& child' " who "were both on fire, continuously" in Book 1, for example. Others, like the story in Book 3, of how there came to be two sexes, seem half myth, half explication of myth, what Lawrence might call "myth in the head." The speaker is a headless woman, "our first mother":

> "In the beginning" "of the world" "there was a whole" "edgeless
> entity," "sea of dreaming," "of floating" "changeable shape"
> "After awhile" "was differ-" "entiation," "as if pieces of sea,"
> "of water," "became fish" "As if air" "became birds-" "I can't
>   remember"
>
> "It keeps escaping me" "But the sexes came to be" "in pleasure,"
>   "in
> glee" "There was much of" "what you'd call" "obscenity" "at the
> beginning" "Much orgasmic" "sensation" "permeated" "the
>   primal entity;"
> "& when there came to be" "two human sexes," "that was a
>   sharpening,"
>
> "a clarifying" "of the pleasures" "of existing" "The edges" "of our
> forms" "made us shiver & gasp—" "This sounds so" "vague, I
>   guess"

---

* *The Descent of Alette* has just been reprinted by Penguin.

"Then something happened" "to the male—" "perhaps because
   he"
"didn't give birth" "He lost his" "connection" "to the beginning"

"of the world," "to freshness" "of sensation" "To sensation's"
"being soul" "Became a fetishist" "A thinker" "A war-maker" "&
   ruler"
"Made me dance naked alone" "before all men—" "any man—"
   "on a
stage, a" "spotlit stage" "Made lewdness" "lose its" "mutuality"

"its holy aura". . . .

Is it just the man in me who who frowns and thinks of Keats and Merrill, Olson and Berrigan? All of them are as hot for " 'freshness' 'of sensation' " as Notley, and as aware of " 'sensation's' / 'being soul.' " What I like here isn't the story, but the nibble and stroke of its telling: the sudden casualness of " 'This sounds so' 'vague, I guess' "; the juicy assonance of " 'lewdness' 'lose its' 'mutuality.' "

The Descent of Alette is an ambitious work, and I have hardly done it justice. As I write these paragraphs, in fact, I feel abashed. Tugging at my sleeve is Notley's early poem, "Jack Would Speak Through the Imperfect Medium of Alice," which appears both in the *Selected* and as an afterward to Penguin's new volume of Kerouac's poetry, *Book of Blues.* "You, pedant & you, politically righteous & you, alive" her Kerouac complains,

> you think you can peal my sober word apart from my drunken
>   word
> my Buddhist word apart from my white sugar Thérèse word my
> word to comrade from my word to my mother
> but all my words are one word my lives one
> my last to first wound round in finally fiberless crystalline skein
>   . . . .
>
>   I write perfectly lovingly
>   one & one after the other one

> But you—you can only take it when it's that one & not
> some other one
> Or you say "he lost it" as if I (I so nothinged) could ever
> lose the word

This is, perhaps, every writer's gripe against the critic, especially the one inside him or herself. If the poet judges the world, as Whitman attests, "not as the judge judges, but as the sun falling around a helpless thing," why shouldn't we read her in the same gracious way, not sifting collagist sheep from epic goat?

The answer, of course, is that poets are not helpless. In their best poems neither Notley nor Berrigan demands that our mercy overcome our stern judgment as we read. I haven't seen the last of my copy of *The Descent of Alette*—or of "Beginning with a Stain," the long lyric that precedes it in *The Scarlet Cabinet,* which for now both attracts and eludes me. Notley deserves a critic who will help her readers find the pleasures in this poem that I've learned to take in her earlier work. No doubt Berrigan had his Muse as much as his wife in mind, but lines from "She (Not to be confused with she, a girl)" keep coming to mind as I think of what it's like to read Notley at her best. "She is always slightly breathless, or / Almost always slightly. She is witty. She owns a proud & lovely / Dignity, & She is always willing to see it through. / She is an open circle, Her many selves at or near the center, & / She is here right now." That's more exultant than I'd grant myself as a critic; more ample and awkward and sentimental. But then, it may be more "truthtelling," too.

ERIC MURPHY SELINGER

The Autodidact

And when I spoke, the people seemed to hear as
though they were far away, and they would do whatever I asked.

—MALCOLM X

I began with aardvark and lacking
Captain Cook's bolus of squills I spelled
Myself sick tracing the loops and dives
Of these simplified ideographs

Until I reached "X ray." Imagine
My surprise at finding my own name
A spectrum of violent bombardment
Which casts bones like television snow.

I wondered what my father would say,
That prophet of repatriation.
"Well, dog my cats!" He has since boarded
What used to be known as the soul train.

MICHAEL EILPERIN

Satin Sphinx

James Tate. *Selected Poems.* Wesleyan University Press 1991. 239 pp. $14.95 (paper)

James Tate. *Worshipful Company of Fletchers.* The Ecco Press 1994. 82 pp. $20.00

In one of his many vivid and nearly forgotten film reviews of the 1960s, Manny Farber makes a sly distinction between what he calls "White Elephant Art" and "Termite Art." White elephant art takes its name from the "enameled tobacco humidors and wooden lawn ponies bought at white elephant auctions decades ago," and hews to the "square, boxed-in shape and gemlike inertia of an old, densely wrought European masterpiece." Creators of termite art by contrast have "no ambitions towards gilt culture," pursuing instead "a kind of squandering, beaverish endeavor" that "goes always forward eating its own boundaries."

Farber thought the masterpiece-oriented painters of his time (he mentions Warhol, De Kooning, Jim Dine) could learn something from the "termite-art tendencies" of the movies (silents, especially, or Howard Hawks and Faulkner having their way with Chandler's *The Big Sleep*), thus freeing them from the white elephant idea of art as "an expensive hunk of well-regulated area." Since the white elephant idea of gilded, well-regulated poetry is alive and well today, it might be salutary to take a look at the methods of James Tate's corrosive poems.

Indeed, it's hard to think of a more termite-like poet, in theme and method, than James Tate, or a more welcome nibbler at the foundations of our current white elephant poetry of sonnets, villanelles, and—God help us—sestinas. "Before the break-up of my country," one of Tate's rodent-like personae remarks in his new book of poems *Worshipful Company of Fletchers,* "I was content to lie under the kitchen sink / and gnaw on busted pipes . . . When the military planes flew / too low over my house, / I would stagger out into the yard / and sprinkle Tabasco sauce on their dreamy vapor trails" ("The Nitrogen Cycle"). Termite art may seem deliberately ineffectual—the pipes are already broken, the bombers are on their way—but it resolutely refuses the self-righteous posturing and miming of authority of the white elephants.

Some poets resemble stand-up comics. Leering or poker-faced, they deliver the goods to the waiting, paying, drinking, televised audience, who laugh uproariously (they're on camera too, performing the role of audience). James Tate's wit, everywhere on display in his new work, is more subterranean, gnawing at the pipes. He's capable of one-liners, sometimes funny—"I opened a resort, a last resort. . . ." ("A Manual of Enlargement")—sometimes less so, in a Marx Brothers mode ("All it wanted was a fair shake, / or a chocolate shake" ("A Glowworm, a Lemur, and Some Women"). His best poems have a narrative levity, like a long joke skillfully spun out with a melancholy punchline.

Tate's poems (as pretty much everyone has noticed) have the surface polish and cool parodic wit of John Ashbery; like Ashbery's poetry, their associative vigor often flirts with nonsense—what Tate calls, in his new poem "Abandoned Conceptions," "a kind of satiny, sphinxian un-utterableness." He has learned from Gertrude Stein the art of the mock epigram, à la *Tender Buttons:* "sincerest regrets / are always best"; "what's a picnic without pathos?" ("Like a Scarf"); "Sleep is an excellent method for tracking down the jewel thieves" ("Back to Nature"). Like Stein and Ashbery, he enjoys fiddling with the readymade language of clichés and archaisms: "It's the same old story, but I don't remember it" ("More Later, Less the Same"). And Tate, like his New York School mentors, has always been interested in the poetic effects of relentless repetition, as in the spectacular example of his earlier "Lewis and Clark Overheard in Conversation," which consists of twenty-three lines of the identical phrase, "then we'll get us some wine and spare ribs" (in *Hints to Pilgrims*, 1971).

But Tate is twenty years younger than his New York School prede-cessors; he has inherited the Beat legacy as well, with its outsider anger and humor—"Only one Disorderly Person was reported / (No one cared enough to report me.)." ("Annual Report")—as well as something of the wired diction of Sixties rock-and-roll ("Bob Dylan is coming to our town," he announces, "and we are subcutaneously prepared, / that is, our fingernails are on edge" ("I Got Blindsided"). The slightly offputting, archaizing title of his new book (a fletcher is the guy who puts feathers on arrows) sets the winking, sphinxian tone of Tate's best work.

Some poets return again and again to a world of fullness and celebration, giving the madeleine one more dip in the tea; Tate's poems circle a moment that was all loss and emptiness. He was born in Kansas City, in 1943; five months later his father's plane was reported missing over Germany, on what was supposed to have been his last mission. Tate's precocious early poetry tried to fill that absence (*Absences* is one of his book titles). To the astonishment of his classmates at the University of Iowa, Tate's first book of poems, *The Lost Pilot,* won the Yale Series of Younger Poets award for 1967.

The title has a double meaning, designating both the pilot's demise and the son's loss of a directing presence in his life. In the title poem, the lost father is both perfectly preserved in Tate's imagination ("Your face did not rot / like the others—the co-pilot, / for example, I saw him / / yesterday. His face is corn- / mush . . .") and perfectly inaccessible. "I feel dead," Tate confesses towards the end of the poem, but his deadness and his father's are miles apart:

> I feel as if I were
> the residue of a stranger's life,
> that I should pursue you.
>
> My head cocked toward the sky,
> I cannot get off the ground,
> and, you, passing over again,
>
> fast, perfect, and unwilling
> to tell me that you are doing
> well, or that it was a mistake
>
> that placed you in that world,
> and me in this; or that misfortune
> placed these worlds in us.

The poem has a slightly academic cast, with its well-behaved trimeter tercets (showing Stevens' influence), and carefully plotted enjambments. The plain diction is unobtrusive, and allows for the fine paradoxes of the last three lines, and the effective placing of "mistake" and "misfortune." Some of Tate's early titles, such as "For Mother on Father's Day," are themselves heartbreaking; the poem of that title, in the same prosody as "The Lost Pilot," is almost too plangent and unrelieved ("You never got to recline / in the maternal tradition, / I never let you . . .").

Tate's later books shied away from this material. He developed his own distinctive version of the dream-heavy, nouveau surrealism of the Sixties. He never went in for the spare, pared-down diction of his older contemporaries James Wright or Robert Bly or W. S. Merwin. Instead (in this regard like the early work of Mark Strand and Charles Simic), he gave their "deep image" symbols of darkness and moon and forest a parodic twist: "The darkness you cast off seeks me, / eats a hole through the chocolate forest that separates us. . . ." ("Amherst to Easthampton").

Edgy, funny, bleakly satirical, some of Tate's best poems of these years were in the bastard genre of the prose poem. Poems like "Deaf Girl Playing" (1972) and "Goodtime Jesus" (1979) still pack a punch. When Tate won the Pulitzer Prize for his *Selected Poems* in 1991, some alums of the University of Massachusetts, where Tate teaches, took offense when "Goodtime Jesus" (" . . . It was a beautiful day. How 'bout some coffee? Don't mind if I do. Take a little ride on my donkey, I love that donkey. Hell, I love everybody.") was reprinted in the alumni magazine. Tate's more recent "The List of Famous Hats," with its discourse on Napoleon's private bathing cap, is a fine poem in the same vein: "The second eccentricity was that it was a *tricorn* bathing cap. Scholars like to make a lot out of this, and it would be easy to do. My theory is simple-minded to be sure: that beneath his public head there was another head and it was a pyramid or something."

Tate's new book of poems, *Worshipful Company of Fletchers*, returns, in a different mood, to the fraught territory of his first one. It carries an epigraph from a hair-raising prose fragment of Emily Dickinson: "I always ran Home to Awe when a child, if anything befell me. He was an awful Mother, but I liked him better than none." Tate surely appreciates the weird wit of that "awful," as well as the sex-change of the mother. Tate's Pelham house is down the road from Dickinson's in Amherst, and his *Selected Poems* includes a dream encounter with her: " 'Tears are my angels now,' she said to me / around 4 A.M. 'But are they interested / in Cedar Rapids?' I asked. 'I'm not qualified / to say,' was her sorry reply. And so it went, / the sound of a crossbow humming. . . ." ("Thoughts While Reading *The Sand Reckoner*"). Like his contemporaries Charles Wright and Charles Simic, Tate has shared in the rediscovery of Dickinson's surrealist side.

The figure of the lost child appears in many poems, including the first poem of the book, an envoi called "Go, Youth," where the speaker encounters a child's shoe "glistening" in the middle of the road: "I walked around it. / It woke me up a little. The child had disappeared. Some / mysteries are better left alone. Others are dreary, distasteful, / and can disarrange a shadow into a thing of unspeakable beauty. / Whose child is that?"

You'd expect an early, shattering loss like the one Tate experienced to inspire a poetry of elegy and gloom—"The Lost Pilot," for example. But Tate's new poetry is exuberant, as though his early losses had finally swept the slate clean, given him a place all his own from which to start. It's striking how many of these new poems suggest the precise moment of setting out, of newness, what the New York School poet James Schuyler called "the morning of the poem." Here are some of Tate's titles from *Worshipful Company of Fletchers*: "A New Beginning," "The New Work," "The Early Years," "Abandoned Conceptions," "The New Chinese Fictions," "The Morning News." And other poems typically begin at the beginning, so to speak: "Early on / I did some hopeful scratching / in my garden patch." ("A Manual of Englargment"); "It is important to forget, if possible. / And to advance as a pioneer." ("Color in the Garden"). It is as though Tate wants to signal to his readers that *Worshipful Company* is itself a kind of "first book."

A poetry of beginnings is bound to seem, at times, wavering, groping, uncertain. Not all the poems in *Worshipful Company* seem successful to me; I'm not crazy about "50 Views of Tokyo," despite the jacket copy's explanation that in it "an aged Japanese officer recalls his youth and World War II." But all these new poems have an exploratory genuineness that never seems cheap or facile.

In his essay on Jane Freilicher's Bonnard-like paintings of interiors and backyards (the best piece I know on the link between the new poetry and painting of the Fifties), John Ashbery says Freilicher's work first struck him as "tentative, a quality I have since come to admire and consider one of her strengths, having concluded that most good things are tentative, or should be if they aren't." In the same essay he says her paintings "do not look as if they took themselves for granted . . . each is like a separate and valuable life coming into being." And finally: "The artists of the world can be divided into two groups: those who organize and premeditate, and those who accept the tentative, the whatever-happens-along." Ashbery's opposition of the tentative and the premeditated nicely aligns with Farber's termites and elephants.

As aesthetic categories go, "tentativeness" (like "termite art") may not seem very promising, but it's a quality much in evidence in Tate's strongest work (and *Worshipful Company of Fletchers* is his best book). There is, for example, the sense of starting out perilously in these poems, "a separate and valuable life coming into being." We watch the poem itself struggling into life, sometimes, as in "Where Were You?", quite explicitly:

> The poem has passed.
> It was here, in this room,
> several hours ago.
> Its sleeve brushed my cheek,
> and I hesitated . . .
> Then someone spoke my name
> and I ran through all the rooms
> desperate for an explanation . . .

The poem ends powerfully:

> Something, someone, was trying to find me,
> an assassin, my twin or redeemer,
> who would keep me awake nights on end
> with his labyrinthine, lachrymose tales
> of triumphs and defeats, the narrow
> mountain passes and the women who waited,
> and the children who disappeared without a trace.
> And then the benighted mumbling,
> the sighs and barely audible slivers of song.

The success of the passage depends on Tate's uncanny mixture of parody and loss—the grandiloquent word "lachrymose" hiding the emotion invited by those lost children. These lines seem to echo, may even allude to, Ashbery's great poem "At North Farm," from *A Wave*: "Somewhere someone is traveling furiously toward you, / At incredible speed, traveling day and night, / Through blizzards and desert heat, across torrents, through narrow passes. / But will he know where to find you . . . ?" But where Ashbery's "someone"—Love or Death—remains portentous, Tate's seems more specific to the task of writing poems; it's a Muse figure he's invoking. The poem concludes: "A shawl covered our knees / and we rocked back and forth / as if some raggedy sense had snuck back into our lives."

Tentative, too, is Tate's tendency to interrupt the coming-to-life of a poem with wry asides. In "The New Work," he instructs himself to "start with a little thing, like his socks, and then, with some luck, we'll build from there." When he gets those socks striding "across the ancient war-torn cities," he pauses to remark: "This is very promising: I can see he is a noble figure / out of his mind with grief—the very stuff of poetry!" That sense of modest, tentative building, starting small and taking what's at hand (Ashbery's "whatever happens along"), is the premise of many of these poems, such as "In My Own Backyard" ("I've seen fox, deer, wild turkey, pheasant, skunk, / snakes, moles, guinea hens. I've thrown a boomerang / that never came back. . . .") and the wonderfully titled "Porch Theory" ("Lots of wicker and baskets, a Victorian / birdcage, on rainy nights children sleeping / but not really sleeping under quilts / telling ghost stories.").

If we usually think of the essay as a didactic mode, a public forum for the well regulated expression of ideas, "tentativeness" is akin to another and deeper aspect of the essay form, for both *essayer* and *tenter* are French words for "attempting," or "trying out" something. The great essayists—Montaigne, Emerson, Valéry—give us a vivid sense of the groping, nibbling, exploratory mode of the imaginative mind, in the process of making art that, as Manny Farber writes, "goes always forward eating its own boundaries." In his own way, James Tate has perfected an essayistic poetry that gives as rich a sense of the coming into being of a poem as I know. In taking nothing for granted he reminds us, as Ashbery says of Freilicher's canvases, "that we shouldn't take ourselves for granted either."

CHRISTOPHER BENFEY

Notes on Blasphemy

"The governor dissolved us as usual"
—Thomas Jefferson

"Society is a sea"
—Ralph Waldo Emerson

1. The Centenarian Recalls an 1854 Auction

In the first generation, the usual things: the future
grandfather stripped quickly for the block,
his thirty years like wine raised in the auctioneer's voice, his color
enriched by oils. His eyes harden. He trembles in arm and thigh
as his price rises from mouth to slaver's mouth, like stock
in some oil company whose fields are in flower. His soul, a die,
bounces on the spit-streaked ground between the feet
of bidders.
                    The patient queue, the flower
of freedom, examines him from eyeteeth to bunghole.
Behind the bidding, in a pale harbor clad scantily
in dissolving foam, a slaveship—Guinea-
bound Cinderella—gets outfitted. Its rigging is like a soul
creaking in the sun as the bidding comes to climax
and the muscular sailors pause on its decks
to see the buyer scoop a life up deftly
and pocket it.
                    The bought heart smokes like a coal;
its beats pile up in a chest ringing like a till;
the thoughts in the head multiply like interest
in the new master's accounts. His smith's skill
is harvested. His will clutches the ground like the plant
without its cotton.

His purchaser, a spit-shined senator,
dreams aloud of the annexation of Cuba and Mexico.
But—"Like the sun, we already hold them in our power,"
is what his friend says. "Their best things will flow

northwards in our gravity. We everyday become the gods
of this hemisphere, just as our federal notes are the gods
of these little towns. See this new boy? Those nations will be studs

that beget our strength; their sunburnt histories our plugs
of sweet tobacco. Ha! We'll milk their mountains like his mammy's
 dugs,

we'll teach their scrawny independence to speak
good English. We'll tell their seas what beaches to lick."
The senator leans on the slave and laughs: "You make me weak."

2. Baptism

The first night on the plantation he was seized by God.
Mud behind the cabins just seemed
to yank him to his knees.
Every child could see his heart had opened
like a bible on Sunday. They took him directly
to the Mississippi and right there in the water
he saw the Lord: light like the rainbow hoop
the moon stamps on clouds. No human face at all.
He said the three-part God wandered
in that light aimlessly, forever.

He tore himself from the priest's grip, twisting like a fish,
and told the wet congregation "get the hell out my face."
A whip
splitting the perfect skin
of a young girl's back does not cause
such shock.

He said he'd heard the truth about things:
the whole song of sorrows that moves in human hearts.
He swore all his time on earth—and he lived another 90 years—
he would break up baptisms, scandalize deacons,
and cuss "that damned ring of light
in which I don't believe."

3. Reply to Jesus

My Lord, leave me alone,
my Lord, go home. . . .

My life's hard as the rocks
long chain gangs strain to break,
hard as the rocks, lord,
that break up ships at sea,

Why come now, King Jesus,
and snatch me from the chaff?
Why drag me by the hair
up the neck of your cross?
Why fling me so far past myself,
farther than the hardest liquor on the barroom shelf?
Why lock me up in fate's stare?
Why hang me up on God's laugh?

My life's hard as the moment
when the troops move and the battles start.
My luck's hard and evil
as bombs falling in the dark,
yes, wound up tight and evil
as lynch mobs in the dark.
Don't come here telling me
to eat sweetmeats and live;
Don't come here telling me
to learn sweet words, and forgive—

Don't you know I'm pickled in the world's curses?
Many days I've wished you'd let me die.
My days fly like flags on the devil's hearses.
I caught disease from your sky.

You say skip my heart across that lightning lake,
that sky, and it'll fly down the throat of the sun—
you say my heart beating deep in the sun,
fire burned in fire, will shine on men. . . .
Down on earth you say my brimstone
heart will bring the torturers down,
and break the wars like eggs.

Lord, the only fire I know is Satan's.
I was beaten on his forge like a metal curse—
made in fire like an iron word.
I'd make your Jordan steam and hiss—
brain white-hot like a just-forged cross—
I'd make those waters shout and twist like branded slaves;
I'd make your Jordan run hide in my people's graves. . . .

Take your hope away, King Jesus,
hug your heaven close
to your chest and carry it home.
That rose you gave it—earth—is death-cell dry.
I say lay it down in hell, Lord, and let it lie,
because my life's hard as the rocks
long chain gangs strain to break,
hard as the rocks that split quick ships at sea.
Busted wood and bodies on the rocks's cracked lips
is all that's left of my floating ships.

4. Jesus Responds

You have learned nothing from my book
where there are no explanations.

You have learned nothing from the dead
over whom you walk, all the deaths
over which you walk as I once
walked the salt waves that wanted
nothing to do with a God
but held me up in sunlight all the same.
In my day no one gave God a "no" for an answer.
Look at me: I swallowed down death.
I was born between thighs, nailed
between thieves, and tore free,
robed in the lightning, and *then* began to live,
and *then* went that starlet, Aphrodite, one better:
A rank wave spat her up one day,
but I was born from the air. . . . Molecule
sought molecule. . . . My right wrist took an age
to form, and then it bobbed high in a matriarchal oak,
wind-tossed, lighter than life, for centuries
frightening climbing children: yea, one or two
fell to nasty deaths. And molecule sought molecule. . . .

My midsection formed all at once—boom!
and a black sea rushed over it,
and not even the wide-mouthed sharks nibbled it,
for from the first the seat of my appetites
was outside nature: My dear, I was
beyond reproach. The whole tossing sea
moaned, infested with immortality. . . . "You, moon,
I am god!" is its cry every sleepless night. . . . My eyes opened
in a cliff face. My blood
hung drop by drop in rainclouds.
My brain was hammered out in the waves:
And the thoughts that passed through it!
Plans to catch the wriggling nations in a net,
plots to feed the opposition to the bombs!

And what did I have to do with it all, I who passed
across the world like a small alternative?

Isn't it enough that I stretch like darkness on the eyes of praying
   congregations,
that I'm squeezed under all those eyelids, unheard in all those
   murmurs,
corroding all those spires with brackish immortality? . . .

See how the nations shed me like tears. . . .

Eternity, unscatter! I say.
Will I never be at peace,
in one piece?
Gather me up in your song.
An old god grows weak, fed on bitter prayers.

MICHAEL COLLINS

THORNTON M. DOSSETT
Evers

Sturdy Boxcars and
Exploding Pickle Jars

Thylias Moss. *Small Congregations: New and Selected Poems.* The Ecco Press 1995. 158 pp. $22.95

Reading Thylias Moss is always dangerous and exhilarating, because one never knows exactly when the poem that rests so matter-of-factly on the page might explode and leave its reader marked forever. In her *Small Congregations: New and Selected Poems,* such treachery is all the more powerfully and deliciously subversive. While most volumes of selected poems these days seem to serve the rather humdrum purpose of announcing their authors' arrival at the higher echelons of literary accomplishment, Moss's is intent instead on dragging the whole grand firmament of poetry down to the level of what truly matters. Like Marilyn Hacker, June Jordan, Yusef Komunyakaa, and Adrienne Rich, who have provided a generation of young American poets a widening space in which to investigate the possibility of empathy in a world of clashing human identities, Moss just as fiercely addresses such issues as spirituality, race and racism, sexual diversity, poverty, and social justice. A visionary and a healing poet, she can turn washing discarded bread in a river into absolution and transcendence or show us how her mother quietly making another woman's bed embodies pure rage.

Moss's authority when she speaks stems from her uncanny ability to locate herself in the consciousness of other people. She can illuminate the thoughts of her loathsome adversaries as deftly and compassionately as she can those of her childhood playmates. Take, for example, her brilliant, harrowing poem "The Lynching," where she enters the impervious consciousness of a Klansman's daughter:

> They should have slept, would have
> but had to fight the darkness, had

to build a fire and bathe a man in
flames. No

other soap's as good when
the dirt is the skin. Black since
birth, burnt by birth. His father
is not in heaven. No parent

of atrocity is in heaven. My father chokes
in the next room. It is night, darkness
has replaced air. We are white like
incandescence

yet lack light. The God in my father
does not glow. The only lamp
is the burning black man. Holy
burning, holy longing, remnants of

a genie after greed. My father
baptizes by fire same as Jesus will.
Becomes a holy ghost when
he dons his sheet, a clerical collar

out of control, Dundee Mills percale,
fifty percent cotton, dixie, confederate
and fifty percent polyester, man-made, man-
ipulated, unnatural, mulatto fiber, warp

of miscegenation.
After the bath, the man is hung as if
just his washed shirt, the parts
of him most capable of sin removed.

Charred, his flesh is bark, his body
a trunk. No signs of roots. I can't leave
him. This is limbo. This is the life after
death coming if God is an invention as were

> slaves. So I spend the night, his thin moon-begot
> shadow as a mattress; something smoldering
> keeps me warm. Patches of skin fall onto me
> in places I didn't know needed mending.

The conflicts raging in her subject's mind are almost lovingly given expression in the poem's haunting images: The black man who is murdered by her father is both "darkness" and "dirt," and yet "the only lamp," source of warmth and light; the sheet in which her father cloaks himself is "fifty percent cotton" but also "fifty percent polyester, man-made, man- / ipulated, unnatural;" her father is both a hateful racist and a redeeming agent of Jesus Christ; even God is both "holy longing" and the pagan "genie after greed." What little protest this witness can muster is abruptly cut off in the precipitously enjambed line break ". . . flames. No / / other soap's as good . . ." where the reader plummets from the first stanza into the chasm of the rest of the poem. Love and hate, the poet thus instructs us, are as much innate and all-consuming as they are actively imagined, constructed, and struggled against by us.

It is not enough for Moss simply to interrogate the various identities of her characters, complicating their motives with religious, economic, and sexual impulses. She wades even more deeply into the swamps of our humanity with the poem's devastating conclusion. The white daughter who does not stop the lynching, the defense of whose virtue the reader begins to suspect might have even prompted the brutal attack, ultimately sleeps with the black man, upon his dark "shadow as mattress." Though she is warmed by "something smoldering" (the most sexually suggestive phrase in the poem), the physical union of white and black remains somehow incomplete without a corresponding emotional bond. Then the poet masterfully makes us whole again, restoring us through the soft yet unthinkable touch of the burned man's ashes falling like pieces of ethereal skin "onto me / in places I didn't know needed mending." Thus elusive empathy—impossible as it may be to define, I can think of no better word for what Moss creates in the reader by this stunning image—ultimately triumphs over our differences.

Laying bare the intersection of places, names, and people is another way Moss performs her poetic feats. Consider the rumbling force, heralded by its long title, of the poem "She's Florida Missouri but She Was Born in Valhermosa and Lives in Ohio":

> My mother's named for places, not Sandusky
> that has wild hair soliciting the moon like blue-black
> clouds touring. Not Lorain with ways too benevolent
> For lay life. Ashtabula comes closer, southern,
> evangelical and accented, her feet wide as yams.
>
> She's Florida Missouri, a railroad, sturdy boxcars
> without life of their own, filled and refilled with
> what no one can carry.
>
> You just can't call someone Ravenna who's going
> to have to wash another woman's bras and panties, who's
> going to wear elbow-length dishwater to formal gigs,
> who's going to have to work with her hands, folding and
> shuffling them in prayer.

The blunt language here chugs along like boxcars hurtling down railroad tracks that are the poem's central image. The stanzas are ungainly and square, deliberately and defiantly space-occupying; like her mother (or the other boxcars, it is not too great a stretch for Moss to invoke, that transported Jews to their deaths in concentration camps "filled and refilled with / what no one can carry") the poem itself becomes a sturdy container for painful experience, neither pretty nor polite. This poem wrests its pathos out of the functional, ugly, and plainly recognizable facts of human suffering. As if inured to the chore of conveying meaning, like almost all the poems collected in this volume, it shuns the merely lovely, the aurally pleasing, the connoisseurish, the world-weary. We know that this train will never stop for sightseeing in Vienna; its conductor is too intent on making startling, hard-earned observations like "You just can't call someone Ravenna who's going / to have to wash another woman's bras and panties, who's / going to have to wear elbow length dishwater to formal gigs."

Nor can Moss be bothered with the formalities of meter and rhyme, of mannered diction or even the tiresome rules of proper grammar; indeed, sometimes she asks outright whether her own chosen medium of the poem can accommodate her heavy freight of disenfranchisement and resentment. This question of purpose leads also to what is most problematic about Moss's work. She seems to disavow art constantly, yet undeniably what she writes is serious poetry. This unhappy union is enacted in the poem "Interpretation of a Poem by Frost":

A young black girl stopped by the woods,
so young she knew only one man: Jim Crow
but she wasn't allowed to call him Mister.
The woods were his and she respected his boundaries
even in the absence of fence.
Of course she delighted in the filling up
of his woods, she so accustomed to emptiness,
to being taken at face value.
This face, her face eternally the brown
of declining autumn, watches snow inter the grass,
cling to bark making it seem indecisive
about race preference, a fast-to-melt idealism.
With the grass covered, black and white are the only options,
polarity is the only reality; corners aren't neutral
but are on edge.
She shakes off snow, defiance wasted
on the limited audience of a horse.
The snow does not hypnotize her as it wants to,
as the blond sun does in making too many prefer daylight.
She has promises to keep,
the promise that she bear Jim no bastards,
the promise that she ride the horse only as long
as it is willing to accept riders,
the promise that she bear Jim no bastards,
the promise to her face that it not be mistaken as shadow,
and miles to go, more than the distance from Africa to Andover,

more than the distance from black to white
before she sleeps with Jim.

No one, white or black (or even gay and Latino!), would disagree that this poem is astounding, more for the courageous challenge it poses to a perceived poetry establishment that still neglects non-white writers than for the vitality of its language *per se*. As she does so successfully elsewhere, Moss slyly injects herself into another's imagination; this time, she penetrates Frost's famous poem, immediately fixing her attention on "his boundaries." In the matter of a few lines, all the conventions of formal poetry, the whole tradition in which Frost so expansively wrote, are equated dramatically with the stark narrowness of Jim Crow laws, the dividing lines between white and black.

Moss admits, in one of the poem's most moving moments, that "Of course, she delighted in the filling up / of his woods, she so accustomed to emptiness, / to being taken at face value." Beauty *is* present, but how to get at it, especially when Moss's heroine has been banished from her own domain? The reader feels the chafe of her yearning as the young black girl stares into the woods, perhaps wishing to explore but kept out "even in the absence of fence." The inaccessibility is so total that even as she shakes off the snow in an effort to find her own mode of expression, no one pays attention and her defiant act is "wasted on the limited audience of horse." Worse than the world's disheartening lack of interest, the very elements themselves seem dead-set against her, at least in this frozen New England landscape, with its white snow and "the blond sun . . . making too many prefer daylight." Here Nature conspires to silence her, depriving her (in its inhospitable conception by a white man) of the sense of place so integral to Moss's poems.

Finally, the poet becomes her own most insurmountable obstacle, with all her "promises to keep, / the promise that she bear Jim no bastards, / the promise that she ride the horse only as long / as it is willing to accept riders, / the promise that she bear Jim no bastards / the promise to her face that it not be mistaken as shadow, and miles to go. . . ." The repetition of the chilling phrase "that she bear Jim no bastards" captures what every aspiring young poet dreads, and what so many minority writers even more acutely feel: that his or her product is unworthy of its literary parents, and that the very act of making poetry (or at least endeavoring to "hypnotize," as she seems to believe Frost does) distorts authenticity. The poem becomes shameful, monstrous, and incapable of accurately describing the individual's intentions, meanings, and personal histories; the limitations of art become even more apparent through the judgmental eyes of others the vulnerable young poet can all-too-easily imagine.

Whereas in her best poems Moss responds to the terrors of unseemliness and disconnection with gorgeous gestures toward uncovering empathic bonds, here she chooses another, more-travelled road: Rejection and blind anger are her solutions. She ends the poem dismissively, proclaiming that it will be "more than the distance from Africa to Andover, / more than the distance from black to white / before she sleeps with Jim." With her allusion to forced sex Moss stresses that her writing as a black woman is as much at risk of being appropriated as the slave girl's body, that her objections to taking up the pen will be just as callously suppressed. By not daring to question the inevitability of such a relationship between black and white, she does all of poetry a great disservice. Heartwrenching as her plight may be—after all, as her phrasing astutely implies, she has no choice but to sleep with Jim—she leaves less eloquently stated how she makes her peace with poetry. Though she strikes again the chord of longing for human kinship, primarily in her echoing of the Frost poem, here she fails to overcome enmity.

As a non-white poet ideologically aligned with Thylias Moss, yet enamored of meter and rhyme, I am disturbed that such a gifted poet should widen any such rifts. In my estimation, it is precisely the universality of the body's rhythms—irrespective of culture of origin or skin color, the same heart beats iambically in all of us—that makes poetry like Frost's so compelling. Exerting the pressures of our own language and bodies and experience against what might naively be construed as rigid "rules" of prosody creates even more rich opportunities for poets of color to write themselves across, to *transgress* what Moss emphatically points to as "boundaries." (To enter the realm of the ostensibly impermissible, but which is obviously in practical terms unpossessable by anyone, I encourage my students to write their own versions of snarling sonnets or villainous villanelles.) Because the music of the body belongs to all people, it has a vast potential for uniting us, the very enterprise with which Moss is so passionately concerned.

Unfortunately, Moss also transmits her distrust of poetry to her reader, via lackluster writing. Indeed, the greatest problem in her work, and one others have commented on, is that of its difficult music; at times, her methods are not equal to her message. Whether it was the distraction of the interminable din coming from the O. J. Simpson trial or the raucous bigotry and misogyny of the Million Man March, or any of the other contentious soundings on race and gender relations in America, for a long time I found I was deaf to these poems. I first blamed myself for a poem's falterings, as though I shared the reader/master's bias in "Interpretation of a Poem by Frost," until I realized that I was no more a member of the persecuting majority than Moss herself. Then I thought: If her poems fail to sound beautiful, perhaps it is because it hurts the eyes so much to read them, to see the awful truths that they reveal. I had only to think again of Marilyn Hacker and June Jordan, of Thom Gunn and Adrienne Rich, to know that this was even a less convincing excuse.

An example of Moss's less impressive work is "Passover Poem," which seems oddly to lament the diversity she elsewhere celebrates:

> God wipes his eyes.
> God blinks as we do to resolve blur and disbelief.
> He looks at the Jews he chose. They need a messiah.
> He looks at my mother. Christ bought her with his blood.
> Christ owns her. She is not free.
> He looks at a million Latino boys called *Jesús*. Jesus.
> And recognizes not one of them as his son.
> He looks at Asian eyes and tries to steady his hands.
> The bomb didn't do it all.
> He looks at the blood smeared on Sharon Tate's doors and walls.
> "Safe," he says, more umpire than God.
> Yet death does not pass over.
> God blinks again. The earth is still there unchanged.
> And poor God cannot pass the buck, he made the buck.

While the monotonous tone of the poem may heighten the tedium and disdain with which its God views his feuding creation, there seems no obvious purpose to dead-end, half-articulated lines like "The bomb didn't do it all." Moss seems unable to animate this divine consciousness, that of an incomprehensible God who permits evil and suffering to dwell among his many-hued people, as fully and easily as she can those of her fellow mortals. She fails to capitalize on her intriguing premise, and so we never come to understand this God who regrets what he has made; instead, the poem verges on sounding like its maker's own bitter complaints and misgivings about other people, the swarms of identical Latino *Jesúses* and all those Asians who survived the bomb, while her own mother remains mired in servitude. Whether God is tearful or merely tired when he "wipes his eyes" at the beginning of the poem, by its uninspired and hackneyed end Moss seems to care very little.

Despite such only partially realized efforts, and over her own remonstrances to poetic craft, most of what Moss presents in this volume is well worth taking in. It is fitting to end with the last three stanzas from the longer poem "The Day Before Kindergarten: Taluca, Alabama, 1959" at the point where a store that previously refused her mother service is burning to the ground:

> When the store starts burning
> I'm on Mama Lelia's porch
> wanting to see
> how the red
> melts off peppermint.
> I know it's like that.
> One by one
> each thing burns.
> Pickle jars explode.
> Mama Lelia asks me:
> *Do it look like rain?*
> No'm, it don't.
> *Ain't God good!*
> She laughs.
>
> Later,
> while it's still smoking
> I go poking with a stick.
> Ashes look like nappy

nigger hair. Smells
like when the hot comb
gets too hot
and burns Mama's neck.
This smell's so big
must have come
from a hundred necks.

Holding my doll,
I look at the smoke,
could be a black man
running down the road;
then run some ashes
on her face
'cause I ain't scared
no more
of nothing.
Maybe I should be
but I ain't.

The same tough lessons Moss learned at such a tender age is the education she now offers us. The pickle jars that explode in her work are the preserved traditions for which she has so little patience; the fire that burns down the white people's store is all the frenetic, volatile, and obliterating power of her words. She recognizes that her furious imagination can hurt her own folks, like the too-hot comb that singes her mother's neck. Yet Moss still goes "poking" among the wreckage and finds in the ashes her own identity, which she rubs on our faces as she does on her doll, making us part of her quest. In the end, after reading these strident, enraged, but stubbornly humane poems, there may be nothing left in the smoke for any of us to fear in the other.

RAFAEL CAMPO

Contributors

ALICE AYCOCK is an artist living in New York City. Her most recent show was at the John Weber Gallery.

HAROLD BEAVER lives in Holland. His latest book is *Moby Dick, Anatomy of a Whale.*

CHRISTOPHER BENFEY, who teaches at Mt. Holyoke College, is writing a book about Degas, Reconstruction, and New Orleans.

RAFAEL CAMPO's first book of poems, *The Other Man Was Me* (Arte Publico Press), was a National Poetry Series winner in 1994. A second book of poems, *What the Body Told,* will be published this year by Duke University Press. He has also published a book of essays, *The Poetry of Healing: A Doctor's Education in Empathy, Identity, and Desire* (Norton). He teaches at Harvard Medical School. He is the recipient of a $20,000 Echoing Green Foundation Award.

ANNE CARSON is a Classicist and poet who teaches at McGill University. Her two most recent books of poems are *Plainwater* (Alfred A. Knopf) and *Glass, Irony, and God* (New Directions).

MARTY COHEN's essays on literature and graphics have been published in *The Threepenny Review* and *American Book Review.* He is the Director of Policy Studies at the Work in America Institute.

MICHAEL COLLINS, an assistant editor at *The New Leader,* has published poetry and prose in *Parnassus, Callaloo,* and *Salamander.*

CLAUDIA DEMONTE is an artist living in New York. She teaches at the University of Maryland and has won numerous awards for her sculpture.

THORNTON M. DOSSETT, a self-taught artist, was born in Georgiana, Alabama in 1938.

BEN DOWNING is Managing Editor at *Parnassus.*

MICHAEL EILPERIN is a teaching fellow at the Johns Hopkins Writing Seminars and a doctoral student at Yale. His poetry appears in the Spring issue of *The Paris Review.*

ROGER FANNING teaches in the MFA Program for Writers at Syracuse University. His book *The Island Itself* was selected for the National Poetry Series in 1990 and published by Viking Penguin in 1991.

JOHN FOY's poems have appeared most recently in *Pivot, Poetry, The New Yorker,* and *Graham House Review.* He lives and works in New York City.

LEE FRIEDLANDER's photographs are in major museum collections across the country.

SIDNEY GOODMAN's work is the subject of a major retrospective at the Philadelphia Museum of Art and an exhibition at the Terry Dintenfass Gallery.

SEAMUS HEANEY, the distinguished Irish poet and critic, won the 1995 Nobel Prize in Literature.

RODNEY JONES's *Apocalyptic Narrative and Other Poems* was published in 1993 by Houghton Mifflin, who will be bringing out his *Things That Happen Once* later this spring.

MARY KARR is the author of two books of poems, *Abacus* (Wesleyan) and *The Devil's Tour* (New Directions). She has also published a memoir about her childhood, *The Liars' Club* (Viking).

JOY KATZ is pursuing an M.F.A. in poetry at Washington University in St. Louis.

X. J. KENNEDY's most recent book of poems is *Dark Horses* (Johns Hopkins University Press).

DAVID KIRBY is W. Guy McKenzie Professor of English at Florida State University. His books include *Saving the Young Men of Vienna,* which won the University of Wisconsin's Brittingham Prize in Poetry, and a critical study entitled *Mark Strand and the Poet's Place in Contemporary Culture* (University of Missouri Press). His poems have appeared in *Kenyon Review, Southern Review, Chicago Review,* and *Ploughshares.*

WAYNE KOESTENBAUM, an Associate Professor of English at Yale, is the author of *Jackie Under My Skin: Interpreting an Icon* (Farrar, Straus & Giroux), *The Queen's Throat: Opera, Homosexuality, and the Mystery of Desire* (Poseidon), and two volumes of verse, *Rhapsodies of a Repeat Offender* and *Ode to Anna Moffo and Other Poems* (Persea).

JAY LADIN's poems have appeared in *Parnassus,* as well as many other magazines and anthologies. He currently teaches literature at the University of Massachusetts at Amherst and is a Ph.D candidate at Princeton University.

WILLIAM LOGAN is the author of three books of poems and the long-forthcoming *Vain Empires* (David R. Godine). His book of essays and reviews, *Reputations of the Tongue* (David R. Godine), will appear in the fall. He lives in Florida and in Cambridge, England.

ED MCGOWIN is an artist living in New York. He teaches at State University of New York—College at Old Westbury, and his most recent show was at the Grey Gallery at New York University.

JOHN FREDERICK NIMS has translated other poems of Catullus in his *Sappho to Valery: Poems in Translation* (University of Arkansas Press). His most recent book of poems is *The Six-Cornered Snowflake* (New Directions). In 1993 he was given the Folger Shakespeare Library's O. B. Hardison Poetry Prize.

CARL PHILLIPS, on leave from Washington University in St. Louis, currently teaches creative writing at Harvard. His book of poems, *Cortège* (Graywolf), was nominated for a National Book Critics Circle award.

ERIC MURPHY SELINGER teaches at DePaul University and writes regularly on poetry for *The Boston Phoenix.*

DIANN BLAKELEY SHOAF's first book of poems, *Hurricane Walk,* was published by BOA Editions in 1992. Recent poems have appeared or are forthcoming in *Antioch Review, Bloomsbury Review, Colorado Review, Ploughshares,* and *Southern Review.* She teaches at a girls' prep school and at an adult arts institute in Nashville, where she also works as a dance critic.

RICHARD SIEBURTH teaches French and Comparative Literature at New York University and is currently preparing a translation of Gerard de Nerval's *Selected Prose and Poetry* for Penguin Classics.

WILLARD SPIEGELMAN, Hughes Professor of English and editor of the *Southwest Review* at Southern Methodist University, is the author of several books, including *The Didactic Muse: Scenes of Instruction in Contemporary American Poetry* (Princeton University Press), and most recently, *Majestic Indolence: English Romantic Poetry and the Work of Art* (Oxford University Press). He was a Guggenheim Fellow in 1994–1995.

SALLY TITTMANN is an artist living in New York City. She teaches carpentry and Latin at the Brearley School.

ELIZABETH VANDIVER is a peripatetic Classicist who has taught Greek and Latin language, literature and history in Georgia, Louisiana, Utah, and Italy.

HELEN VENDLER is Porter University Professor at Harvard. A book of her essays on contemporary poetry, *Soul Says,* has recently been published by the Harvard University Press, along with two sets of lectures: *The Given and the Made* (The T. S. Eliot Memorial Lectures) and *The Breaking of Style* (The Richard Ellman Memorial Lectures). She is finishing a commentary on Shakespeare's *Sonnets.*

MICHAEL VITTI is a photographer living in Brooklyn.

GYORGYI VOROS teaches creative writing at Virginia Tech. Her book on Wallace Stevens and nature is forthcoming from the University of Iowa Press.

DAVID YEZZI is the Assistant Editor of *The New Criterion.*

ARTWORK CREDITS

Publishers

ANOTHER CHICAGO PRESS
P.O. Box 11223
Chicago, IL 60611

BEACON PRESS
25 Beacon St.
Boston, MA 02108

COPPER CANYON PRESS
Box 271
Port Townsend, WA 89368

COUNTERPOINT PRESS
1627 I St. N.W., Suite 850
Washington D.C. 20006

JOHN DANIEL & CO./
FITHIAN PRESS
P.O. Box 1525
Santa Barbara, CA 93102

ECCO PRESS
100 W. Broad St.
Hopewell, NJ 08525

FARRAR, STRAUS, & GIROUX
19 Union Square West
New York, NY 10003

THE FIGURES
5 Castle Hill Ave.
Great Barrington, MA 01231-1552

DAVID R. GODINE
Box 9103
9 Lewis St.
Lincoln, MA 01773

HARCOURT BRACE
1250 Sixth Ave.
San Diego, CA 92101

HOUGHTON MIFFLIN
215 Park Ave. South
New York, NY 10003

LOUISIANA STATE UNIVERSITY PRESS
Baton Rouge, LA 70893

MACMILLAN PUBLISHING CO.
866 Third Ave.
New York, NY 10022

NEW DIRECTIONS PRESS
80 Eighth Ave.
New York, NY 10011

W. W. NORTON
500 Fifth Ave.
New York, NY 10110

OXFORD UNIVERSITY PRESS
200 Madison Ave.
New York, NY 10016

PANTHEON
201 E. 50th St.
New York, NY 10022

PARAGON
90 Fifth Ave.
New York, NY 10011

PENGUIN
375 Hudson St.
New York, NY 10013

SHEEP MEADOW PRESS
P.O. Box 1345
Riverdale-on-Hudson, NY 10471

STORY LINE PRESS
Three Oaks Farm
Brownsville, OR 97327-9718

SWALLOW PRESS
c/o OHIO UNIVERSITY PRESS
Scott Quadrangle 220
Athens, OH 45701

TALISMAN HOUSE
Box 1117
Hoboken, NJ 07030

TRIQUARTERLY/NORTHWESTERN
UNIVERSITY PRESS
625 Colfax Ave.
Evanston, IL 60201

UNIVERSITY OF ARKANSAS PRESS
Fayetteville, AK 72701

UNIVERSITY OF CALIFORNIA PRESS
2120 Berkeley Way
Berkeley, CA 94720

UNIVERSITY OF CHICAGO PRESS
5801 Ellis Ave.
Chicago, IL 60637

UNIVERSITY OF GEORGIA PRESS
Athens, GA 30602

UNIVERSITY OF ILLINOIS PRESS
54 E. Gregory Dr.
Champaign, IL 61820

UNIVERSITY OF MISSOURI PRESS
2910 LeMone Blvd.
Columbia, MO 65201

WESLEYAN UNIVERSITY PRESS
110 Mt. Vernon St.
Middletown, CT 06457

ZOLAND BOOKS
384 Huron Ave.
Cambridge, MA 02138

Highlights of Volumes 1–20

Prices: $40.00 Per Volume ($20.00 Per Issue) for Libraries
$20.00 Per Volume ($10.00 Per Issue) for Individuals available
in 16 mm microfilm, 35 mm microfilm, 105 mm microfiche.
Article copies Thru:
UMI (University Microfilms International)
300 North Zeeb Road
Ann Arbor, MI 48106-1346
(313) 761-4700

Volume 5 · No.2—*Fifth Anniversary Issue:* Poems by Margaret Atwood, Carolyn Forché, Cynthia Macdonald, James Reiss, David St. John, and others; Carolyn Forché on Louise Glück; Michael Wood on Auden; X. J. Kennedy on Wagoner; Alfred Corn on Montale; John Hollander on Bishop; *Special Tribute to Virgil Thomson* with Thomson, Ivan Tcherepnin, Donal Henahan, Jack Larson, and others

Volume 6 · No.1—Alicia Ostriker on Contemporary Women's Poetry; Denis Donoghue on Derek Walcott; Tess Gallagher on Jensen; Donald Hall on Heaney, Montague, Calvin Bedient on Ashbery; Rosellen Brown on Simic, Hacker; John Bayley on Hardy

Volume 6 · No.2—Terrence Des Pres on Poetry and Politics; Rachel Hadas on Ritsos; Donald Davie on Allen Tate; Stephen Yenser on James Wright; Marjorie Perloff on Beckett

Volume 7 · No.1—Octavia Paz: A Poem for Donald Sutherland; Nicholas Kilmer on Hall; Philip Dacey on Bly; Rosemary Johnson on May Swenson; Robert Von Hallberg on Metcalf; Kelly Cherry on Darr, Inez; Leonard Nathan on McHugh, Dacey

Volume 7—No.2—Richard Howard on Milosz; Carol Muske on Rich; M. I.. Rosenthal on Charles Wright, James Tate; Diane Ackerman on Berryman; Calvin Bedient on Olson; David Lehman on Delmore Schwartz; Willard Spiegelman on Charles Tomlinson

Volume 8 · No.1—Seamus Heaney on Walcott; Donald Davie on Hecht, Miles; Rosemary Johnson on Sexton; Joseph Brodsky: An Essay on Tyranny; Judith Gleason on Rilke; Bonnie Costello on Levertov; Gregory Rabassa on Vallejo; Paul Berman on Ginsberg; Calvin Bedient on Heaney; X. J. Kennedy on Sissman

Volume 8 · No.2—Terrence Des Pres on Brecht; William Harmon on Merrill; Guy Davenport on Cummings; Michael McFee on Dave Smith; Turner Cassity on James Dickey; Elizabeth Macklin on Paz; Ben Howard on Ted Hughes; R. W. Flint on Kinnell, Wagoner

Volume 9 · No.1—Joseph Brodsky on Tsvetayeva; Ross Feld on Apollinaire; Katharine Washburn and Margaret Guillemin on Celan; John Bayley on Brodsky; Calvin Bedient on Glück; John D. Engle on Thomas Kinsella; Paul West on Hans Magnus Enzenberger

Volume 9 · No.2—William Harmon on Robert Morgan; Calvin Bedient on Walcott; R. W. Flint on John Logan; Linda Gregerson on Mark Strand; Sydney Lea on Wendell Berry and Philip Booth; Harold Beaver on Ashbery

Volume 10 · No.1—*Tenth Anniversary Issue:* Judith Gleason on Forché; R. W. Flint on Leopardi; Calvin Bedient on Charles Wright; Darryl Pinckney on Ginsberg

Volume 10 · No.2—*Words and Music Issue:* Virgil Thomson: On Writing Operas and Staging Them; Ned Rorem: Art Song; Interviews with David

Del Tredici, Donald Gramm, and Phyllis Curtin; essays on Handel, Berlioz, Berg, Britten, Tippett, Wagner, Strauss; Auden as Librettist, Elliott Carter's Songs

Volume 11 • No.1—Seamus Heaney on Miroslav Holub; R. W. Flint on Carruth; Ross Feld on Montale; Kathy Callaway on James Wright; Ammiel Alcalay on Hebrew Poetry; Joan Retallack on Gertrude Stein and John Cage; Richard Howard on Amy Clampitt

Volume 11 • No.2—*International Poetries Issue:* Ross Feld on Baudelaire; David McDuff on Akhmatova; Terrence Des Pres on Breytenbach; John Ahern on Pasolini; Annie Dillard on Modernist Poetry; R. W. Flint on Louis Simpson; Helene J. F. de Aguilar on Milosz; Poems by Walcott, Mayakovsky, Khlebnikov, Ratushinskaya; Racine's Phèdre, translated by Richard Wilbur

Volume 12 • No.1—William Harmon on Robert Frost; Harold Beaver on John Berryman; Sven Birkerts on Modern Sequences; Ross Feld on Robert Creeley; Joan Retallack on Language Poets; Mary Jarrell on Jarrell and Warren letters

Volume 12 • No.2 / Volume 13 • No.1—*Women and Poetry Issue* (Double Issue): May Swenson on Emily Dickinson; Tess Gallagher on Marianne Moore; David McDuff on Tsvetayeva; Catharine Stimpson on Adrienne Rich and Lesbian/Feminist Poetry; retrospectives on Bishop, Bogan, Sexton, Niedecker, the tradition of black female poets; a symposium on Plath; poems; artwork

Volume 13 • No.2—Selected poems from Peter Viereck's *Archer in the Marrow;* Alan Williamson on Montale; Marjorie Perloff on Hölderlin; Richard Tillinghast on Allen Ginsberg; Peter Viereck on Pound and Williams; Poems by Robert Creeley, John Frederick Nims, Robert Morgan

Volume 14 • No.1—Poems by Zbigniew Herbert; Zbigniew Herbert on Petrarch; Seamus Heaney on Zbigniew Herbert; Rita Dove on Derek Walcott; Baron Wormser on Adam Zagajewski; Diane Ackerman on Dylan Thomas; Stephen Jay Gould on Darwin and Poetry; Charles Rowan Beye on Horace; Donald Davie on Lorine Niedecker; Miroslav Holub on Jaroslav Seifert; Poetic Prose by Marianne Hauser, Guy Davenport, and Paul West

Volume 14 • No.2—Hugh Kenner on Magics and Spells; Judith Gleason on B. Wongar; Eavan Boland on Elizabeth Bishop; Nina Cassian on Paul Celan; Inea Bushnaq on Arabic Poetry; Marjorie Perloff on Paul Blackburn

Volume 15 • No.1—*Fifteenth Anniversary Issue:* Alice Fulton on Emily Dickinson; Paul West on Djuna Barnes; Paul Christensen on Ethnopoetics; Sven Birkerts on Prose Poetry; Susan Mitchell on Julia Budenz and Constance Hunting; Amy Clampitt on Howard Moss

Volume 15 • No.2—Eavan Boland on the Contemporary Lyric; Zbigniew
Herbert on Atlas; Sven Birkerts on Les A. Murray; Suzanne Fox on Colette
Inez; Baron Wormser on Czeslaw Milosz; John Ahern on Italian Dialect
Poetry; Jonathan Williams on Geoffrey Grigson; Poetry by Zbigniew
Herbert, Aleksandr Kushner, and Gyorgi Petri; and Poetic Prose by
Yankowitz, West, Rogoff, King, and Davis

Volume 16 • No.1—Paul West on Djuna Barnes; Ross Feld on Primo Levi;
Harold Beaver on Seamus Heaney; Calvin Bedient on Medbh McGuckian
and Paul Muldoon; Russell Edson on La Fontaine; John Felstiner on
Celan's translations of Shakespeare; Michael Wood on Philip Larkin;
William Logan on W. D. Sndograss; Sherod Santos on C.K. Williams;
William Harmon on Carnegie Mellon Poets; K.E. Duffin on science and
poetry; Paul Schmidt on food and poetry; Poems by Tess Gallagher and
Seamus Heaney; Prose Poems by Russell Edson; Three Previously Unpub-
lished Poems by May Swenson; A tribute to May Swenson by Mona Van
Duyn

Volume 16 • No.2—Memoirs by Harold Beaver, Wendy Gimbel, Melissa
Green and Michael Heller; Reviews of Biographies and Autobiographies
by: Sven Birkerts on Randall Jarrell; Suzanne Gardinier on Marianne
Moore; William Logan on W.H. Auden; Evelyn Reilly on Allen Ginsberg;
Rodney Jones on James Wright; Essays on Poetics by Ben Belitt, Alice
Fulton, Barry Goldensohn, Mary Karr, Jann Pasler, Marjorie Perloff;
Poetry by: Judith Ortiz Cofer, Alice Fulton, Elton Glaser, Debora Greger

Volume 17 • No.1—*Multicultural Issue:* Garrett Hongo: *America Singing, An
Address to the Newly Arrived Peoples;* Suzanne Gardinier on Thylias Moss
and Marilyn Nelson Waniek; Manini N. Samarth on Frank Chin, Gish
Jen and David Wong Louie; Suzanne Fox on Lorene Cary and Sara
Lightfoot Lawarence; Fiction by Robert Antoni, Michelle Cliff; A Memoir
by Ekoneskaka; Poetry by Jack Agüeros, Marilyn Chin, Safiya Henderson-
Holmes, Enid Shomer, Julio Marzán; New Voices in American Poetry:
Blyden, Cader, Catacalos, Czury, Farmer, Fujimoto, Garcia, Gloria,
Guevara, Joseph, Kricorian, Ladin, Lau, Lee, Liu, Martínez, Ryals,
Shankar-Perez, Slomkowska, Uschuk, Vasquez, Vazirani, Vega,
Yamanaka

Volume 17 • No.2 / Volume 18 • No.1—*Long Poem Issue:* Long Poems by
William Logan, Alice Fulton, Jorie Graham, John Tranter, Albert Gold-
barth, Ronald Johnson, Peter Viereck, James McManus, Ruth L.
Schwartz, Steve McCaffery, Mei-mei Berssenbrugge and David Gordon.
Thom Gunn on Basil Bunting; Evelyn Reilly on John Ashbery; Marianne
Boruch on Sylvia Plath; David Barber on Deborah Larsen, Brendan
Galvin, Pamela Alexander, and Andrew Hudgins; William Harmon on
Hart Crane; Paul West on Paul Hoover; Thomas M. Disch on David
Budbill, Mark Jarman, Charlotte Mandel, Les Murray, and Frederick

Rafael Campo on Lucy Grealey, Reynolds Price, Marc J. Straus, and Paul West; Mark Doty on Diane Ackerman; Sven Birkerts on the Prose of W. S. Merwin; Wayne Koestenbaum on Gertrude Stein; Robert Pinsky on William Carlos Williams; Wendy Walker on Harry Matthews; Eric Murphy Selinger on Susan Howe; David Yezzi on Thomas M. Disch; Carol Muske on Sandra Cisneros and Rita Dove; Daniel Kunitz on James Lasdun; Colette Izez on Jack Agüeros; and Karen Zusman on Judith Ortiz Cofer; Poetic Fiction by Rikki Ducornet and Patricia Eakins; Prose Poetry by Albert Goldbarth, April Bernard, Marie Harris, and Maurice Kilwein Guevara; Poems by David Kirby, Judith Yamamoto, Brenda Hillman, Cynthia Macdonald, Diann Blakely Shoaf, Lucie Brock-Broido, Rafael Campo, Seamus Heaney, Ben Downing, Gwyneth Lewis, Lynn Emanuel, Martin Espada, and Lee Ann Roripaugh; Mary Karr on Memoir; and Essays on The Differences Between Poetry and Prose by Tom Disch, Suzanne Gardinier, and Margaret Atwood.

SHENANDOAH

THE WASHINGTON AND LEE UNIVERSITY REVIEW

Betty Adcock

David Baker

Kathryn Stripling Byer

Hayden Carruth

Peter Cooley

Nicholas Delbanco

John Engels

Margaret Gibson

Eamon Grennan

Susan Hahn

Robin Hemley

Michael Longley

Kent Nelson

Mary Oliver

Deborah Pope

Reynolds Price

William Matthews

Scott Russell Sanders

Reginald Shepherd

SHENANDOAH

45/4 $3.50

WINTER 1995

One year (4 issues): $11.00
Sample: $3.50

Name _____

Address _____

City/State _____

Zip _____
                          P

SHENANDOAH
Troubadour Theater, 2nd Floor
Washington and Lee University
Lexington, VA 24450-0303

Studies in 20th Century Literature

A journal devoted to literary theory and practical criticism

Volume 20, No. 2 (Summer, 1996)
Special Issue: The Object in France Today
Guest Editor: Martine Antle

Special Issues in preparation:
Special Issue on Contemporary German Poetry
Guest Editor: James L. Rolleston

Illness and Disease in 20th Century Literature
Guest Editor: Sander L. Gilman

Silvia Sauter, Editor
Eisenhower 104
Kansas State University
Manhattan, KS 66506-1003
Submissions in:
German and Russian

Marshall Olds, Editor
1111 Oldfather
University of Nebraska
Lincoln, NE 68588-0318
Submissions in:
French and Spanish

Subscriptions—add $5 for Air Mail
Institutions—$20 for one year ($35 for two years)
Individuals—$15 for one year ($28 for two years)